W9-AHG-203

# ABSOLUTE
# BEGINNER'S
# GUIDE

## TO

# Microsoft® Excel
# 2002

Joe Kraynak

201 West 103rd Street,
Indianapolis, Indiana 46290

# Absolute Beginner's Guide to Microsoft® Excel 2002

Copyright © 2003 by Que Publishing

All rights reserved. No part of this book shall be reproduced, stored in a retrieval system, or transmitted by any means, electronic, mechanical, photocopying, recording, or otherwise, without written permission from the publisher. No patent liability is assumed with respect to the use of the information contained herein. Although every precaution has been taken in the preparation of this book, the publisher and author assume no responsibility for errors or omissions. Nor is any liability assumed for damages resulting from the use of the information contained herein.

International Standard Book Number: 0-7897-2920-2

Library of Congress Catalog Card Number: 2002113718

Printed in the United States of America

First Printing: February 2003
Reprinted with corrections: April 2003

06    05    04    03        4    3    2

## Trademarks

All terms mentioned in this book that are known to be trademarks or service marks have been appropriately capitalized. Que cannot attest to the accuracy of this information. Use of a term in this book should not be regarded as affecting the validity of any trademark or service mark.

## Warning and Disclaimer

Every effort has been made to make this book as complete and as accurate as possible, but no warranty or fitness is implied. The information provided is on an "as is" basis. The author and the publisher shall have neither liability nor responsibility to any person or entity with respect to any loss or damages arising from the information contained in this book.

**Associate Publisher**
Greg Wiegand

**Acquisitions Editor**
Stephanie J. McComb

**Development Editor**
Mark Cierzniak

**Managing Editor**
Charlotte Clapp

**Project Editor**
Tricia Liebig

**Copy Editor**
Margo Catts

**Indexer**
Chris Barrick

**Proofreader**
Kellie Cotner

**Technical Editor**
Lovisa J. Bedwell

**Team Coordinator**
Sharry Lee Gregory

**Interior Designer**
Anne Jones

**Cover Designer**
Anne Jones

**Graphics**
Tammy Graham

# Contents at a Glance

# Table of Contents

# About the Author

**Joe Kraynak** has taught hundreds of thousands of novice computer users how to master their computers and their software. His long list of computer books includes *The Complete Idiot's Guide to Computer Basics, Using and Upgrading PCs, CliffsNotes Buying Your First PC, More Easy Windows 98,* and *The Complete Idiot's Guide to Microsoft Office XP.*

Joe graduated from Purdue University with a bachelor's degree in creative writing and philosophy and a master's degree in English literature. After college, Joe spent several years as a technical writer and trainer, designing training programs and writing manuals for various manufacturing plants throughout the state of Indiana. Joe's extensive computer and training experiences have helped him develop a knack for making computers, software, and the Internet more easily accessible to beginning users.

# Dedication

*To my wife, Cecie, whose beauty and strength constantly inspire me to do my best work.*

# Acknowledgments

Several people toiled laboriously to create and produce this high-quality publication. I owe special thanks to Stephanie McComb for choosing me to author this book and to my agent, Neil Salkind of Studio B, for handling the assorted details to get this book in gear. Thanks to Mark Cierzniak for guiding the content of this book and keeping it focused on new users. Thanks to Margo Catts for ferreting out all my typos and fine-tuning my sentences. And thanks to Lovisa Bedwell for making sure the information in this book is accurate and timely. Tricia Liebig deserves a round of applause for shepherding the manuscript (and accompanying art) through production. And, last but not least, thanks to Que's production team for transforming a loose collection of electronic files and screen shots into such an attractive, bound book.

# We Want to Hear from You!

As the reader of this book, *you* are our most important critic and commentator. We value your opinion and want to know what we're doing right, what we could do better, what areas you'd like to see us publish in, and any other words of wisdom you're willing to pass our way.

As an associate publisher for Que, I welcome your comments. You can email or write me directly to let me know what you did or didn't like about this book—as well as what we can do to make our books better.

Please note that I cannot help you with technical problems related to the *topic* of this book. We do have a User Services group, however, where I will forward specific technical questions related to the book.

When you write, please be sure to include this book's title and author, as well as your name, email address, and phone number. I will carefully review your comments and share them with the author and editors who worked on the book.

**Email**:    feedback@quepublishing.com

**Mail**:    Greg Wiegand
Que Publishing
201 West 103rd Street
Indianapolis, IN 46290 USA

For more information about this book or another Que title, visit our Web site at www.quepublishing.com. Type the ISBN (excluding hyphens) or the title of a book in the Search field to find the page you're looking for.

# INTRODUCTION

Microsoft Excel is one of the most powerful spreadsheet programs on the market. Using Excel, you can create automated accounting sheets that do everything from tracking income and expenses to analyzing complex financial data. And best of all, Excel executes the most complicated, monotonous chores for you, such as performing calculations and charting (graphing) your data.

But Excel's power does you little good until you know how to navigate Excel and exploit its many features. Fortunately, this *Absolute Beginner's Guide to Microsoft Excel 2002* provides you with all the instructions you need in an easy-to-follow, fully illustrated format. This book begins with a general overview of Excel and of *worksheets* (Excel's name for *spreadsheets*) and then leads you step-by-step through the most essential tasks. Here, you learn how to enter data, insert formulas and functions, create attractive charts, format your worksheets to make them look pretty, print your creations, and much more.

## A Book for the True Beginner

The *Absolute Beginner's Guide to Microsoft Excel 2002* is for novice Excel users, those who have little or no experience with Excel and who know little or nothing about worksheets. Whether you must learn Excel for work, school, or home, or would like to learn about Excel and worksheets for your own personal development, this is the book for you. With its no-frills approach, this book provides instructions on how to master the most basic tasks and then take advantage of the most powerful features that Excel has to offer.

## How This Book Is Organized

The overall structure of this book is designed to feed you information as you're ready for it. The book begins by providing a basic explanation of *worksheets* and instructions on how to move around in Excel and enter commands. Later chapters show you how to enter data, insert formulas and functions, format your worksheets, create charts, and insert clip art. By the time you reach Chapter 10, you should have a completed, printed worksheet. Beyond Chapter 10, you can explore some of Excel's additional features and learn how to customize and automate Excel to work more efficiently.

In addition to progressing from the basics to more advanced techniques, this book is divided into the following four distinct parts to help you easily locate the information you need.

## Part 1: Excel Worksheet Orientation Day

Consider this part to be Excel Worksheets 101, the starting point for those who have no experience with Excel worksheets. Here, you learn what a worksheet is, how it functions, and how people use worksheets in home and business applications. You also learn how to move around in Excel, enter commands, and work with Excel *workbook* files. (A workbook consists of one or more worksheets.)

## Part 2: Creating Your First Worksheet

As soon as you understand worksheets and the basics of navigating Excel, you're ready to create your very own worksheet. Here you learn how to enter *labels* (text) and *values* (numbers) in the various *cells* (boxes) that make up a worksheet. You also learn how to control the size of the cells by adjusting the worksheet's row heights and column widths. Finally, you learn how to enter formulas and functions that perform calculations on the numbers you entered.

## Part 3: Formatting, Charting, and Printing Your Worksheet

A worksheet can appear very plain at first. In this part, you learn how to give your worksheet a makeover by changing the fonts (typestyles) and adding shading and borders to cells. Here you also learn how to create charts (graphs), insert clip art images, and print your completed worksheets and charts.

## Part 4: Going Beyond the Basics

You've mastered the basics and yearn for more. Welcome to Part 4, where you learn how to manage a database with Excel, customize Excel for the way you work, automate tasks with Excel's macros, take advantage of Excel's Web-based features, and use Excel's speech and handwriting recognition features to streamline your data entry. By the time you finish this part, you can consider yourself an Excel power user!

# Conventions Used in This Book

This book explains the essential concepts and tasks in an easily digestible format. At the beginning of each chapter is a bulleted list of *In This Chapter* highlights that provides you with a framework for what you are about to learn. At the end of each chapter, under the heading *The Absolute Minimum*, you can review the main points covered in the chapter.

In addition, several icons appear throughout the book to direct your attention to a *note* that provides more detailed information, a *tip* that can help you perform a step more efficiently, or a *caution* to help you steer clear of a potential problem. Following is a brief description of each icon:

**note**

Notes provide additional information about the subject matter covered in a particular section. You can safely skip these notes and still learn the basics.

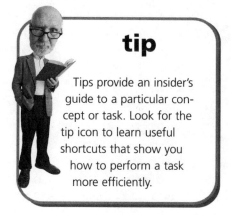

**tip**

Tips provide an insider's guide to a particular concept or task. Look for the tip icon to learn useful shortcuts that show you how to perform a task more efficiently.

**caution**

Cautions point out common user errors and problem areas, so you can avoid the problems that hundreds of other users already have made. To avoid trouble and stay on the right track, read the cautions.

# PART

# i

# Excel Worksheet Orientation Day

1

# UNDERSTANDING EXCEL WORKSHEETS (SPREADSHEETS)

# What Is a Worksheet?

Excel is an application that is commonly known as a *spreadsheet program*. As such, Excel enables you to use your computer to create automated accounting sheets, called *worksheets* or *spreadsheets*, on which you can enter text, dates, values, and other entries. ("Worksheet" is Excel's name for a *spreadsheet*, so from now on, to avoid confusion, we will refer to spreadsheets as worksheets.)

A worksheet is an oversized "page" consisting of *rows* and *columns* that intersect to form tiny boxes, called *cells*. Into each cell, you can type labels (text entries), values (numbers), dates and times, or formulas (which perform calculations on the values). Open your checkbook register, or just look at Figure 1.1, to see a very basic model of a worksheet. Each column in a checkbook register specifies a particular entry: check number, date, transaction description, payment, deposit, balance, and so on. Each row represents a specific transaction. The rows and columns intersect to form little boxes into which you scribble each piece of data: the check number, the date and description of the transaction, the amount of the transaction, and the new balance.

Though each Excel worksheet contains more than 16 million cells, a basic worksheet may use only a few hundred.

**FIGURE 1.1**

A checkbook register is a simple model of a worksheet.

| TRANS TYPE or CHECK NO. | DATE | DESCRIPTION OF TRANSACTION | PAYMENT/ DEBIT (−) | | FEE (IF ANY) (−) (✓) | DEPOSIT/ CREDIT (+) | | BALANCE | |
|---|---|---|---|---|---|---|---|---|---|
| | | | | | | | | $ 3,250 | 00 |
| 101 | 7/17 | House Payment | $ 1,047 | 15 | | | | 2,202 | 85 |
| 102 | 7/19 | Kroger Groceries | 150 | 75 | | | | 2,052 | 10 |
| 103 | 7/19 | Shell Gas | 24 | 32 | | | | 2,027 | 78 |
| — | 7/20 | Deposit Pay | | | | 756 | 03 | 2,783 | 81 |
| 104 | 7/22 | Kroger Groceries | 30 | 47 | | | | 2,753 | 34 |
| 105 | 7/25 | 500 Auto | 357 | 02 | | | | 2,396 | 32 |
| 106 | 7/26 | Noah's Animal Hospital | 60 | 50 | | | | 2,335 | 82 |
| | | | | | | | | | |
| | | | | | | | | | |
| | | | | | | | | | |
| | | | | | | | | | |
| | | | | | | | | | |

An Excel worksheet functions in the same way on your computer. As shown in Figure 1.2, a worksheet consists of numbered rows and lettered columns that intersect to form the small boxes called cells. What you see on the screen and in Figure 1.2, however, is only a small portion of the entire worksheet. Excel worksheets can have 256 columns and 65,536 rows, for a grand total of 16,777,216 boxes (or cells).

Figure 1.2 shows a blank slate, an empty worksheet, as you see it when you first start Excel. As such, the worksheet does you little good. It becomes useful only after you enter some data into it. Figure 1.3 shows a sample worksheet complete with data. This worksheet is designed to track sales figures for a small business. A worksheet can contain any or all of the following six types of entries:

- Labels (text entries)
- Values (numbers)
- Dates
- Times
- Formulas
- Functions

**note**

For more information about the types of data you can enter into worksheet cells, see "Understanding Types of Data Entries," in Chapter 4, "Entering and Editing Labels and Values."

**FIGURE 1.2**

A worksheet consists of columns and rows that intersect to form cells.

Worksheet

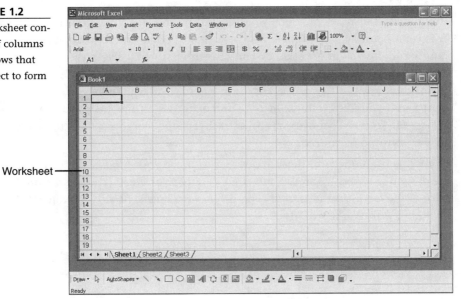

Labels    Values    Formula results

**FIGURE 1.3**

Worksheets serve
a useful function
only after you
enter data.

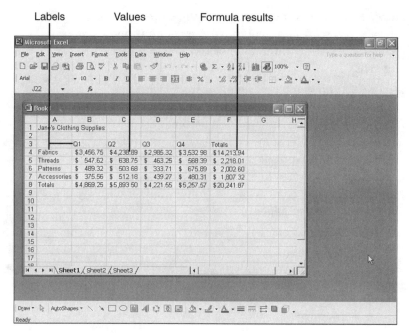

# What Is a Workbook?

Though Excel displays only one worksheet at a time, every file you create and save
in Excel is actually a workbook file, consisting of one or more worksheets. When you
start Excel, the opening workbook contains three worksheets. In the lower left corner
of the workbook window are three worksheet tabs, labeled Sheet1, Sheet2, and
Sheet3, as shown in Figure 1.4. For many people and uses, one worksheet is sufficient, but if you need to track income and expenses for several businesses or want to
spread out your budget over several worksheets, the workbook model can help you
keep everything organized.

To change from one worksheet to another, you use your mouse to click the tab for
the desired worksheet. You can insert additional worksheets, change the name and
color of the worksheet tabs, and even delete worksheets, as explained in Chapter 3,
"Working with Workbook Files."

Worksheet

**FIGURE 1.4**

A workbook initially has three worksheets.

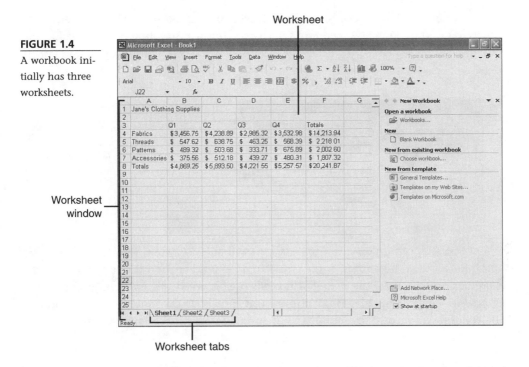

Worksheet window

Worksheet tabs

# Examining Columns, Rows, and Cells

As mentioned earlier, a worksheet consists of 256 vertical columns and 65,536 horizontal rows that intersect to form 16,777,216 cells. As such, a worksheet is little more than a huge table, a grid that keeps entries aligned vertically and horizontally on a page. If you have ever worked with tables in a word processing program, you know that they can be powerful tools in helping you align text on a page. This is one of the primary features of worksheets, as well.

The gridlines in Excel worksheets are displayed primarily for your benefit, so you can see the cell boundaries as you work. When you print your worksheet, the gridlines do not appear on the printout. However, Excel does enable you to *format* the worksheet to insert horizontal lines between rows, vertical lines between columns,

note

You can also have Excel wrap a long entry to display it on two or more "lines" inside a cell. See Chapter 7, "Formatting Your Worksheet," and read the section named "Changing the Alignment of Entries in a Cell."

boxes around individual cells or groups of cells, and to add shading to the cells. This helps you and anyone else who looks at the spreadsheet to follow a row or column of entries more easily. Figure 1.5 shows a sample worksheet with shading and borders.

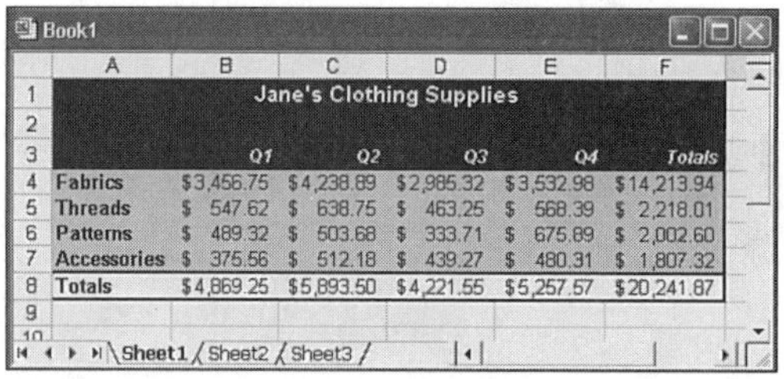

**FIGURE 1.5**

You can add borders and shading to make your worksheet more attractive and easy to follow.

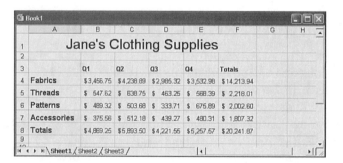

When you start typing entries into cells, you will quickly realize that the cells are too small for some of the entries. Some entries may extend beyond the cell's borders into neighboring cells, or, if the neighboring cells are occupied, the entry might appear *truncated*—part of the entry is not shown. Fortunately, Excel enables you to change the column widths and row heights to accommodate even the longest entries, as shown in Figure 1.6.

**FIGURE 1.6**

Excel can modify cell sizes to make your entries fit.

# Understanding Cell Addresses

To keep track of every entry in every cell, Excel assigns an address to each and every cell in a worksheet. The address consists of the cell's column letter (called the *column heading*) followed by its row number (or *row heading*). The cell in the upper left corner of the worksheet has the address A1, as shown in Figure 1.7. The cell to its right is B1. The cell below A1 is A2.

**FIGURE 1.7**

Excel assigns an address to each and every cell.

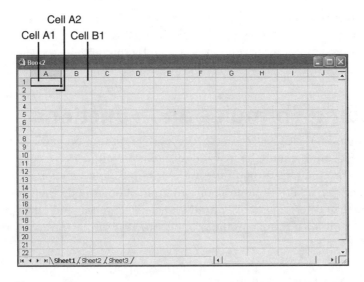

Of course, the rows can be numbered consecutively from 1 to 65,536, but how do you assign letters to 256 columns using a 26-letter alphabet? To accommodate all the columns, Excel doubles up on the letters after Z. So, after Z comes AA, AB, AC, and so on up to AZ; after AZ comes BA, BB, BC, and so on up to BZ; and the column letters continue in this manner, all the way through the letter I, up to IV, giving each and every column a unique single- or double-letter designation. Cell addresses become very important when you begin to enter formulas and functions, as explained in the following section.

Excel can also reference entire blocks of cells (called *ranges*) by using the address of the cell in the upper-left corner of the block, followed by a colon and the address of the cell in the lower right corner. For example, the reference for the range highlighted in Figure 1.8 would be B3:E9.

**FIGURE 1.8**

Excel can reference an entire range of cells.

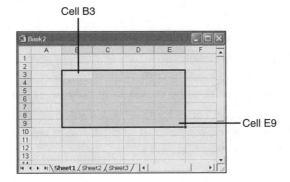

Using addresses, Excel can even keep track of cells on other worksheets. To reference a cell on another worksheet in the same workbook, Excel uses the worksheet name, followed by an exclamation point, followed by the cell address. For example, the address of cell H9 on Sheet3 would be Sheet3!H9.

# Understanding Formulas and Functions

The major difference between a checkbook register and an Excel worksheet is that a worksheet can calculate the new balance for you and perform countless other mathematical calculations through the use of formulas and functions. Excel uses formulas to perform addition, subtraction, multiplication, and division on the entries in a worksheet to determine totals, grand totals, percentages, and other practical results. Figure 1.9 shows a sample formula in action. This simple formula totals the values in cells B4 to E4.

Formula, as typed in cell F4

**FIGURE 1.9**

Formulas automate calculations in a worksheet.

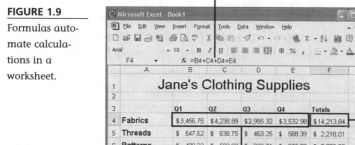

Formula calculates and displays total

Formula totals these values

The following are some helpful facts about formulas that should help you understand how formulas operate in a worksheet:

- You enter a formula in the cell in which you want the *result* to appear. Excel performs the specified calculation and then displays the result in this cell.

- All formulas start with an equal sign (=). If you start a formula with a letter, Excel assumes you are entering a label. If the formula begins with a number, Excel interprets the entry as a value.

- Formulas typically include cell addresses that reference values contained in other cells in the worksheet. For example, the formula =B4+C4+D4+E4 calculates the total of the values contained in cells B4, C4, D4, and E4.

- Formulas can also include numbers. For example, if a spreadsheet displays your monthly income in cell H10, and you want to calculate your annual income, you can enter the formula =H10*12, which tells Excel to multiply the value in cell H10 by 12.

- Formulas use the following symbols, called *arithmetic operators*:

  + Addition

  – Subtraction

  * Multiplication

  / Division

  ^ Raise to the ___ power of

  % Percentage

- Excel follows the standard order of operations for calculating equations, performing all multiplication and division first and then addition and subtraction. You can control the order of operations by using parentheses to group the operations you want Excel to perform first. For example, to determine the average of the values in cells B4, C4, D4, and E4, you would enter the formula =(B4+C4+D4+E4)/4. This forces Excel to perform addition before division. See "Learning the Order of Operations" in Chapter 6, "Automating Calculations with Formulas and Functions," for details.

- A formula automatically re-calculates its result whenever you change a value in one of the cells that the formula references. For example, if a cell contains the formula =B4+C4+D4+E4, and you change the value in cell D4, Excel automatically re-calculates the result and displays it in the cell that contains the formula.

Functions can be a little more complex than formulas, but functions act as a sort of mathematical shorthand. For example, the function AVERAGE can calculate the average of a range of numbers without requiring you to enter the cell address of every value you want included in the average. In the preceding example, for instance, you could save time by using the AVERAGE function: Rather than type **=(B4+C4+D4+E4)/4**, you could simply enter **=AVERAGE(B4:E4)**.

Excel features a wide selection of functions, most of which are more complex than the AVERAGE function. Excel has functions designed specifically for financial calculations, engineering applications, statistics, and much more. Figure 1.10 shows a financial function in action. This function determines the monthly payment for a loan, based on the loan amount, the term of the loan, and the interest rate.

Every function consists of the function itself followed by an *argument*. The argument consists of the values that the function uses to calculate the result and must be entered in the proper *syntax* (order). In Figure 1.10, for instance, the worksheet uses the function =PMT(rate,nper,pv,fv), where PMT is the function used to determine the payment due on a loan, rate is the interest rate, nper is the number of payment periods, pv is the present value of the loan, and fv is the future value of the loan (which is zero, when it is finally paid off). (In the argument (rate,nper,pv,fv), rate, nper, pv, and fv are merely placeholders. When you type the argument, you use cell addresses or actual values in place of the placeholders.)

Function as entered in cell

**FIGURE 1.10**

Functions can perform advanced calculations on the values in a worksheet.

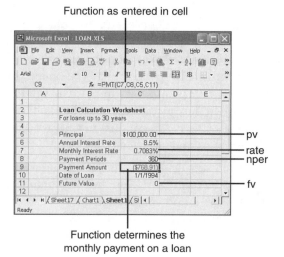

pv
rate
nper
fv

Function determines the
monthly payment on a loan

Fortunately, you don't need to learn and memorize the functions to use them effectively. Excel comes equipped with the Function Wizard, which leads you step-by-step through the process of choosing the function you need and then selecting the cells that make up the argument. Figure 1.11 shows the Function Wizard in action.

**FIGURE 1.11**

Excel's Function Wizard simplifies the process of entering functions.

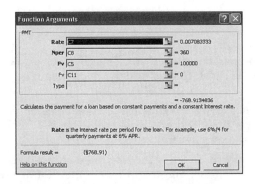

# Making Data Graphical with Charts

When most people look at a page of numbers, they see abstract values. To give that data meaning and make it more understandable, Excel provides tools for charting (graphing) the data. Charts provide a way to transform your data into a picture that more effectively illustrates the significance of the data. For example, a bar chart is commonly used to illustrate how profits have grown or shrunk over time. A non-profit organization might use a pie chart to illustrate how much money is allocated to each of its various programs. Or you might use a line chart to examine how your investments have performed over the last 12 months.

Excel features a wide selection of chart types to help display data in various ways. The type you choose depends on the data you are charting and how you want that data presented. Table 1.1 lists Excel's most common chart types, along with a description of each type. Figure 1.12 shows the most common chart types in action. (Excel features some less common chart types, as well, including surface charts, radar charts, and bubble charts, not listed in the table.)

## **TABLE 1.1**  Common Excel Chart Types

| Chart Type | Description |
| --- | --- |
| Bar | A chart consisting of horizontal rectangles of varying lengths. Bar charts are useful for comparing values at a given point in time, such as the total monthly sales at three different stores. |
| Column | A chart consisting of vertical rectangles of varying heights. Bar charts are commonly used to compare values as they change over time, but can be used in place of bar charts. |
| Pie | A round chart that shows values as slices of a pie. Pie charts are useful for illustrating the relationship between parts of a whole, such as where various percentages of your paycheck are spent. |

**TABLE 1.1**   (continued)

| Chart Type | Description |
| --- | --- |
| Doughnut | A pie chart with the middle scooped out. This chart looks like a doughnut and is used, like a pie chart, to illustrate the relationship between parts of a whole. |
| Line | A chart that looks like a connect-the-dots picture. Line charts illustrate changing values over time. You might use a line chart to plot the growing value of your portfolio over several years. |
| Area | A line chart that's colored in below the line. Area charts illustrate the amount of change over time, and might look somewhat like sand drifts. |
| XY Scatter | Plots two or more sets of data as collections of dots on a graph to compare the distribution of the data sets. |
| Stock | Displays the high, low, and close price of stocks in a given day. |

**FIGURE 1.12**

Excel features several different chart types.

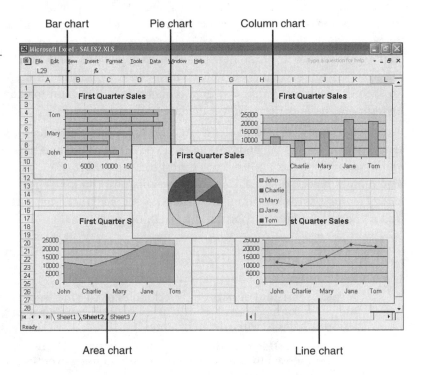

Bar chart   Pie chart   Column chart

Area chart   Line chart

Excel has three-dimensional versions of most of the basic chart types. For instance, the bars in bar charts can be made to look like blocks rather than flat rectangles. This 3D look can make a great impact in reports and presentations.

At first, you might think that charting data would be a complicated task, but Excel actually features a Chart Wizard that greatly simplifies the process. All you need to do is select the cells that contain the data you want to chart, start the Chart Wizard, and follow its instructions. The Chart Wizard leads you step-by-step through the process, prompting you to select the desired chart type and enter any other preferences you have. After you have answered all the Wizard's questions, it creates the chart according to your specifications. You can then tweak the chart as desired to further customize it. All this and more is explained in greater detail in Chapter 8, "Charting (Graphing) the Worksheet Data."

> **tip**
>
> If you use PowerPoint to create presentations, you can copy charts from Excel and paste them on slides in your PowerPoint presentation.

# The Absolute Minimum

In this chapter, you learned all the basic concepts and terminology required to start working with Excel worksheets. Congratulations! You now have a solid understanding of how worksheets are structured, what they do, and how they do it.

- You know that worksheets consist of columns and rows that intersect to form cells.

- You know that you can type text, values, or formulas into cells to create a functional worksheet.

- You know that you can chart your data to make it more graphical with Excel's Chart Wizard.

At this point, you also have a clear picture of how Excel uses cell addresses to determine the location of cells and how Excel uses cell addresses in its formulas and functions. Of course you're not ready to start entering formulas and functions, but with the knowledge you have at this point, you're way ahead of the game and well prepared to get some hands-on experience with Excel in the next chapter.

IN THIS CHAPTER

- Starting Excel for the first time.
- Navigating the Excel program window.
- Understanding the parts of the workbook window.
- Using Excel's menus, dialog boxes, and toolbars.
- Entering preferences in Excel's task panes.
- Obtaining help while working with an Excel worksheet.

# 2

# STARTING AND NAVIGATING EXCEL

# Starting Excel

During its installation, Excel places its name on the Windows Start, Programs menu or the Start, All Programs menu, depending on which version of Windows you are running. To start Excel, you select its name from the menu. When you are ready to start Excel, take the following steps:

1. Click the Windows **Start** button. The Start button is located in the lower left corner of the Windows screen, as shown in Figure 2.1. The Start menu opens.

2. Point to **All Programs** or **Programs**. The name of this menu varies depending on the version of Windows that is installed on your computer.

3. Click **Microsoft Excel**.

**note**

In Windows XP, when you first run a program, Windows places a shortcut for the program directly on the Start menu, so you don't need to open the All Programs submenu next time.

**FIGURE 2.1**

You can select Excel from the Windows Start, All Programs menu.

Click Start

Point to All Programs

Click Microsoft Excel

If you have Excel as a part of the Microsoft Office collection of programs, you may be able to use the Microsoft Office Shortcut bar to run Excel. This bar contains buttons for each Office program installed on your computer. To determine whether the Microsoft Office Shortcut bar is installed and to turn it on if it is installed, take the following steps:

1. Click the Windows **Start** button. The Start menu opens.

2. Point to **All Programs** or **Programs**. The All Programs or Programs submenu opens.

3. Point to **Microsoft Office Tools**. The Microsoft Office Tools submenu opens, as shown in Figure 2.2.

4. Click **Microsoft Office Shortcut Bar**. If this option is not displayed, the Shortcut bar is not installed on your computer.

> ## tip
>
> You can easily create a shortcut icon for running Excel from the Windows desktop (the opening screen that your computer displays on startup). Click the **Start** button, point to **All Programs** or **Programs**, and then use your right mouse button to click **Microsoft Excel**. This opens a *context menu*, which displays commonly chosen commands for this object. Point to **Send To**, and then click **Desktop (create shortcut)**. Now you can run Excel by double-clicking its icon on the Windows desktop.

Microsoft Office Tools submenu

**FIGURE 2.2**

You can turn on the Microsoft Office Shortcut bar for quick access to your Office applications.

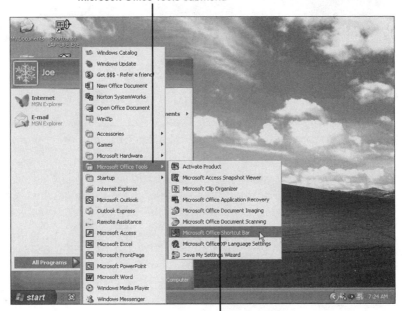

Click Microsoft Office Shortcut Bar

Assuming the Microsoft Office Shortcut Bar option is available and you selected it, the Shortcut bar pops up on your screen, typically at the top or on the right side of the screen, as shown in Figure 2.3. To run Excel, simply click its button in the Shortcut bar. (If the Shortcut Bar is not installed, insert the Microsoft Office or Excel CD into your computer's CD drive and follow the installation instructions to install the Shortcut Bar.)

**FIGURE 2.3**

The Microsoft Office Shortcut Bar displays a button for each installed Office application.

Click the Microsoft Excel button

# Touring Excel's Program Window

Whichever way you choose to run Excel, when Excel starts it displays a program window like the window shown in Figure 2.4. This window contains the following components:

- **Title bar** at the very top of the window displays the name of the program followed by a dash and the name of the workbook, which Excel refers to as Book1, until you name and save the workbook. On the far right of the title bar are three buttons that give you control over the window: the Minimize, Maximize/Restore, and Close buttons. The following section, "Maximizing, Minimizing, and Restoring Windows," explains how to use these buttons.

- **Menu bar** just below the title bar displays the names of Excel's menus. When you click a menu's name, the menu opens, revealing available options. You can then click the desired option, as explained later in this chapter in the section "Selecting Commands from Menus." At the right end of the menu bar is the Ask a Question box. To get help, click in this box, type your question, and press the Enter key. See "Getting Help," later in this chapter, for details.

- **Toolbars** appear below the menu bar. Initially, two toolbars appear: the Standard toolbar and the Formatting toolbar. Toolbars provide buttons for commonly entered commands, enabling you to bypass the somewhat clunky menu system. You learn how to turn on additional toolbars later in this chapter in the section "Turning on Other Toolbars."

- **Workbook window** is where Excel displays the actual workbook, complete with columns, rows, and cells. This is where you will begin to type entries. You learn more about this window later in this chapter in the section "Touring Excel's Workbook Window."

- **Formula bar** just above the workbook window contains the *name* box, which displays the address of the currently selected cell or range of cells, and the *formula bar*, which displays the contents of the selected cell. When you begin to type an entry in a cell, two buttons appear to the left of the formula bar: one with a red X on it and the other with a green check mark. You can click the X to cancel (erase) the entry or click the check mark to accept it.

- **Task pane** is a new feature in Excel 2002 and all other Microsoft Office applications. Initially, Excel displays the New Workbook task pane, which enables you to open a workbook you previously worked on or create a new workbook from scratch or by using a template. However, the task pane automatically changes whenever you perform certain tasks. If you enter the command for inserting a clip art image, for instance, the Clip Art task pane appears, providing you with the controls you need to choose an image. You can close the task pane at any time by clicking the X button in the upper right corner of the pane.

- **Status bar** at the bottom of the window displays information about the current activity, including helpful information and keyboard and program modes. For example, if you press the Scroll Lock key on your keyboard, SCRL appears in the status bar.

Title bar    Formula bar    Menu bar    Toolbars

FIGURE 2.4

**FIGURE 2.4**

When you start
Excel, the Excel
program window
appears.

Workbook
window

Status bar

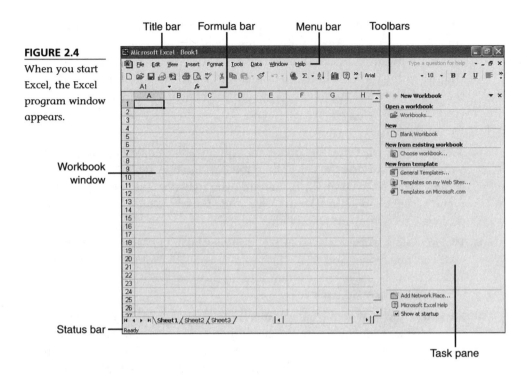

Task pane

## Maximizing, Minimizing, and Restoring Windows

In the upper-right corner of every window are three buttons that give you control
over the size of the window: the Minimize button, the Maximize/Restore button, and
the Close button. The following list provides a brief description of each button.

The Minimize button makes the
window disappear. To bring the
window back into view, click its button in
the Windows taskbar (at the bottom of the
Windows desktop).

The Maximize button makes the
window as large as it can be—full
screen. After you click the Maximize button, it transforms itself into the Restore
button, described next.

When a window is not
maximized, you can drag its
title bar to move it. You cannot
move a maximized window.

The Restore button changes the window back to whatever size it was before you clicked the Maximize button.

The Close button closes the window. If you click the Close button for a workbook window, Excel closes the workbook. If you click the Close button for Excel's program window, Excel shuts down, removing itself from the screen.

Examine the upper right corner of Excel closely, and you should see that Excel has two sets of buttons for controlling its windows, as shown in Figure 2.5: a set for the program window (Excel's window) and a set for the workbook window (called the document window). The document window is actually a window inside Excel's program window. Most applications have this feature, so you can have two or more documents open at the same time in a single application.

**FIGURE 2.5**

Excel has two sets of window-control buttons.

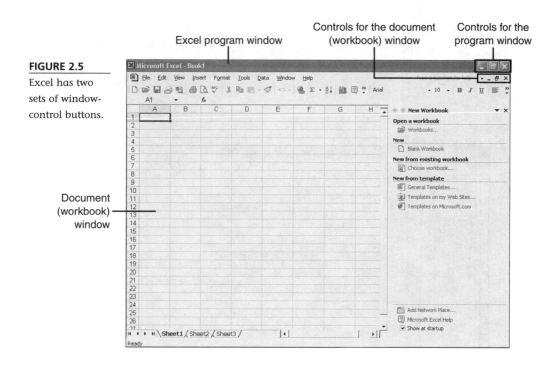

## Resizing Windows

Though the window control buttons give you single-click control over a window's size, they do not enable you to set a custom size. To manually adjust the size of a window, first you must make sure that the window is *not* maximized; you cannot change the size of a maximized window. If the Restore button is displayed, the window is maximized, so click the Restore button to de-maximize the window.

After the window is de-maximized, move the mouse pointer over the lower-right corner of the window so that the mouse pointer turns into a double-headed arrow. Hold down the left mouse button and drag the corner of the window until the window is the desired size and dimensions, as shown in Figure 2.6. You can also drag the window's right or bottom border to change only one dimension of the window.

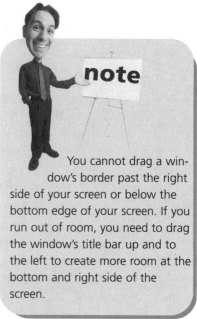

**note**

You cannot drag a window's border past the right side of your screen or below the bottom edge of your screen. If you run out of room, you need to drag the window's title bar up and to the left to create more room at the bottom and right side of the screen.

**FIGURE 2.6**

You can control the size and dimensions of Excel's program window.

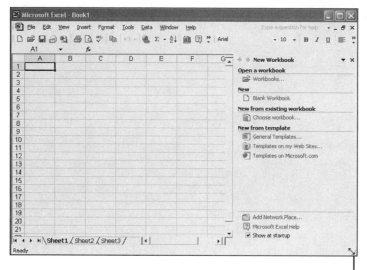

Drag this corner to resize the window

# Touring Excel's Workbook Window

Inside the Excel program window is a workbook window that displays the current worksheet in front. In this window, you enter the labels, values, and formulas that make up each worksheet. Figure 2.7 illustrates the various components of the workbook window. Table 2.1 lists and describes each component.

**TABLE 2.1** Workbook Window Components

| Component Name | Purpose |
| --- | --- |
| Tabs | Provide a way to switch from one worksheet to another. Click the tab for the desired worksheet. |
| Tab scrolling buttons | Enable you to scroll through the worksheets in a workbook. |
| Scroll bars | Enable you to bring into view a section of the current worksheet that is not displayed. |
| Column headings | Identify the columns by letter. |
| Row headings | Identify the rows by number. |
| Selector | Outlines the currently selected cell. |
| Split bars | Split the worksheet window into two panes so you can view two different portions of the same worksheet. |

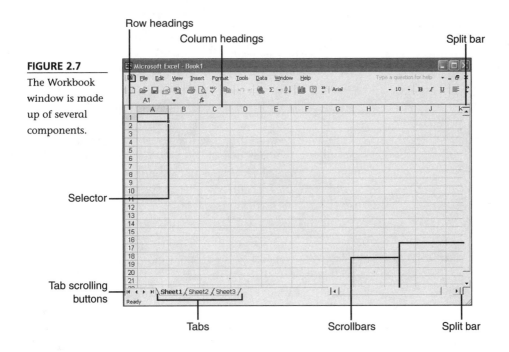

**FIGURE 2.7**

The Workbook window is made up of several components.

# Using the Toolbars

Below Excel's menu bar are two toolbars that place the most common commands right at your fingertips: the Standard toolbar and the Formatting toolbar. Instead of searching through Excel's menus and submenus to locate commands, you can save time by learning the buttons first. The following sections can help you identify the buttons on the Standard and Formatting toolbars when you're first starting to learn them.

> **tip**
>
> To view the name of a button in one of the toolbars, rest the mouse pointer (no clicking) on the button for a second or two. A tiny box called a *ScreenTip* appears, displaying the button's name.

## Exploring the Standard Toolbar

The Standard toolbar contains buttons (called *tools*) for general commands, such as commands for creating and saving a workbook, printing the current workbook, and copying and pasting selections. Table 2.2 lists the buttons and explains the purpose of each tool.

**TABLE 2.2**   Standard Toolbar Buttons

| Button | Tool Name | Purpose |
|---|---|---|
| | New | Displays the New Workbook task pane, so you can start a new project. |
| | Open | Opens an existing workbook file. |
| | Save | Saves the currently open workbook to a disk. |
| | Email | Displays an email message header, so you can send the workbook to someone else via email. |
| | Search | Displays the Search task pane, enabling you to search your computer for a particular file or search the current workbook for a specific data entry. |
| | Print | Prints the current worksheet, workbook, or chart. |
| | Print Preview | Displays a version of the worksheet or workbook or chart as it will appear in print. |
| | Spell Check | Checks for typos and spelling errors in the current workbook. |

| Button | Tool Name | Purpose |
|---|---|---|
| | Cut | Moves the selected data to the clipboard, from which you can paste the data somewhere else. |
| | Copy | Places a copy of the selected data on the clipboard, so you can paste a copy of the data somewhere else. |
| | Paste | Inserts the current contents of the clipboard into the selected cell or cells. |
| | Format Painter | Copies the formatting of the selected cell or cells, so you can apply the formatting to other cells. |
| | Undo | Reverses your last action. |
| | Redo | Reinstates the previous action you chose to undo. |
| | Insert Hyperlink | Inserts a hyperlink (live link) to another file or to a Web page. |
| | AutoSum | Calculates the total of the values in the currently selected cells. Also provides averages or a count of entries in the cells. |
| | Sort Ascending | Arranges the entries in a selection alphabetically from A to Z, or numerically from the smallest number to the highest. |
| | Sort Descending | Arranges the entries in a selection alphabetically from Z to A, or numerically from the highest number to the smallest. |
| | ChartWizard | Starts the ChartWizard, which leads you step by step through the process of creating a chart. |
| | Drawing | Toggles the Drawing toolbar on and off. The Drawing toolbar features additional buttons for adding basic shapes to your worksheets and charts. |
| 100% | Zoom | Adjusts the screen magnification. |
| | Microsoft Excel Help | Displays Excel's Help window on the right side of the screen, so you can get assistance or answers to your questions. |
| | Toolbar Options | Displays additional buttons that do not fit on the toolbar as it is currently displayed, and provides options for adding or removing buttons from the toolbar or displaying the toolbars in such a way that more buttons are visible. |

## Exploring the Formatting Toolbar

The Formatting toolbar contains buttons for changing the appearance of a selection; for example, you can use the Formatting toolbar to change the text style and size, add borders and shading to cells, and make numbers appear as dollar amounts. Table 2.3 lists the Formatting buttons and provides a brief description of each tool.

**TABLE 2.3**   Formatting Toolbar Buttons

| Button | Tool Name | Purpose |
| --- | --- | --- |
| Arial | Font | Lets you pick a different type style for the selected cells. |
| 10 | Font size | Changes the text size of selected cells. |
| B | Bold | Boldfaces entries in the selected cells. |
| I | Italic | Italicizes entries in the selected cells. |
| U | Underline | Underlines entries in the selected cells. |
| ≣ | Align Left | Aligns entries along the left side of selected cells. |
| ≣ | Center | Centers entries in the selected cells. |
| ≣ | Align Right | Aligns entries with the right side of selected cells. |
| ⊞ | Merge and Center | Merges the selected cells to create a single cell and then centers the entry in that cell. |
| $ | Currency Style | Displays numerical values as dollar amounts. |
| % | Percent Style | Displays numerical values as percentages. |
| , | Comma Style | Adds a comma to values of 1000 and above. |
| +.0 .00 | Increase Decimal | Adds decimal places to values in selected cells. |
| .00 +.0 | Decrease Decimal | Removes decimal places from values in selected cells. |
| ⊑ | Decrease Indent | Reduces the distance that entries are indented in selected cells by the width of one typewritten character in the standard font (Arial 10-point by default). |

| Button | Tool Name | Purpose |
|---|---|---|
| | Increase Indent | Increases the distance that entries are indented in selected cells by the width of one typewritten character in the standard font (Arial 10-point by default). |
| | Borders | Adds the specified border type to selected cells. |
| | Fill Color | Shades selected cells with the specified gray shade or color. |
| | Font Color | Transforms text in selected cells from black to the specified color. |
| | Toolbar Options | Displays additional buttons that do not fit on the toolbar as it is currently displayed, and provides options for adding or removing buttons from the toolbar or displaying the toolbars in such a way that more buttons are visible. |

## Taking Control of the Toolbars

Excel is initially set up to display both the Standard and Formatting toolbars on a single line, giving the workbook window more room. Unfortunately, this limits the number of buttons each toolbar can display. To access a button that is not displayed on one of the toolbars, you must click the Toolbar Options button. This opens a tiny palette with the remaining buttons and you can click the desired button. When you click a button on the Toolbar Options palette, Excel moves the button to the main toolbar area, making it more accessible in the future.

You can customize the toolbars for the way you work. You can move a toolbar to its own separate line, for instance, to provide it with more room for displaying buttons. Note that at the left side of a docked toolbar (one that's nested at the top of a program window) is a light gray vertical bar. This bar is called the *move handle*. Move the mouse pointer over the move handle until the mouse pointer appears as a four-headed arrow, as shown in Figure 2.8. Now hold down the left mouse button and drag the toolbar up or down to the desired position.

## tip

The Excel program window has four toolbar docking areas: just below the menu bar, on the left side of the window, on the right side of the window, and just above the status bar. Try dragging a toolbar to one of these locations.

By dragging one toolbar directly below another and then dropping it in place, you can position both toolbars in the *docking area*, each on a line of its own. (The docking area is any location where a toolbar can "snap" in place.) If you move the toolbar beyond the docking area, it becomes a *floating toolbar*, which acts as though it lives in its own window. Floating toolbars tend to get in the way, so most users prefer keeping them docked.

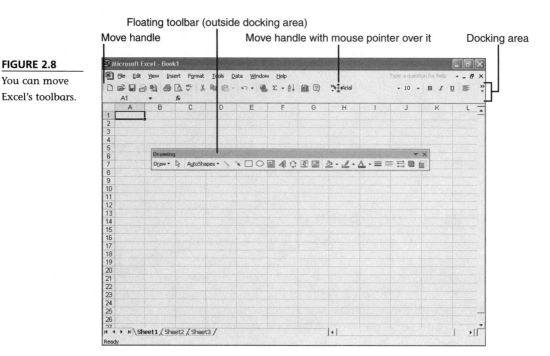

Floating toolbar (outside docking area)

Move handle          Move handle with mouse pointer over it        Docking area

**FIGURE 2.8**

You can move Excel's toolbars.

## Turning on Other Toolbars

Though the Standard and Formatting toolbars provide most of the tools you need on a daily basis, Excel provides more than a dozen other toolbars for special tasks. These include the Borders, Chart, Drawing, Picture, Web, and Word Art toolbars. To turn a toolbar on or off, perform one of the following steps:

- Open the **View** menu, point to **Toolbars**, and click the name of the desired toolbar. (A check mark next to a toolbar's name indicates it is on.)

- Right-click any toolbar or the menu bar and then click the name of the desired toolbar.

- If the toolbar is a floating toolbar, click its Close (X) button.

# Selecting Commands from Menus

Although toolbars provide the most convenient access to commands, they do not supply buttons for every Excel command. Excel's menus, however, provide a complete selection. To enter a command from one of the menus, click the name of the desired menu and then click the desired command, as shown in Figure 2.9. For example, to print a worksheet, workbook, or chart, you would click **File** in the menu bar and then click **Print**.

Click the name of the desired menu

**FIGURE 2.9**

Enter commands by selecting them from pull-down menus.

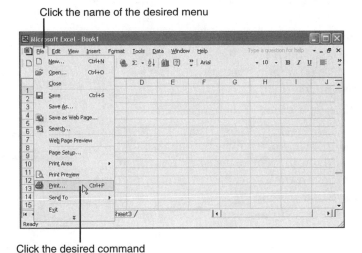

Click the desired command

That seems straightforward enough, but menus do exhibit a few quirks that can be a little confusing at first. To ease the transition, read through the following list of menu hints and techniques:

- A command you're looking for may not appear on the main menu; some are listed on submenus. In such a case, rest the mouse pointer on the submenu's name to open it, and then click the desired command. You can tell whether a menu item represents a submenu if the item's name is followed by a right-pointing arrow.

- Excel features *Smart Menus*, a Microsoft innovation that hides all but the most commonly used menu commands. If you open a menu and don't see the command you expected, click the double-headed arrow at the bottom of the menu to see additional commands. (After you select a particular command for the first time, Excel "remembers" the command you chose and displays it on the main menu the next time you open the menu.)

- Commands that appear light gray are not available. If you open the Edit menu, for instance, and you have not yet chosen to copy or cut a selection, the Paste command appears gray, because Excel has nothing to paste.

- A command that is followed by ellipses (…) displays a *dialog box*, which prompts you to provide additional details. When you open the File menu and click Print, for instance, Excel displays the Print dialog box, which prompts you to specify the pages you want to print, the number of copies, and so on.

- Many of the most common commands have shortcut keystrokes assigned to them that enable you to enter commands quickly by pressing a key combination. You can save a workbook, for instance, by pressing Ctrl+S—holding down the Ctrl key while pressing the S key. To help you learn these timesaving keystrokes, Excel displays the keystrokes on the menus.

**tip**

You can open a menu by holding down the Alt key while typing the underlined letter in the menu's name. You can then move from one menu to the next by using the left and right arrow keys. To select a command from an open menu, type the underlined letter in the command's name or use the up or down arrow key to select the command and press **Enter**.

Excel employs another clever device for enabling you to select commands from menus: *context-sensitive* menus. These menus are called context-sensitive because the commands that each menu contains relate only to the selected object. For example, if you right-click one of Excel's toolbars, the menu that appears provides a list of options for turning specific toolbars on or off. (See Figure 2.10.) These menus remain hidden. To bring a particular context menu into view, simply right-click the desired object—a selection of cells, a chart, a piece of clip art, or some other object.

Click the desired command

Right-click an object

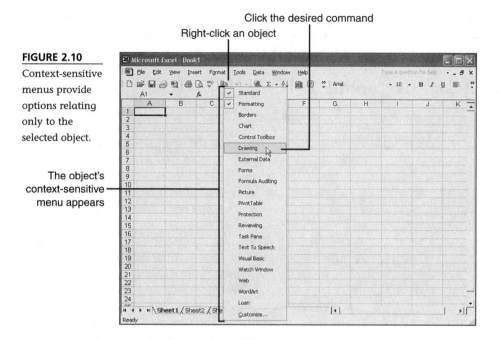

**FIGURE 2.10**

Context-sensitive menus provide options relating only to the selected object.

The object's context-sensitive menu appears

# Making Selections in Dialog Boxes

Excel executes many commands as soon as you enter them. If you choose to cut data, Excel instantly removes it from the workbook. For some commands, however, Excel requires additional input from you. If you open the File menu and select Save As, for instance, Excel displays the Save As dialog box, as shown in Figure 2.11, asking you to type a name for the workbook and specify the disk drive and folder in which you want it saved.

**FIGURE 2.11**

Dialog boxes request additional information.

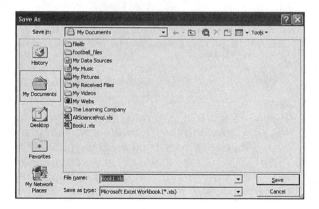

To respond successfully to a dialog box, you should know the various controls they contain. Table 2.4 lists the types of controls typically found in dialog boxes, along with a brief explanation of each control's purpose.

**TABLE 2.4** Dialog Box Controls

| Control | Control Type | What It Does |
| --- | --- | --- |
| View \| Calculation | Tabs | Enables a single dialog box to have two or more sets of options. Click a tab to change from one set of options to another. |
| | Text box | Acts as a fill-in-the-blank box, enabling you to type a specific entry, such as a file name. |
| None | Option buttons | Provide a user with a group of options, only one of which can be chosen. Choosing one option in a group deselects all other options in that group. |
| Gridlines | Check boxes | Provide a user with a group of options from which the user can select none, some, or all options in the group. |
| File, Edit, View, Insert, Format, Tools, Data, Window and Help, Drawing, AutoShapes | List box | Presents a list of options or preferences, only one of which the user can choose. |
| Automatic | Drop-down list | Presents a hidden list of options from which a user can choose only one item. To view the items in a drop-down list, you click a downward-pointing arrow to the right of the list. This opens the list, like a menu. |
| 10 minutes | Spin box | Offers values or settings that you can change incrementally by clicking the up or down arrow to the left of the box. In some cases, you can click inside the spin box and type an entry. |
| OK | Command button | Provides a way for executing or cancel-ing the dialog box. Most dialog boxes have three command buttons: OK to confirm, Cancel to quit, and Help to get more information. |

# Maneuvering in Excel's Task Panes

In Excel 2002, Microsoft introduced *task panes* to place even more controls within easy reach. Task panes appear alongside the workbook window and help you do everything from opening workbooks and searching for files to inserting clip art and managing the clipboard. If no task pane is displayed, open the **View** menu and click **Task Pane** to turn on a task pane. Excel features four task panes:

- **New Workbook** appears whenever you start Excel. It displays a list of the four workbooks you most recently opened and displays commands for opening a workbook, creating a new blank workbook, creating a workbook from an existing workbook, and creating a workbook from a template.

- **Clipboard** displays a list of items you recently cut or copied, so you can choose what you want to paste.

- **Search** provides a form you can fill out to search for a file by name.

- **Insert Clip Art** displays a form you can use to find a particular clip art image. For example, you might want to add a picture to a worksheet to make it more graphically appealing.

A task pane is a cross between a dialog box and a Web page (on the Internet). Task panes contain text boxes, command buttons, lists, and other controls that are very similar to those you find in dialog boxes. They also contain hyperlinks (which appear as blue text entries) that call up other features and dialog boxes. When you move the mouse pointer over a hyperlink, the mouse pointer transforms into a pointing-hand icon, and you can click the hyperlink to execute it.

In the upper-right corner of each task pane are two buttons, as shown in Figure 2.12: the Close (X) button, for closing the task pane, and the Other Task Panes button (the button with the downward pointing arrow on it), which displays a menu that lists the other three task panes. In the upper left corner of the task pane is a Back button, which you can click to view the previous task pane, and the Forward button, which you can click to view the next task pane.

> **note**
>
> The task pane's Back button becomes functional only after you pick a different task pane; then you can back up to the previous pane. The Forward button becomes functional only after you back up to a previous task pane.

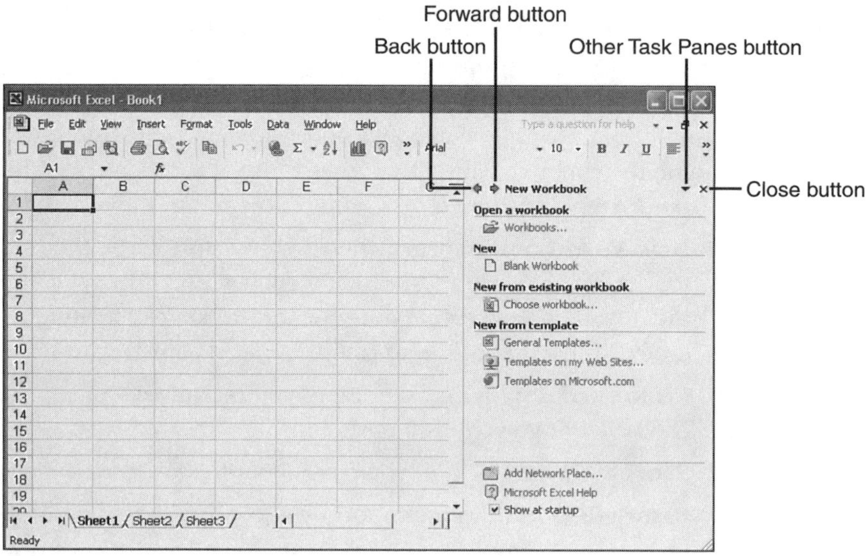

Forward button

Back button · Other Task Panes button

**FIGURE 2.12**

The task pane title bar displays buttons for controlling the task panes.

Close button

# Getting Help

In Excel 2002, help is just a click away. On the far right end of Excel's menu bar is the Ask A Question box (the box that contains the text "Type a question for help"), where you can type a question or one or two key words to quickly track down the help you need. Whenever you need help, take the following steps to ask your question:

1. Click in the Ask a Question box.

2. Type one or more words to describe what you're trying to do or what you would like to learn more about.

3. Press **Enter**. This opens a menu with several topics that match your search entry, as shown in Figure 2.13.

4. Click the desired topic. This opens Excel's Help window, which typically displays several links on topics that match your search entry.

5. Click a link for the specific help you need. (See the next section, "Navigating Excel's Help System," for details.) Excel's Help window displays the requested information, as shown in Figure 2.14.

**FIGURE 2.13**
Use the Ask a
Question box to
get help.

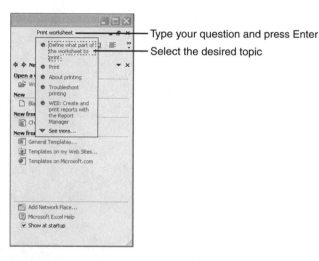

Type your question and press Enter

Select the desired topic

**FIGURE 2.14**
Excel's Help win-
dow provides
answers to your
questions.

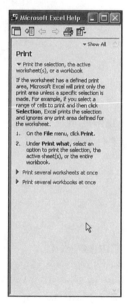

## Navigating Excel's Help System

You can access Excel's help system at any time by asking a question, as explained in
the previous section, or by opening Excel's Help menu and clicking Microsoft Excel
Help, or by pressing the F1 key on your keyboard. Whichever method you employ,
Excel displays help in a separate window on the right side of the screen and automatically scoots Excel's program window to the left to make room. This places the

program window and the Help window side by side, so you can continue working while viewing the help system's instructions.

Near the top of the Help window are several buttons that control the size and orientation of the Help window, enable you to print helpful information and instructions, and let you set preferences. The following list describes these buttons:

**Auto Tile/Untile** automatically resizes the program and helps windows to keep them side by side. Use this button to turn Auto Tile on and off.

**Show/Hide** displays or hides the Help window's left pane, which provides tabs for accessing the Help system's Contents, Answer Wizard, and Index.

**Back** displays the previous help screen, if you advanced from one help screen to another.

**Forward** displays the next help screen, if you backed up to a previous help screen.

**Print** prints the currently displayed information or instructions.

**Options** opens a menu that contains the Show Tabs option, the Back and Forward options, and other options that control how the Help system functions.

**note**

If you press F1 or open the Help menu and choose Microsoft Excel Help, and an animated character appears onscreen—instead of the Help window—the Office Assistant is activated. See "Obtaining Context-Sensitive Help," later in this chapter, to learn how to use the Office Assistant and how to disable it, if it becomes *too* helpful.

Excel's help system provides three different ways for you to find help. You simply click the tab for the type of help you want (Contents, Answer Wizard, or Index) and then use the controls on that tab to search for specific topics. (If the tabs are not displayed, click the Show button as explained earlier.) The following list explains the three tabs and three different ways you can search for help:

■ **Contents** displays a table of contents for using Excel, as shown in Figure 2.15. (If the table of contents does not appear, click the plus sign next to Microsoft Excel Help to expand the list.) Click the plus sign next to a topic to display a list of subtopics. Continue clicking plus signs until you find the desired topic, and then click the topic's name. The right pane displays information relating to the topic. (When you expand a topic list by clicking a plus sign, a minus sign appears next to the topic. Click the minus sign to hide the subtopic list.)

- **Answer Wizard** works just like the Ask a Question box. In the **What would you like to do?** box, type your question or one or more key words that describe the desired topic and click the **Search** button (or press **Enter**). Under **Select Topic to Display**, the Answer Wizard displays a list of topics that match your search text. Click the topic that best describes the help you need. Related information or instructions appear in the right pane.

**tip**

The right pane often appears too skinny to display information. To change the relative sizes of the left and right panes, use your mouse to drag the bar that separates them.

- **Index** provides a searchable index of Excel help topics. In the **Type Keywords** text box, type a few letters of the topic for which you're looking. As you type, the list of keywords scrolls down to show topics whose names match what you have typed so far. Double-click the desired keyword. Scroll down the **Choose a Topic** list and double-click the desired topic.

Information and instructions appear here

**FIGURE 2.15**

Excel Help's Contents tab displays a complete table of contents for the help system.

Click a plus sign to view subtopic

Click the desired topic

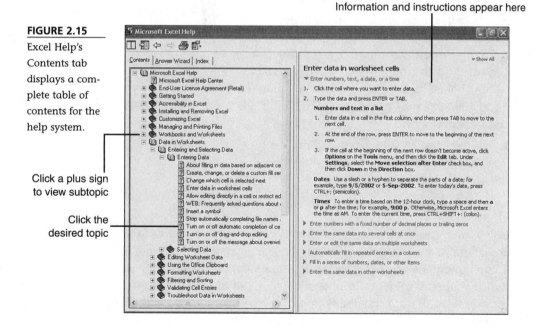

If you're lucky, the first help screen you see provides the help you need. In most cases, however, you need to probe a little further. Many help screens display a bulleted list of topics, with the bullets appearing as downward-pointing triangles. You must click the bullet or the topic's name to expand the information below the bullet. Some help screens contain links to other related topics, as well. These links typically appear as blue text; when you position the mouse pointer over a link, the pointer transforms into a pointing-hand icon, and the topic's name appears underlined. Click the topic to display its information.

If you probe too deep into the help system and want to go back to a previous screen, click the Back button, near the top of the Help window.

## Viewing ScreenTips

Toolbar buttons and other objects can seem as cryptic as Egyptian hieroglyphics to a novice user. To help, Excel features screen tips that pop up whenever you rest the mouse pointer on an object. ScreenTips appear in their own tiny boxes and display the name of the selected object. See Figure 2.16.

## Obtaining Context-Sensitive Help

Excel's help system features an animated tutor, called Clippit, who can help answer your questions. In previous versions of Excel, Clippit was a central character, popping up whenever you needed help, and sometimes when you didn't. In Excel 2002, Microsoft chose to make Clippit a little less intrusive.

> **tip**
>
> To view information about any object on the screen, open the **Help** menu and choose **What's This?** or press **Shift+F1**. A question mark appears next to the mouse pointer, indicating you can now click on an object to learn more about it. Click the desired object.

If you feel comforted by having Clippit on hand, you can activate this Office Assistant by performing the following steps:

1. Open the **Help** menu.
2. Click **Show the Office Assistant**. Clippit pops up.

As you work in Excel, Clippit occasionally asks whether you need help performing a task. Simply give your okay, and Clippit jumps in to lend a hand. You can also ask Clippit questions whenever you want. Click Clippit, type your question, and press **Enter**. Clippit displays a list of possible topics of interest, just as if you had used the Answer Wizard. Click the desired topic. To make Clippit go away, right-click Clippit and choose **Hide**. To bring him back, press the **F1** key.

ScreenTip

**FIGURE 2.16**

Rest the mouse pointer on an object to view its ScreenTip.

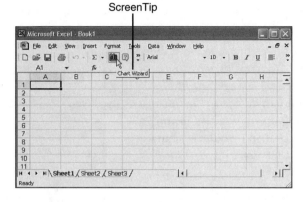

**FIGURE 2.17**

Clippit provides context-sensitive help and answers your questions.

# Obtaining Help in Dialog Boxes

Dialog boxes can be packed with confusing options and preferences. Fortunately, help is just a click or two away. In the upper-right corner of most dialog boxes is a button with a question mark on it. To get help, click that question mark button and then click the option for which you need help. Alternatively, you can right-click the option and then click **What's This?** A small text box appears, displaying a description of the option.

# Exiting Excel

When you are finished working in Excel, you should save any work you have completed and then shut down the program. (To learn how to save workbook files, see Chapter 3, "Working with Workbook Files.") If you do not save your workbook before shutting down, you risk losing your workbook, or at least losing whatever changes you made since you last saved it.

To exit Excel, take one of the following steps:

- Open the **File** menu and choose **Exit**.
- Click the Excel program window's Close (**X**) button.
- Press **Alt+F4**. (Hold down the **Alt** key while pressing the **F4** key.)

**caution**

If you shut down Excel before saving changes to a workbook, Excel beeps and displays a dialog box asking whether you want to save your workbook before exiting. Click **Yes** to save it, **No** to lose your changes, or **Cancel** to continue working in Excel.

# THE ABSOLUTE MINIMUM

In this chapter, you learned how to take control of Excel and make it work for you. Congratulations on becoming a master of the Excel interface! You now have a solid understanding of Excel's program window, workbook window, menus, toolbars, dialog boxes, and help system.

- You can successfully start up Excel when you're ready to work and shut it down at the end of the day.

- You know the name of every part of Excel's program window, and you can explain its purpose and show how to use it.

- You know how to enter commands by clicking toolbar buttons or selecting commands from menus.

- You can successfully navigate any dialog box and Excel's four task panes.

- You know how to get help when you need it.

This chapter may not have been the most fun, but it has taught you the basic moves you need to know to move around in Excel and enter commands. In other words, you just completed the driver's education portion of your Excel training program. You are now fully qualified to begin using Excel to create your very own worksheets and workbooks.

3

# WORKING WITH
# WORKBOOK FILES

# Starting with an Excel Workbook Template

Each time you start Excel, it opens a blank workbook, so you can begin entering data immediately. However, you might be able to save yourself a considerable amount of time by creating a new workbook based on one of the many *templates* included with Excel. Excel features templates for creating expense statements, invoices, purchase orders, income statements, and other commonly-used worksheets. Each template is professionally designed and contains the formulas and functions required to perform the necessary calculations. Rather than start from scratch, you can open a workbook template and then customize the workbook, or, if the workbook is exactly what you need, simply start adding your data.

To open an Excel template, take the following steps:

1. Open the **File** menu and choose **New**. The New Workbook task pane appears.

2. Under **New from Template**, click **General Templates**. The Templates dialog box appears.

3. Click the **Spreadsheet Solutions** tab. Excel displays a small collection of spreadsheet templates, as shown in Figure 3.1.

4. Click the desired template and click **OK**. Excel installs the selected template and then opens it, so you can begin working. (If prompted, insert the Excel or Office installation CD and click **OK**.)

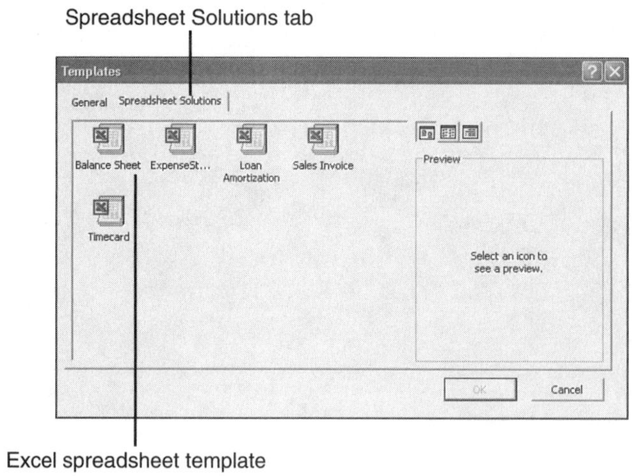

Spreadsheet Solutions tab

**FIGURE 3.1**

To save time, use one of Excel's sample spreadsheet templates.

Excel spreadsheet template

If you have an Internet connection, you can connect to Microsoft's Templates Gallery and obtain dozens of other useful templates for both home and business applications. The Templates Gallery features templates for all Microsoft Office applications, including Excel, Word, Access, and PowerPoint. Each template is marked with an icon for the program used to create it, so you can determine which templates are designed exclusively for Excel. Excel's New Workbook task pane provides easy access to these templates, as these steps demonstrate:

1. Open the **File** menu and choose **New**. The New Workbook task pane appears.

2. Under **New from Template**, click **Templates on Microsoft.com**. Excel automatically runs your Web browser, which connects you to Microsoft.com. The opening Web page prompts you to select a country.

3. Click the link for the desired country. This connects you to the Templates Gallery for the selected country.

4. Scroll down the page and click the desired template category, as shown in Figure 3.2, to display a list of subcategories, including the number of templates available in each subcategory.

Click the desired template category

**FIGURE 3.2**

With an Internet connection, you can obtain templates online.

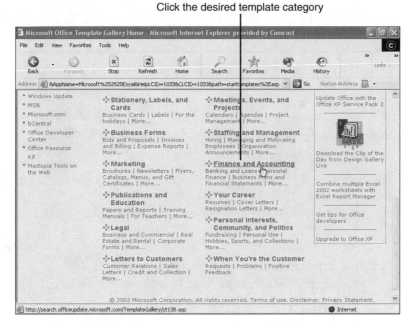

5. Click the link for the desired subcategory to display a list of available templates, as shown in Figure 3.3. Note that the icon next to each template name indicates the application used to create it: Excel, Word, Access, or PowerPoint.

**FIGURE 3.3**

The Template Gallery features templates for all Office applications.

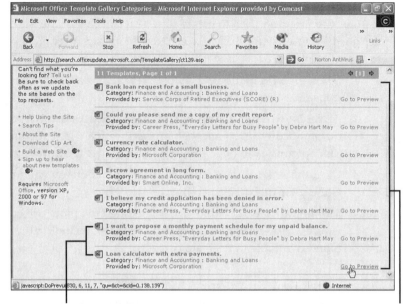

Icons indicate template type                                                                 Available templates

6. Click the **Go to Preview** link next to the desired template, so you can check it out before downloading (copying) it. The first time you choose to preview a template, a Security dialog box pops up asking whether it is okay to run a Microsoft program on your computer.

7. Click **Yes** to give your permission. The End User License Agreement appears, notifying you of your rights and responsibilities in using this template.

8. Read the License Agreement, and (assuming you agree), click **Accept**. Your Web browser displays a preview of the template, as shown in Figure 3.4.

9. To open the template in Excel, click **Edit in Microsoft Excel**. Your Web browser downloads the template and opens it in Excel, so you can start using it or modifying it.

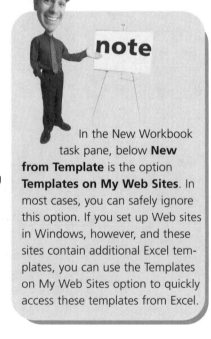

**note**

In the New Workbook task pane, below **New from Template** is the option **Templates on My Web Sites**. In most cases, you can safely ignore this option. If you set up Web sites in Windows, however, and these sites contain additional Excel templates, you can use the Templates on My Web Sites option to quickly access these templates from Excel.

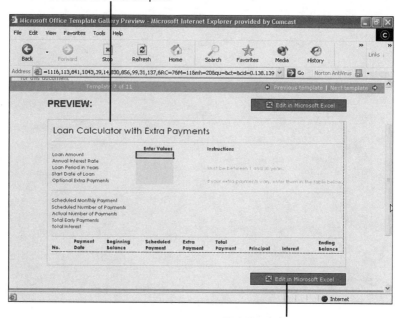

Preview of Excel template

**FIGURE 3.4**

The Template Gallery lets you preview a template before opening it.

Click Edit in Microsoft Excel

# Creating Workbooks from Scratch

If you can find a template that perfectly suits your needs, use it. However, if you're a diehard do-it-yourselfer or if you have a custom workbook in mind, you might prefer (or need) to create a workbook from scratch. In such a case, you open a blank workbook and type the labels, values, dates, formulas, and functions yourself, as explained in Part 2, "Creating Your First Worksheet."

Whenever you start Excel, it automatically opens a blank workbook, so you can start creating a workbook immediately. You can also create a new, blank workbook at any time by using the File, New command. Whenever you need a blank workbook, take the following steps to create it:

1. Open Excel's **File** menu and choose **New**. The New Workbook task pane appears.

2. Under New, click **Blank Workbook**, as shown in Figure 3.5. Excel creates a new blank workbook, named Book#, where # is the next workbook number. (When Excel starts, it opens Book1. If you create a second blank workbook, it is named Book2. A third is named Book3, and so on.)

Click Blank Workbook

**FIGURE 3.5**

You can start a workbook from scratch by creating a blank workbook.

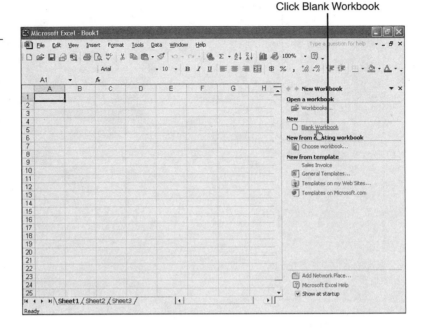

# Saving and Naming Your Workbook

As you create and edit your workbook, your entries and changes are stored only temporarily, in your computer's memory. If you exit Excel or shut down your computer, or if the power blips off for only a second, you risk losing any of the work you have done. To prevent data loss, you should save and name your workbook soon after creating it and then save it at least every ten minutes.

**tip**

To open a new, blank workbook with a single click, click the **New** button on the far left end of the Standard toolbar.

When you choose to save a workbook for the first time, Excel displays the Save As dialog box, which you use to name the workbook and specify where you want it stored. Unless you specify otherwise, Excel saves all workbooks in the My Documents folder. I strongly recommend that you store all workbooks in My Documents, so you know where to look for them later.

Assuming you are saving your workbooks in the My Documents folder, the steps for saving a workbook are very straightforward:

1. Open Excel's **File** menu and choose **Save**. The Save As dialog box appears, as shown in Figure 3.6, displaying the contents of the My Documents folder.

2. Click in the **File Name** text box.

3. Type a descriptive and unique name for your workbook.

4. Click the **Save** button. Excel saves your workbook to disk and assigns it the file name you typed.

**FIGURE 3.6**

Use the Save As dialog box to save your workbook for the first time.

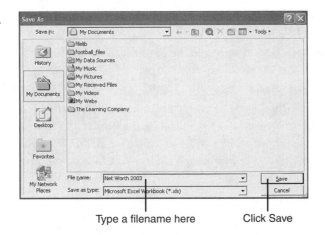

Type a filename here          Click Save

If you have created your own folders for managing your documents, you need to know a little more about how to use the various controls in the Save As dialog box. These controls can seem a little confusing at first. The following list explains the various controls to help you better understand them and expertly navigate the drives and folders on your computer:

**Navigation bar**, which runs down the left side of the dialog box, displays commonly accessed locations, including the History folder, the My Documents folder, the Windows Desktop, your Favorites list, and My Network Places (shared drives and folders on your network). To quickly open a location, click its button.

**Save In** drop-down list, near the top of the dialog box, displays the name of the currently opened disk drive or folder. To change to a different disk drive or folder, open the Save in drop-down list and click the letter of the disk drive or name of the folder.

**Folder/File** list  (the largest portion of the dialog box) displays the contents of the selected disk drive or folder. In this list, you can double-click a folder to open it and display its contents.

**Back** button displays the contents of the previous file/folder list.

**Up One Level** button displays the contents of the folder or drive that holds the currently displayed folder. For example, if you open the My Documents folder on drive C and then click the Up One Level button, you open your *username* folder (where *username* is the name you enter to log in to Windows).

**Search the Web** button displays a screen that helps you track down a particular Web site.

**Delete** button removes the currently selected file or folder and places it in the Windows Recycle Bin.

**Create New Folder** button creates a new, empty folder on the currently selected drive or in the currently opened folder. For example, if My Documents is selected, click Create New Folder to make a folder inside the My Documents folder. When you click Create New Folder, the Create New Folder dialog box appears, asking you to type a name for the folder. Type a name that's unique and descriptive—but brief—and click **OK**.

**Views** button displays a list of available ways the Save As dialog box can display the contents of the currently selected disk drive or folder— List (file names), Details (file names, sizes, and dates), Properties (file names and information), Preview (file names and a tiny picture of each document), or Arrange Icons (by name, file type, or date).

**Tools** button provides options for deleting the selected item, renaming it, adding it to your Favorites list, and performing other housekeeping chores.

**File Name** text box provides a space in which you can type a name for the file.

**Save as Type** drop-down list provides options for saving the workbook as an Excel workbook or a template.

**Save** button tells Excel to save the workbook in the selected folder, using the file name you typed.

note

To enable the Save As or Open dialog box to display a one-page preview of a workbook, you must turn on the Preview option for the workbook. With the workbook open in Excel, open the **File** menu and click **Properties**. Click the **Summary** tab and click the **Save Preview Picture** check box. Click **OK**.

**Cancel** button cancels the save operation and closes the dialog box without doing anything.

After you have saved and named a workbook, Excel assumes you always want to save this workbook in the same folder, using the same filename. This saves time when you save your changes later. Rather than select a folder and type a filename, you simply open the **File** menu and choose **Save** or click Excel's **Save** button.

# Saving a Workbook as a Template

Earlier in this chapter, you met some of Excel's templates, the templates included with Excel and those in the Templates Gallery on the Web. After you have created a workbook, you can save your custom workbook as a template, so you can use it over and over again to create new workbooks. Templates store the following information and settings for new workbooks:

**Formatting:** Any borders, shading, character styles, and other formatting is stored in the template. Whenever you type an entry in a cell, that entry takes on the formatting applied to the cell.

**Text and data:** You can choose to have column and row headings and other data saved in the template, so you don't need to retype them when you create a new workbook based on this template.

**Charts:** Any charts or other graphics in a template are saved with the template, making them available in any workbook based on the template.

**Formulas:** Templates contain all the formulas included in the original workbook.

**Toolbars and options:** Any changes you made to customize Excel while you were creating the template are automatically available in any workbook that's based on the template.

> **tip**
>
> To have the first page of your template displayed in the preview area of the Templates dialog box, open the **File** menu and click **Properties**. Click the **Summary** tab and click the **Save Preview Picture** check box. Click **OK**.

Before you save a workbook or worksheet as a template, you must create a custom workbook or worksheet, as explained in Part 2, "Creating Your First Worksheet." You can then save the workbook or worksheet (a one-sheet workbook) as a template.

After you have created a custom workbook or worksheet, take the following steps to save it as a template:

1.  Open Excel's **File** menu and choose **Save As**. The Save As dialog box appears, as you saw in Figure 3.6, displaying the names of all Excel workbook files in the My Documents folder.

2.  Open the **Save as Type** list and click **Template (\*.xlt)**. (When Excel saves a workbook, it adds the extension .xls to the end of the file name, to indicate that the file is a workbook. Templates are saved with the extension .xlt.) The Save As dialog box automatically opens the Templates folder, and Templates appears in the Save In box. (See Figure 3.7.)

3.  If you want to give this template a different name than what is displayed in the File Name box, type the desired filename.

4.  Click **Save**.

> **caution**
>
> You must save your templates in the C:\Documents and Settings\\*username*\ Application Data\ Microsoft\Templates folder for the templates to appear in the Templates dialog box. Whenever you choose to save a workbook or worksheet as a template, the Save As dialog box automatically opens this folder and displays its contents.

**FIGURE 3.7**

You can save your workbook as a template for creating additional workbooks.

Templates appears here

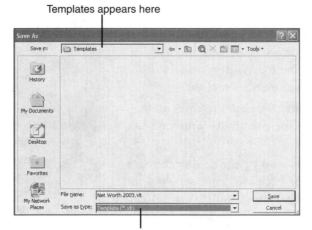

Save workbook as a template

# Opening a Saved Workbook

Whenever you want to work on a particular workbook that you (or someone else) has already created and saved, you must open it in Excel. Assuming the workbook file is stored in the My Documents folder, finding and opening the workbook file is easy:

1. Open Excel's **File** menu and click **Open** or click the **Open** button in the Standard toolbar. The Open dialog box appears, displaying the names of all Excel workbook files in the My Documents folder, as shown in Figure 3.8.

2. Click the name of the Excel workbook file you want to open.

3. Click the **Open** button.

To open a workbook file that is stored on a drive or in a folder other than My Documents, you need to know how to navigate to other drives and folders by using the Open dialog box. First, click the arrow to the right of the **Look in** box, as shown in Figure 3.9. This displays a list of disk drives and other storage areas on your computer and, if your computer is networked, on the network. Click the desired storage location. The contents of this location is displayed in the Folder/File list, as shown in Figure 3.10. Double-click a folder to view its contents. Continue double-clicking folders until you reach the folder that contains the desired workbook, and then double-click the workbook's name.

**tip**

Excel keeps track of the four most recently opened workbooks and lists them at the bottom of the File menu. To open a workbook you have recently worked on, open Excel's **File** menu and click the workbook's name. Or, open the Windows **Start** menu, point to **My Recent Documents** (in Windows XP) or **Documents** (in earlier versions of Windows), and click the workbook's name. (Windows keeps track of the 15 most recently opened documents created in any program.)

**note**

If you pass up a folder while navigating, click the **Back** or **Up One Level** button in the Open dialog box's toolbar to back up to the previous folder or file list.

My Documents

**FIGURE 3.8**

You must open a
workbook file to
use it.

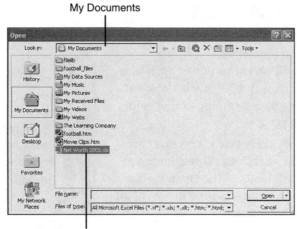

Excel workbook file

Click this arrow

**FIGURE 3.9**

If a workbook is
not in My
Documents, you
may need to
change to the
folder in which it
is stored.

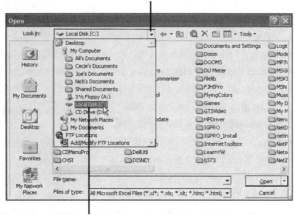

Click the disk drive or network location where the workbook is stored

Double-click a folder to open it

**FIGURE 3.10**

Navigate to the folder in which your Excel workbook files are stored.

Folder/File list

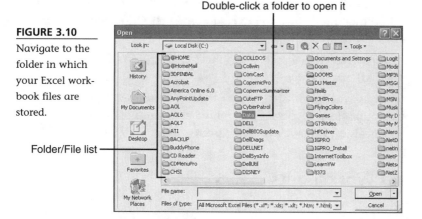

# Managing Worksheets

As you know from Chapter 2, every workbook starts out with three worksheets, named Sheet1, Sheet2, and Sheet3. You also know that each worksheet has its own tab that you can click to bring the worksheet to the front of the stack and display its contents. At this point, however, you probably don't know that you have a great deal of control over the worksheets that make up a workbook. You can group the worksheets, insert and delete worksheets, copy and move worksheets, rename worksheets, and even choose a different color for each tab. The following sections show you how to take control of the worksheets in your workbook.

## Selecting Worksheets

Before you start manipulating worksheets, you need to know how to select one or more worksheets. The following list explains the various methods for selecting worksheets:

- To select a worksheet, click its tab.
- To select multiple neighboring worksheets, click the tab of the first worksheet and then hold down the **Shift** key while clicking the tab of the last worksheet in the group.

- To select two or more non-neighboring worksheets, click the tab of one of the worksheets and then hold down the **Ctrl** key while clicking additional worksheet tabs.

- To select all worksheets in a workbook, right-click any worksheet tab and choose **Select All Sheets**.

- If you select two or more worksheets, they remain a group until you ungroup them. To ungroup selected worksheets, right-click the tab of one of the selected worksheets and click **Ungroup Sheets**.

## Inserting and Deleting Worksheets

In older versions of Excel, each workbook started out with 16 worksheets and had room to add another 240, for a grand total of 256. In Excel 2002, workbooks can handle more than 256 worksheets, but they start up with a more reasonable, manageable number: 3. You can then add or delete worksheets as needed. To insert a single worksheet, take the following steps:

1. Click the tab of the worksheet before which you want the new worksheet inserted. For example, if you want the new worksheet between Sheet1 and Sheet2, click the Sheet2 tab. (You can select more than one tab to have that number of worksheets inserted.)

2. Open the **Insert** menu and click **Worksheet**, as shown in Figure 3.11. Excel inserts a new worksheet immediately and names it Sheet#, where # is the number representing the next worksheet in the series.

> **tip**
>
> To insert a worksheet or chart sheet, right-click the tab before which you want the sheet inserted and click **Insert**. This opens the Insert dialog box, displaying an icon for each type of object you can insert. Click the **Worksheet** or **Chart** icon and click **OK**.

If you insert multiple worksheets, some of the worksheet tabs may not appear onscreen at all times. They scroll outside the worksheet tab viewing area, as do the rows and columns that extend outside the workbook window. To bring worksheet tabs into view, you use the *tab scrolling* buttons, as shown in Figure 3.12. The middle two buttons scroll one tab to the left or right with each click of the mouse. The leftmost button scrolls to the beginning tab, and the rightmost button scrolls to the end. Just to the right of the tab viewing area is a vertical bar, called the *tab split bar*. Drag this bar to the right to view more tabs or to the left to view fewer tabs.

**FIGURE 3.11**

Excel lets you add to a work-book by insert-ing worksheets.

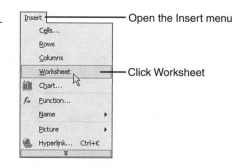

Open the Insert menu

Click Worksheet

**FIGURE 3.12**

The tab scrolling buttons enable you to bring additional tabs into view.

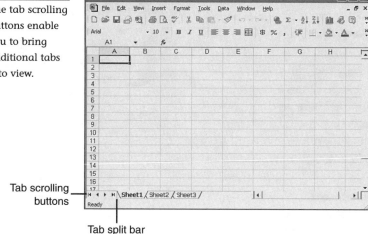

Tab scrolling buttons

Tab split bar

If a workbook contains more worksheets than you need, you can delete the extras. Take the following steps to delete worksheets:

1. Select the tabs of the worksheets you want to delete.

2. Right-click any one of the selected tabs and click **Delete**. If the selected work-sheet(s) is blank, Excel removes the worksheet(s) immediately. If a selected worksheet contains data, Excel displays a dialog box asking you to confirm the deletion.

3. If asked to confirm the deletion, make absolutely sure you do not need any of the data contained on the worksheet. To permanently delete the worksheet(s), click **Delete**, or click **Cancel** to cancel the deletion.

## Copying and Moving Worksheets

If you already created and formatted a worksheet and would like to add a copy of that worksheet as another sheet in the same workbook or as a worksheet in another workbook, you don't need to re-create the worksheet. Just copy or move it. To copy or move a worksheet, perform the following steps:

1. To copy or move one or more worksheets from one workbook to another, make sure both workbooks are open.

2. Click the tab for the worksheet you want to move or copy.

3. Open the **Edit** menu and choose **Move or Copy Sheet**. The Move or Copy dialog box appears, as shown in Figure 3.13.

4. To move or copy the worksheet to a different workbook, open the **To Book** list and choose the name of the destination workbook. If you do not choose a different workbook, Excel assumes you want to copy or move the worksheet to a different location in the same workbook.

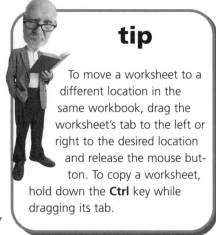

**tip**

To move a worksheet to a different location in the same workbook, drag the worksheet's tab to the left or right to the desired location and release the mouse button. To copy a worksheet, hold down the **Ctrl** key while dragging its tab.

5. In the **Before Sheet** list, click the name of the worksheet before which you want this worksheet inserted.

6. To copy the worksheet, rather than move it, click the check box next to **Create a Copy**.

7. Click **OK**. Excel moves or copies the worksheet to the specified location.

**FIGURE 3.13**

You can move or copy a worksheet to the same workbook or a different workbook.

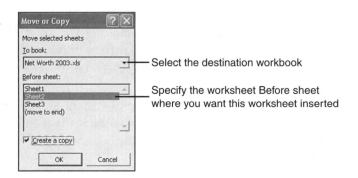

Select the destination workbook

Specify the worksheet Before sheet where you want this worksheet inserted

# Renaming Worksheet Tabs

At first, worksheets have fairly generic names: Sheet1, Sheet2, and Sheet3. To change a worksheet's name to something more descriptive, follow these steps:

1. Right-click the tab you want to rename and click **Rename**. The tab's current name appears highlighted.

2. Type a new, more descriptive name for the tab and press **Enter**.

# Changing a Tab's Color

Excel 2002 introduces a cool feature that makes working with workbooks a little more exciting: color tabs. Initially, every tab wears a drab gray, but you can give each tab its own color by doing the following:

1. Right-click the tab whose color you want to change and click **Tab Color**. The Format Tab Color dialog box appears, displaying a palette full of colors, as shown in Figure 3.14.

2. Click the desired color.

3. Click **OK**. The tab appears in its new color.

**FIGURE 3.14**

The Format Tab Color dialog box features several bright colors.

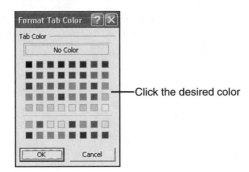

Click the desired color

# THE ABSOLUTE MINIMUM

When you move from this chapter, make sure you walk away understanding this concept: *Every workbook is a file that contains one or more pages called worksheets.* This concept provides a framework for all of the other hands-on skills you acquired in this chapter. You now know how to

Start a project with a pre-designed workbook template rather than starting from scratch.

Open a blank workbook that you can use to design and construct a custom workbook.

Save and name a workbook, so you can open and edit it later.

Save a workbook as a template so you can use it as a model for any workbooks you create in the future.

Select, insert, copy, move, and rename worksheets and change the color of their tabs.

At this point, you know everything you need to know to create and manage the workbooks that hold your Excel worksheets. In the next part, you begin to focus more closely on the worksheets themselves as you begin to enter data, format the data, add formulas, and print your worksheets.

# PART

# CREATING YOUR FIRST WORKSHEET

4

# ENTERING AND EDITING LABELS AND VALUES

# Understanding Types of Data Entries

As you know from Chapter 1, each worksheet consists of multiple rows and columns that intersect to form boxes, called cells. For a worksheet to do something useful, its cells must contain *data entries*: text, numbers, dates, and so on. Following is a list of the various types of data you can enter in the cells, along with a brief description of each type:

- **Labels (text)** are non-numerical entries. Labels are commonly used for worksheet titles, column headings, and row headings. They can include the names of people or places, or any other text that is not to be treated as a number or date.

- **Values (numbers)** are numerical entries, including dollar amounts, percentages, or fractions. Whenever a value begins with a number and contains no text, Excel treats it as a value. When entering values, simply type the number. Later, you can format the cell to tell Excel to treat the number as a dollar amount, percentage, or fraction.

- **Dates** are numerical or text entries that specify a particular day of the year. Dates typically include numbers separated by forward slashes or dashes—for example, 4/15/03 or 2-27-04.

- **Times** are numerical entries that specify a particular time of day. Times typically include numbers separated by a colon—for example, 9:10 for nine o'clock and ten minutes or 10:15:35 for ten o'clock, fifteen minutes, and thirty-five seconds.

- **Formulas** are mathematical strings that tell Excel how to perform an equation that uses values from other cells in the worksheet. For example, the formula =D5+D6+D7 tells Excel to total the values in cells D5, D6, and D7. Excel displays the formula's result in the cell that contains the formula.

- **Functions** are a type of mathematical shorthand that handles complex equations with less input from you. Like formulas, all functions begin with an equal sign.

# Moving from Cell to Cell

To enter data in the various cells that make up a worksheet, you must have a way to move from one cell to another. The most intuitive method is to point and click. Using your mouse, position the mouse pointer over the desired cell and click the left mouse button. The most intuitive method, however, is not always the fastest. As you type entries, your keyboard acts as a more efficient navigational instrument. Table 4.1 lists the various keys you can use to move around in a worksheet.

**TABLE 4.1**   Keystrokes for Navigating a Worksheet

| Press | To Move |
|-------|---------|
| Enter | One cell down after accepting the entry you just typed. |
| Tab | One cell to the right after accepting the entry you just typed. |
| ↓ | One cell down. |
| ↑ | One cell up. |
| ← | One cell to the left. |
| → | One cell to the right. |
| Ctrl+↑ | To the top of a data region (an area of a worksheet that contains entries). |
| Ctrl+↓ | To the bottom of a data region. |
| Ctrl+← | To the leftmost cell that contains an entry in a data region. |
| Ctrl+→ | To the rightmost cell that contains an entry in a data region. |
| PgUp | Up one screen. |
| PgDn | Down one screen. |
| Home | To the leftmost cell in a row. |
| Ctrl+Home | To the upper-left corner of a worksheet. |
| Ctrl+End | To the lower-right corner of the area of a worksheet that contains data. |
| End, ↑ | If the selected cell is blank, moves up to the next blank cell. If the selected cell contains an entry, moves up to the next cell that contains an entry. (Press and release the End key and then press the arrow key.) |
| End, ↓ | If the selected cell is blank, moves down to the next blank cell. If the selected cell contains an entry, moves down to the next cell that contains an entry. (Press and release the End key and then press the arrow key.) |
| End, ← | If the selected cell is blank, moves left to the next blank cell. If the selected cell contains an entry, moves left to the next cell that contains an entry. (Press and release the End key and then press the arrow key.) |
| End, → | If the selected cell is blank, moves right to the next blank cell. If the selected cell contains an entry, moves right to the next cell that contains an entry. (Press and release the End key and then press the arrow key.) |

## Using the Scroll Bars

The workbook window displays only a very small portion of the available columns and rows. If cells you want to see move off screen, you can bring them back into view by using the scroll bars. The vertical scroll bar (on the right side of the workbook window) enables you to scroll up and down. The horizontal scrollbar (near the lower-left corner of the workbook window) enables you to scroll left and right. The following picture and list illustrate basic scroll bar moves:

**Scroll arrows:** Click once on a scroll arrow to scroll one cell in the direction of the arrow. Hold down the mouse button to scroll continuously in the direction of the arrow until you reach the end or release the mouse button.

**Scroll box:** Drag the scroll box inside the scroll bar in the direction you want to scroll. The box's position inside the scroll bar represents the area of the worksheet. If, for example, you drag the box to the middle of the scroll bar, the workbook window displays the middle of the *data area* (the area on the worksheet that contains data).

**Scroll bar:** Click once inside the scroll bar on either side of the scroll box to scroll one screenful at a time. If you're using the vertical scroll bar, this is the same as pressing the PgUp or PgDn key.

> **tip**
>
> To quickly jump to a specific cell by using its address, open the **Edit** menu and choose **Go To** or press **F5**. Type the cell's address and press **Enter** or click **OK**. If the cell is on a different worksheet, type the worksheet name, an exclamation point, and the cell's address—for example, **Sheet3!m25**.

## Splitting the Workbook Window

In large worksheets, you may want to view two parts of the worksheet at the same time. If, for example, the worksheet has column headings that indicate the types of data you need to enter in each column, you may want those column headings to remain onscreen at all times. In other words, you don't want them to scroll off the screen. You can lock headings in place using the Freeze Panes feature, as explained in Chapter 5, "Controlling Rows, Columns, and Cells."

Another way to lock headings in place or view two sections of a worksheet for other reasons is to use the split bars, as shown in Figure 4.1. Drag the vertical split bar down or drag the horizontal split bar to the left to create a two-paned window. Each pane has its own set of scroll bars, so you can scroll inside the pane independently of the other pane.

Split bar

**FIGURE 4.1**

Drag the split
bar to the
desired location
to create a two-
paned window.

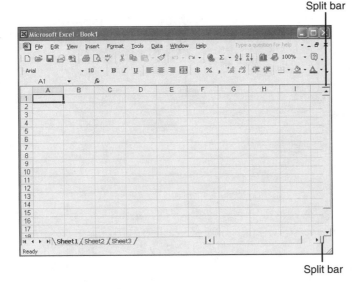

Split bar

# Entering Data

The steps you take to enter data are basically the same regardless of the type of data
entry: text, value, date, or time. Following are the steps you take to type a data entry
into a cell:

1. Select the cell in which you want to type the
   entry.

2. Type the entry. As you type, the entry
   appears both in the cell and in the formula
   bar, as shown in Figure 4.2.

3. Accept the entry by doing one of the
   following:

   Press **Enter** to accept the entry and move to
   the next cell down.

   Press **Tab** to accept the entry and move to
   the next cell to the right.

   Click the **Enter** button (the green check
   mark), to the left of the formula bar to
   accept the entry and keep the current cell
   selected.

**note**

To cancel an entry
before you accept it, press
the **Esc** key or click the **Cancel**
button (the red **X**), to the left of
the formula bar.

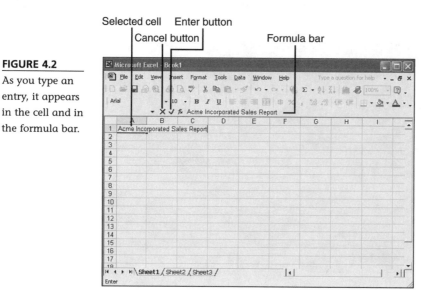

**FIGURE 4.2**

As you type an
entry, it appears
in the cell and in
the formula bar.

Selected cell   Enter button

Cancel button

Formula bar

Though the basic steps for entering data in a worksheet are easy to master, the various types of data entries must be typed in a specific format that indicates to Excel the type of data each cell contains. The following sections cover the peculiar formatting requirements for the various data types.

## Entering Text Labels

Text entries are the easiest to master. A text entry is any entry that contains text only (non-numeric characters) or a combination of text, spaces, and numbers (as in a mailing address). Unlike numeric entries, which Excel aligns to the right, text entries are aligned with the left side of the cell.

In some cases, you may want a numerical entry, such as a ZIP code, treated as a text entry rather than as a numeric entry. To format a numeric entry as text, type a single quote before the entry—for example, you might type '60629 to have a ZIP code treated as text.

If you type a text entry that is longer than the cell is wide, and the cells to the right are blank, Excel displays the entire entry. If, however, the neighboring cells to the right contain entries, Excel *truncates* (displays only part of) the entry. You can drag the right side of the column heading to widen the column, as shown in Figure 4.3, and/or choose to have Excel *wrap* the text to display it on more than one line. See Chapter 5, "Controlling Rows, Columns, and Cells" for additional options and detailed instructions on how to widen columns, increase row heights, and wrap text in cells.

Drag the column heading border

**FIGURE 4.3**

You can quickly widen a column to give your entries more room.

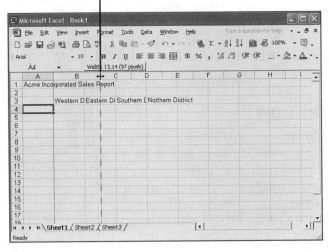

## Entering Numbers

Numerical entries (values) can contain any of the numerals 0 to 9 and these special characters: + - ( ) , . $ %. No spaces are allowed. All values are right-aligned, unless you specify otherwise when you format the cells (as explained later in this chapter in the section called "Adjusting Number Formats").

When typing values, the most important point to keep in mind is to allow Excel to handle the formatting. In other words, don't worry about typing a dollar sign or percentage symbol. Instead of typing $700.00, simply type 700. Later (as you will learn in "Adjusting Number Formats"), you can format the cell to display the currency format. Excel then will add the dollar sign and two decimal places to make the value look like a dollar amount.

If you type a number that is longer than the cell is wide, Excel expands the cell a little to accommodate the number. If you later reduce the cell width so that the number no longer fits, Excel displays the entry as a series of number signs, like this: #######. Excel doesn't display just a portion of a

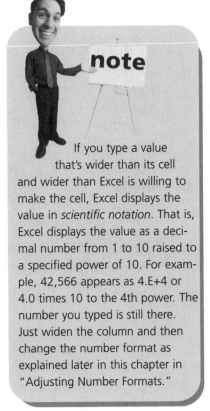

**note**

If you type a value that's wider than its cell and wider than Excel is willing to make the cell, Excel displays the value in *scientific notation*. That is, Excel displays the value as a decimal number from 1 to 10 raised to a specified power of 10. For example, 42,566 appears as 4.E+4 or 4.0 times 10 to the 4th power. The number you typed is still there. Just widen the column and then change the number format as explained later in this chapter in "Adjusting Number Formats."

value (as it does with text entries), because if it did display a portion of the number, you might glance at the number and think you were looking at the entire number. To have Excel display the number in its entirety, widen the column, as shown in Figure 4.3.

## Entering Dates and Times

Most dates and times are in a numeric format, but unlike values, dates and times require some special characters. Fortunately, Excel accepts times and dates entered in a variety of formats. Table 4.2 illustrates some of the more common valid formats for dates and times. Like numbers, you can enter dates in a generic format, such as 9-3-06 or 9/3/06, and then change the cell format later to have Excel display the date in whichever format you prefer.

**tip**

As you type entries in a column, Excel keeps track of those entries. If you start typing an entry that's similar to an entry you already typed, Excel's AutoComplete feature completes the entry for you. If the AutoComplete entry is correct, press **Enter** to accept it. If the AutoComplete entry is incorrect, continue typing the entry as you want it to appear. If AutoComplete tacks on additional characters, press **Del** to remove them and then press **Enter** to accept your entry. To disable AutoComplete for values, open the **Tools** menu, click **Options**, and click the **Edit** tab. Click **Enable AutoComplete for Cell Values** to remove the check mark.

**TABLE 4.2**    Common Date and Time Formats

| Format | Example |
|---|---|
| MM/DD/YY | 4/8/06 |
| MMM-YY | Jan-06 |
| DD-MMM-YY | 28-Oct-06 |
| DD-MMM | 06-Sep |
| HH:MM | 16:50 |
| HH:MM:SS | 8:22:59 |
| HH:MM AM/PM | 7:45 PM |
| HH:MM:SS AM/PM | 11:45:16 AM |
| MM/DD/YY HH:MM | 11/8/06 4:20 |
| HH:MM MM/DD/YY | 4:20 11/18/06 |

Dates and times can be a little quirky. The following list alerts you to some of the more unexpected attributes of times and dates:

■ When typing dates, separate the day, month, and year with a dash (-) or forward slash (/).

- Avoid starting a date with the name of the month, such as April 8, 2006. Excel treats such dates as text entries. Instead, type 8-Apr-2006 or 8-4-2006.

- To avoid confusion, use all four digits to specify a year. For example, type 2006 instead of 06. Excel generally interprets two-digit years from 00 to 29 as falling in the 21st century (2000 to 2029) and years 30-99 as falling in the 20th century (1930-1999).

**tip**

To enter today's date, press **Ctrl+;** (the Ctrl key plus the semicolon key). To enter the current time (as recorded on your computer's clock), press **Ctrl+Shift+:** (Ctrl plus Shift plus the colon key).

- Excel is on military time (a 24-hour clock), so its day consists of 24 hours, not two twelve-hour periods. In military time, you don't need to say a.m. or p.m. You know that 8:30 is in the morning and 19:30 is at night. When typing times, either type the military time or follow every entry with a.m. or p.m. For example, if you want to type 8:30 at night, type either 20:30 (military time) or 8:30 PM.

- To Excel, dates are numbers, and Excel started counting on January 1, 1900. Excel treats that date as the number 1. January 1, 2008 is 39448, because it is the 39,448th day from January 1, 1900. Likewise, Excel treats times as decimal fractions of a day. Why? Because Excel uses dates and times in calculations. For example, Excel can determine the date on which a savings bond matures given the date it was issued and the number of years that must pass before it matures.

## Adjusting Number Formats

Every cell in a blank Excel worksheet starts with a General format, which essentially is no format at all. Type a text entry, and Excel moves it to the left. Type a number, and Excel moves it to the right. If you type a date, Excel automatically applies a date format. Type a time, and Excel applies a time format. Other than that, Excel does little to the entries you type, because Excel doesn't need to know whether a number represents dollars, percentage points, or the number of cattle on a ranch.

To you and me, however, values do have significance, and we need to see what those values represent. Fortunately, Excel provides several number formats that clearly show what the values represent. Table 4.3 lists and describes the available number formats.

**TABLE 4.3**   Excel Numbering Formats

| Number Format | Description |
| --- | --- |
| General | Displays numbers just as you type them. |
| Number | Displays the whole number plus two decimal places. If you type 457, the cell displays 457.00. |
| Currency | Displays a dollar sign, followed by the whole number and two decimal places. If you type 457, the cell displays $457.00. Excel can display negative numbers in red, enclosed in parentheses, or both, or insert a minus sign before the number. |
| Accounting | Similar to Currency except it provides no special display for negative values. |
| Date | Provides several options for displaying dates, including MM/DD/YYYY, and DD-YY. |
| Time | Provides several options for displaying the time, including HH:MM:SS and HH:MM AM/PM. |
| Percentage | Displays the number you type, followed by two decimal places and a percentage symbol—for example, 99.99%. |
| Fraction | Displays a fraction as a fraction, rather than as a date or text entry. |
| Scientific | Displays a number in scientific notation. That is, Excel displays the base number, followed by E+#, where E+# indicates the number of decimal places you need to move the point to the right. For instance 42,578 shows up as 4.E+4. |
| Text | Treats numbers as text and left-aligns the number in its cell. |
| Special | Handles formatting for special entries, including ZIP codes, social security numbers, phone numbers, and other numerical entries that are not actually values. |
| Custom | Lets you create your own numeric format. |

To change the number formatting for a particular cell or group of cells, take the following steps:

1. Click the cell or drag over the cells whose number format you want to change. (To select multiple cells, see "Selecting a Cell Range," later in this chapter.)

2. Open the **Format** menu and choose **Cells**. The Format Cells dialog box appears.

3. If necessary, click the **Number** tab to bring it to the front.

4. In the **Category** list, click the general category that best represents the type of number format you want. For example, to display values as dollar amounts, click **Currency**, as shown in Figure 4.4.

5. If you are presented with additional choices, enter your preferences. For example, you may be able to specify the number of decimal places, the symbol (such as $ or %), or the way negative numbers are displayed.

6. Click **OK**. Excel returns you to the worksheet and displays any values in the selected cells according to the newly specified format.

**tip**

To apply common numeric formats quickly, select the cell(s) you want to format and then click the Currency Style, Percent Style, or Comma Style button in the Formatting toolbar. The Increase Decimal button adds decimal places, and the Decrease Decimal button removes decimal places.

For information about additional options in the Format Cells dialog box, see "Using the Format Cells Dialog Box," in Chapter 7, "Formatting Your Worksheet."

Select a format category

**FIGURE 4.4**

The Format Cells dialog box lets you specify how you want values displayed.

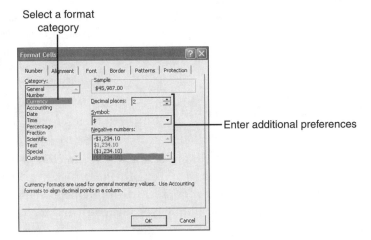

Enter additional preferences

# Having Excel Read Entries Aloud As You Type

If you watch the screen while you type, you can see what you're typing and automatically correct entries on the fly. However, if you're typing numbers from a page, you don't want to keep looking up at the screen. Fortunately, Excel provides a text-to-speech feature that can read your data back to you as you type your entries, assuming, of course, that your computer is equipped with a sound card and speakers. To enable the text-to-speech feature, take the following steps:

1. Right-click any Excel toolbar or the menu bar and choose **Text to Speech**. The Text to Speech toolbar appears, as shown in Figure 4.5.

2. Click the **Speak on Enter** button (the rightmost button on the toolbar).

3. Click in a cell, type an entry, and press **Enter**. Excel reads the entry back to you.

4. To have Excel read back a block of cell entries, drag over the cells to select them and then click the **Speak Cells** button (the leftmost button).

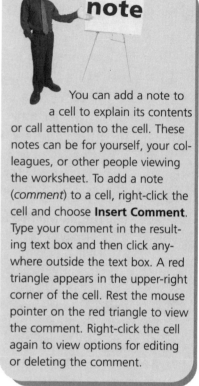

You can add a note to a cell to explain its contents or call attention to the cell. These notes can be for yourself, your colleagues, or other people viewing the worksheet. To add a note (*comment*) to a cell, right-click the cell and choose **Insert Comment**. Type your comment in the resulting text box and then click anywhere outside the text box. A red triangle appears in the upper-right corner of the cell. Rest the mouse pointer on the red triangle to view the comment. Right-click the cell again to view options for editing or deleting the comment.

**FIGURE 4.5**

Excel's text-to-speech feature reads entries back to you as you type them.

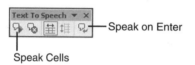

Speak on Enter

Speak Cells

# Entering Data Quickly with AutoFill

Excel features a couple of tricks for quick data entry. It can copy an entry from one cell into as many additional cells as you like, or it can fill several cells with a series of entries, such as the months of a year or a series of numbers that increase incrementally (5, 10, 15, 20, 25...). You simply type one entry and then order Excel to fill in the rest.

The easiest way to fill a series of neighboring cells is to use the cell selector's *fill handle*. The fill handle appears as a tiny dark square in the lower-right corner of the selected cell. To use the fill handle to copy an entry into other cells or to fill neighboring cells with a series of entries, take the following steps:

1. Type your entry or select the cell that contains the entry you want to copy or use as the first item in the series.

2. Move the mouse pointer over the fill handle so that the pointer appears as a cross.

3. Hold down the left mouse button and drag the fill handle up, down, left, or right to highlight the cells you want to fill, as shown in Figure 4.6.

4. Release the mouse button. Excel fills the highlighted cells as follows and displays the AutoFill Options button (below and to the right of the fill handle):

   If the source cell contains a number, Excel copies the number into the selected cells.

   If the source cell contains an entry typically used in a series, such as Jan or January, Mon or Monday, or the like, Excel fills the selected cells with the entries that complete the series. For example, if the original cell contained Jan and you filled it into 5 other cells, those cells would contain Feb, Mar, Apr, May, and Jun.

5. Click the **AutoFill Options** button to display the available options, as shown in Figure 4.7. These options enable you to change the way AutoFill completes the operation. For example, if you intend to copy a value into several cells and AutoFill has filled in a series instead, you can click Copy Cells to have the series replaced with copies of the original entry.

6. Click the desired AutoFill option, or click outside the menu if AutoFill performed the fill exactly as you had wanted.

**caution**

If Speak on Enter is on and you don't hear anything when you type an entry and press Enter, double-click the speaker icon in the Windows System Tray (on the right end of the taskbar). Make sure all volume controls are cranked up and that all Mute boxes are clear (no check mark). If you still don't hear anything, check the volume control on your speakers and make sure the speakers are plugged in to the correct jack on your computer.

Fill handle

**FIGURE 4.6**

Drag the fill handle to highlight the cells you want to fill.

Fill handle

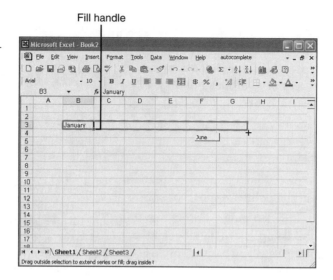

Auto Fill button

**FIGURE 4.7**

The AutoFill button enables you to provide more specific instructions on how to complete the fill operation.

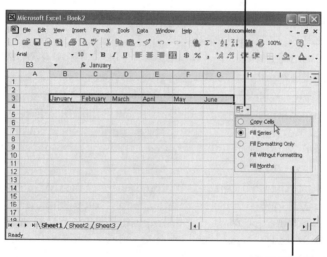

Auto Fill options

AutoFill obtains its information for creating series from lists of commonly used series. You can create your own custom AutoFill lists. Here's what you do:

1. Open the **Tools** menu and choose **Options**. The Options dialog box appears.

2. Click the **Custom Lists** tab.

3. Click the **Add** button, as shown in Figure 4.8. The insertion point moves to the **List Entries** box.

4. Under **List Entries**, type the entries that comprise the list. After each entry, press the **Enter** key to separate the entries.

5. Click **OK**.

You can now fill this list into several cells by typing the first list item in a cell and then dragging the fill handle over additional cells.

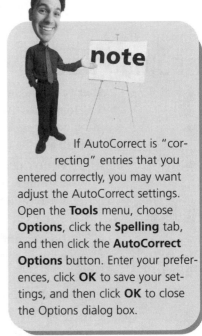

**tip**

Type the first two to three entries of a series (for example, 1, 3, 5). Drag over those entries to select them, and then drag the fill handle to select the cells in which you want the series to continue. When you release the mouse button, Excel completes the series for you.

Add button

**FIGURE 4.8**
You can create your own AutoFill lists.

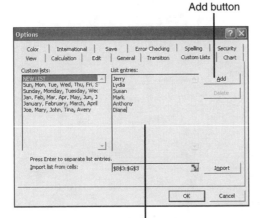

Type list entries here

# Viewing and Using Smart Tags

As you type entries, little button icons might pop up on your screen and then automatically disappear, or a tiny purple triangle might appear in the lower-right corner of a cell. These signs are an indication that Excel's *smart tags* are at work. Smart tags link the entry to other programs (such as a Web browser or email program) that can perform a specific task using the entry. For example, if you enter a stock symbol, such as MSFT, a smart tag appears that enables you to click an option for downloading the stock price from the Internet.

**note**

If AutoCorrect is "correcting" entries that you entered correctly, you may want adjust the AutoCorrect settings. Open the **Tools** menu, choose **Options**, click the **Spelling** tab, and then click the **AutoCorrect Options** button. Enter your preferences, click **OK** to save your settings, and then click **OK** to close the Options dialog box.

If you enter a person's name, you can click the smart tag and click an option for sending that person an email message.

Whenever you type a data entry that Excel recognizes as a candidate for a smart tag, Excel displays a smart tag, which looks like an information icon—a circle with an "i" in the middle of it. Click the smart tag to view a list of options, as shown in Figure 4.9, and then click the desired option.

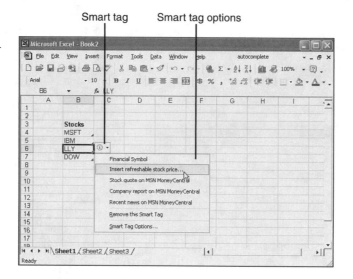

**FIGURE 4.9**
Smart tags connect cells to other programs for performing specialized tasks.

# Editing Data Entries

After you type an entry and press Enter, Excel accepts the entry and places it in the cell. To replace the entry with a different entry, simply click the cell, type the new entry, and press **Enter** or **Tab**. Or, rather than replace the entry, you can edit it, either inside the cell or in the formula bar. To edit an entry, take the following steps:

1. Double-click the cell that contains the entry you want to edit, or click the cell and press the **F2** key. This places an insertion point inside the cell and inside the formula bar, indicating you can now edit the entry. Edit appears in the status bar.

2. Use the arrow keys to move the insertion point to the area of the entry you want to change, or click there with the mouse.

3. To delete characters to the right of the insertion point, press the **Del** key. To delete characters to the left of the insertion point, press **Backspace**. (Or drag over the characters you want to delete and press the **Del** key.)

4. To insert characters, move the insertion point to where you want the characters inserted and type the characters.

5. To accept the new entry, press the **Enter** key or click the Enter button in the formula bar. To reject the new entry and return to the previous entry, press the **Esc** key or click the **Cancel** button.

# Selecting Cells

Whenever you click a cell or press Enter, Tab, or one of the arrow keys to move to a cell, you *select* the cell, and Excel displays a dark outline around the cell, called the *selector*. You typically select a single cell to type or edit an entry. Many times, however, you need to select multiple cells—a *block* or *range* of cells—perhaps to apply the same formatting to several cells or to total the values in multiple cells. The following sections show you how to select and work with cell ranges.

## Selecting a Cell Range

A range consists of any two cells on a sheet—the cells can be neighboring or non-neighboring. The only trick to selecting cells is making sure Excel is not in Edit mode; Excel does not allow you to select cells when you're in the middle of typing or editing an entry. If you are typing or editing an entry, click another cell to exit Edit mode. Then perform one of the following steps to select a range:

■ To select neighboring cells with your mouse, click the cell in the upper-left corner of the range, and then hold down the left mouse button while dragging the mouse pointer down and to the right until it reaches the cell in the lower-right corner of the range. See Figure 4.10.

■ To select neighboring cells with the keyboard, move the selector to the cell in the upper-left corner of the range, and then hold down the **Shift** key and use the down arrow and/or right arrow key to extend the selection to the cell in the lower-right corner of the range.

## tip

To select a range of neighboring cells with the Go To feature, press the **F5** key or **Ctrl+G** to display the Go To dialog box. Type the address of the cell in the upper-left corner of the range, followed by a colon and the address of the cell in the lower-right corner of the range—for example, type **b5:h18**. Press **Enter**.

■ To select non-neighboring cells with your mouse, select the cell or range as explained previously and then hold down the **Ctrl** key while selecting additional cells or ranges.

■ To select an entire row, click the row's number at the far left of the row.

■ To select an entire column, click the column letter at the top of the column.

■ To select the same range on two or more worksheets, select the worksheets before selecting the range. See Chapter 3, "Working with Workbook Files," for instructions on how to select worksheets.

Click here and hold down the left mouse button

**FIGURE 4.10**

You can click and drag to select a range.

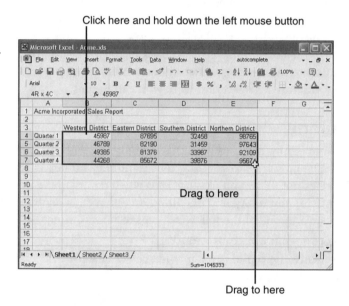

Drag to here

Drag to here

## Naming Cell Ranges

You can treat the individual cells as a group of cells by naming the range. After a range has a name, you can quickly select it using the Go To command. You can also perform mathematical operations on the values contained in the range. For example, if you have a range named Income that contains cells in which you type the amount of each of your paychecks, you can enter the function =SUM(Income) to determine your total pay. (You can name individual cells or ranges.)

To name a cell or range, take the following steps:

1. Select the cell(s) you want to name.

2. Click in the **Name** box on the left end of the formula bar. (This is the box that displays the selected cell's address.)

3. Type a brief, descriptive name for the range, as shown in Figure 4.11. Names can include up to 255 characters (no spaces allowed), but try to use a name that's 10 characters or fewer. You don't want to type a long name whenever you use the Go To feature or use the name in a formula.

4. Press **Enter**. The name appears in the Name box.

Click here and type a name

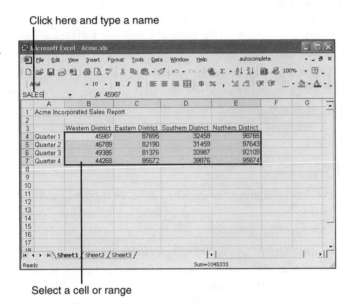

**FIGURE 4.11**

You can name a
single cell or a
range.

Select a cell or range

# Copying and Moving Data

When creating and editing worksheets, you frequently need to move or copy data from one cell or range to another. The Copy option places a duplicate copy of the cell's contents and formatting on the Clipboard. The Cut option moves the contents and formatting of the cell or range to the Clipboard. In either case, you can then use the Paste option to insert the cell contents somewhere else on the same worksheet, on another worksheet, or in another workbook. The following sections show you how to copy and move data.

## Copying a Selection

Excel provides several methods for copying and pasting data. The following list explains the three most common and efficient techniques:

**Ctrl+Drag-and-Drop:** Select the cell or range. Move the mouse pointer over the border of one of the selected cells. (The mouse pointer appears as a four-headed arrow.) Hold down the **Ctrl** key and the left mouse button while dragging the cell or range to where you want the copy placed. Release the mouse button.

**Edit, Copy:** Select the cell or range. Open the **Edit** menu and choose **Copy** (or press **Ctrl+C**). Click the cell into which you want to paste the entry, or, if you copied a range, click the cell in the upper-left corner of the area where you want the copied range pasted. Open the **Edit** menu and click **Paste** (or press **Ctrl+V**).

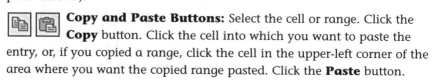 **Copy and Paste Buttons:** Select the cell or range. Click the **Copy** button. Click the cell into which you want to paste the entry, or, if you copied a range, click the cell in the upper-left corner of the area where you want the copied range pasted. Click the **Paste** button.

## Moving a Selection

Moving data is nearly identical to copying data, except that the data is removed from its original location. Likewise, the techniques for moving data are nearly identical to those for copying data:

**Drag-and-Drop:** Select the cell or range. Move the mouse pointer over the border of one of the selected cells. (The mouse pointer appears as a four-headed arrow.) Hold down the left mouse button while dragging the cell or range to where you want it moved. Release the mouse button.

**Edit, Cut:** Select the cell or range. Open the **Edit** menu and choose **Cut** (or press **Ctrl+X**). Click the cell into which you want to paste the entry, or, if you cut a range, click the cell in the upper left corner of the area where you want the cut range pasted. Open the **Edit** menu and click **Paste** (or press **Ctrl+V**).

**Cut and Paste Buttons:**
Select the cell or range. Click the **Cut** button. Click the cell into which you want to paste the entry, or, if you cut a range, click the cell in the upper-left corner of the area where you want the cut range pasted. Click the **Paste** button.

> **tip**
>
> You can right-click a selection for quick access to the Cut, Copy, and Paste commands.

## Erasing Data

Sometimes, rather than move data, you might want to permanently remove it. Excel provides two options for removing data entries:

■ **Clear** enables you to remove data only, formatting only, comments only, or everything (data, formatting, and comments), returning the cells to their pristine state.

■ **Delete** removes the cells and everything in them. Neighboring cells are shifted left or up to fill in the blank space. (You learn how to delete cells in Chapter 5, "Controlling Rows, Columns, and Cells.")

> **tip**
>
> To quickly clear only the contents of cells, select the cells and press the **Delete** key.

To clear a range of formatting, data, comments, or everything, take the following steps:

1. Select the cell or range you want to clear.

2. Open the **Edit** menu, point to **Clear**, and click the desired option, as shown in Figure 4.12:

   **All** to clear formatting, content, and comments.

   **Format** to remove the formatting but leave the data entries and comments in place.

   **Content** to remove the data entries but leave the formatting and comments in place.

   **Comments** to remove the comments but leave the data entries and cell formatting in place.

**FIGURE 4.12**

Use the Edit, Clear options to empty the cells or remove comments or formatting.

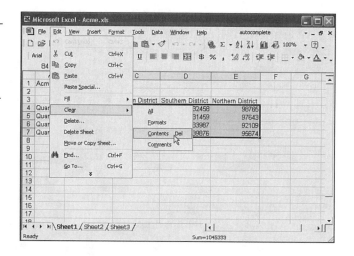

# Undoing Actions and Commands

Whatever you do to your worksheet, you can undo, as long as you don't close the worksheet or exit Excel. To undo your most recent action, simply click the **Undo** button or press **Ctrl+Z**. You can click Undo or press Ctrl+Z several times to back through a series of changes. You can even undo the Undo command by clicking the **Redo** button or pressing **Ctrl+Y**.

Next to the Undo button is a downward-pointing arrow that opens the Undo menu. This menu contains a list of all the actions you performed, starting with the most recent. Contrary to what you might think, the Redo menu does not enable you to pick any action in the list to undo. When you pick an action down the list, that action and all actions that were performed after it are undone. In other words, you can undo the most recent action or the five most recent actions, but you cannot undo only the seventh action. To undo several actions, open this menu and click the last action you want to undo. Excel undoes the selected action and all actions performed after that. (Redo has its own menu, as well.)

# THE ABSOLUTE MINIMUM

The single most important and most time-consuming chore you face when you create a worksheet or workbook is *data entry*, and now that you have completed this chapter, you know everything you need to know, and then some, about entering various types of data in cells. You now know how to

> Move from one cell to another and use the scroll bars to bring additional cells into view.

> Enter labels, values, dates, and times, and adjust the number formats, so the numbers actually look like dollar amounts, percentages, dates, and times.

> Double-check your data entries as you type them by having Excel read them aloud back to you.

> Copy a cell entry into numerous cells and even fill several cells with a series of entries by using AutoFill.

> Replace or edit data entries.

> Select, move, copy, and delete cell entries.

> Undo your most recent edit or command and undo the Undo command.

With the skills you acquired in this chapter, you can create a basic worksheet consisting of labels and values. You can even dress it up a little by formatting numbers as dollar amounts and percentages. You may have found, while working through this chapter, that you have a tough time making all your data entries fit into those tiny boxes. Fortunately, the next chapter shows you how to take control of rows, columns, and cells to give your data more room to spread out.

5

# CONTROLLING ROWS, COLUMNS, AND CELLS

# Changing Column Widths

When you start typing entries, you soon realize how small worksheet cells really are. If you type more than 9 or 10 characters, your entry extends outside the box, and Excel must adjust the column width or truncate the entry to make it fit.

Though Excel does a fairly good job of adjusting column widths to accommodate long entries, you may need to adjust the column widths yourself. Excel offers several methods for changing column widths:

- **Let Excel Adjust the Column Width:** Move the mouse pointer over the right border of the column heading, so the pointer takes on the appearance of a two-headed arrow. (See Figure 5.1.) Hold the mouse steady while double-clicking the left mouse button. Excel automatically adjusts the column width to accommodate the widest entry in the column. (Or, select the column(s) and then open the **Format** menu, point to **Column**, and click **AutoFit Selection**.)

- **Drag and Drop Column Width:** Move the mouse pointer over the right border of the column heading, so the pointer takes on the appearance of a two-headed arrow. Hold down the left mouse button and drag to the left (to make the column skinnier) or to the right (to widen the column).

- **Specify a Precise Column Width:** Select a cell in the column whose width you want to change, or drag over the column headings to select multiple columns. Open the **Format** menu, point to **Column**, and click **Width**. Type a number from 0 to 255 to specify the desired number of characters wide you want the column to be, and then click **OK**. (A column width of 0 hides the column.)

> ## tip
>
> You can change Excel's default column width to specify the column width you want Excel to use for all columns in a workbook.
>
> Right-click a worksheet tab and choose **Select All Sheets**. Open the **Format** menu, point to **Column**, and choose **Standard Width**. In the Standard Column Width text box, type the number of characters wide you want the columns to be. Click **OK**.

- **Match Another Column's Width:** To make one column the same width as another, select a cell in the column whose width you want to match and then click the **Copy** button in the Standard toolbar. Open the **Edit** menu and click **Paste Special**. Click **Column Widths** and click **OK**.

Double-click here

**FIGURE 5.1**

You can have Excel automatically adjust the column width.

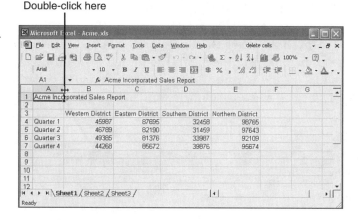

# Changing Row Heights

Initially, row height is set at 12.75 points to accommodate 10-point text and leave a little space between the rows. If you increase the font size, Excel automatically bumps up the row height. If the row height Excel chooses is not the row height you want, you can change the row height yourself by taking one of the following steps:

**Let Excel Adjust the Row Height:** Move the mouse pointer over the bottom border of the row heading, so the pointer takes on the appearance of a two-headed arrow. (See Figure 5.2.) Hold the mouse steady while double-clicking the left mouse button. Excel automatically adjusts the row height to accommodate the tallest entry in the row. (Or select the row(s) and then open the **Format** menu, point to **Row**, and click **AutoFit**.)

**Drag and Drop Row Height:** Move the mouse pointer over the bottom border of the row heading, so the pointer takes on the appearance of a two-headed arrow. Hold down the left mouse button and drag down (to make the row taller) or up (to shorten the row).

**Specify a Precise Row Height:** Select a cell in the row whose height you want to change, or drag over the row headings to select multiple rows. Open the **Format** menu, point to **Row**, and click **Height**. Type a number

**tip**

To select the entire worksheet (to change the width of all columns or height of all rows), click the **Select All** button in the upper-left corner of the worksheet (the gray box directly above the row heading 1 and to the left of the column heading A).

from 0 to 409 to specify the desired number of points tall you want the row to be, and then click **OK**. (A row height of 0 hides the row.)

> **Match Another Row's Height:** To make one row the same height as another, click the number to the left of the row that is the desired height. Click the **Format Painter** button and then click the number to the left of the row whose height you want to change.

Double-click here

**FIGURE 5.2**

You can have Excel automatically adjust the row height.

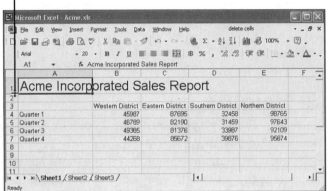

# Wrapping Text in Cells

When you need to insert a long entry into a cell, adjusting the column width and row height may not provide the entry with sufficient room. In such cases, consider having Excel *wrap* the text in the cell. With the wrap feature on, Excel places the entry on two or more lines within the cell, adjusting the row height as needed to accommodate the additional lines. To wrap text in a cell, take the following steps:

1. Select the cell(s) in which you want text to wrap.
2. Open the **Format** menu and choose **Cells**. The Format Cells dialog box appears.
3. Click the **Alignment** tab.
4. Click **Wrap Text** to place a check mark in its box, as shown in Figure 5.3.
5. Click **OK**.

**FIGURE 5.3**

You can choose to have text wrap inside a cell.

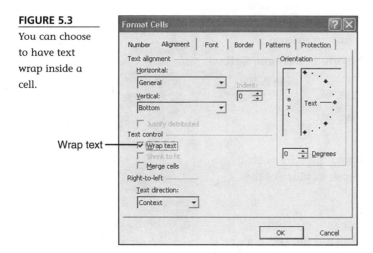

# Merging Cells

Occasionally, you may wish to *merge* two or more cells to create a large cell that spans several columns or rows. This is useful for adding a title to your worksheet or inserting row labels that apply to several rows in a worksheet. See Figure 5.4.

Single cell spans several columns

**FIGURE 5.4**

You can merge two or more cells to create a single, larger cell.

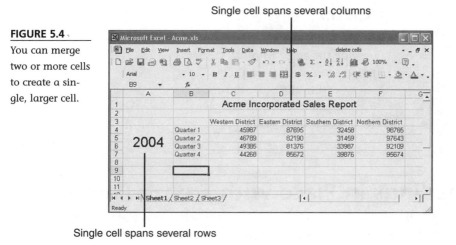

Single cell spans several rows

To merge cells, take the following steps:

1. Select the cells you want to merge.

2. Open the **Format** menu and choose **Cells**. The Format Cells dialog box appears, as shown in Figure 5.5.

3. Click the **Alignment** tab.

4. Click **Merge cells.**

5. Click **OK**. Excel merges the cells and displays a single large cell in place of the smaller cells.

To return the cells to their original (pre-merged state), repeat the steps, removing the check mark from the Merge cells box.

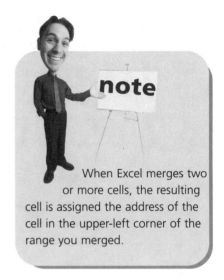

note

When Excel merges two or more cells, the resulting cell is assigned the address of the cell in the upper-left corner of the range you merged.

**FIGURE 5.5**

You can choose to merge the selected cells.

Click Merge cells

# Locking Headings in Place with Freeze Panes

In most worksheets, you type a label at the top of each column or to the left of each row to indicate the type of data in each cell. When you're typing data entries in a column or row, these labels help you figure out what you need to type in each cell. Unfortunately, as you scroll down or to the right, your column and row headings scroll outside the viewing area. To keep them onscreen, you can freeze the columns or rows by taking the following steps:

1. Click the cell that's directly below the row(s) you want to freeze and to the right of the column(s) you want to freeze, as shown in Figure 5.6.

2. Open the **Window** menu and choose **Freeze Panes**. A dark line appears below the frozen rows and to the right of the frozen columns. The frozen rows and columns remain onscreen at all times.

To unlock the panes, first make sure the worksheet with the frozen panes is displayed. (The cell selector can be anywhere on the worksheet.) Open the **Window** menu and choose **Unfreeze Panes**.

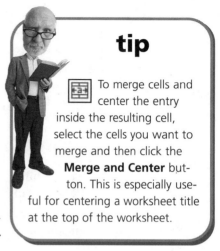

**tip**

To merge cells and center the entry inside the resulting cell, select the cells you want to merge and then click the **Merge and Center** button. This is especially useful for centering a worksheet title at the top of the worksheet.

These columns will be frozen

These rows will be frozen

**FIGURE 5.6**

Choose the cell below the rows and to the right of the columns you want to freeze.

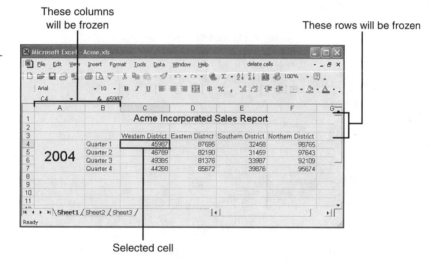

Selected cell

# Inserting Rows and Columns

Given the fact that every worksheet contains 256 columns and 65,536 rows, you would think that you would never need to add columns or rows to a worksheet, and that's true. However, you might need to insert a row or column between two rows or columns that already contain data. In such cases, you can use Excel's Insert command to add rows and columns right where you need them.

## Inserting One or More Columns

When inserting columns, keep in mind that new columns are inserted *to the left* of the currently selected cell or column. To insert a column, take the following steps:

**tip**

To insert a new column quickly, right-click the column letter to the left of which you want the new column inserted and choose **Insert**.

1. Click a cell in the column that is to the right of where you want the new column inserted. Or click the column's heading—the letter at the top of the column. (The new column will be inserted to the *left* of the selected column.)

2. Open the **Insert** menu and click **Columns**, as shown in Figure 5.7. Excel inserts a single column to the left of the currently selected column and adjusts the column letters accordingly.

New column will be inserted to the left of this column

Choose Insert, Columns

**FIGURE 5.7**

You can insert a column to the left of the current column.

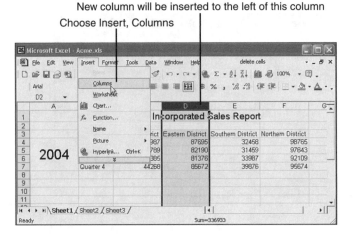

To insert multiple columns, drag over the same number of column headings as the number of columns you want to insert—for example, to insert three columns, drag over three column headings. Then, choose **Insert**, **Columns**. Excel inserts the new columns to the left of the selected columns.

## Inserting One or More Rows

When inserting rows keep in mind that new rows are inserted *above* the currently selected cell or row. To insert a row, take the following steps:

1. Click a cell in the row that's below where you want the new row inserted. Or click the row's heading—the row number at the far left of the row. (The new row is inserted *above* the selected row.)

2. Open the **Insert** menu and click **Rows**, as shown in Figure 5.8. Excel inserts a single row above the currently selected row and adjusts the row numbers accordingly.

**tip**

To insert a new row quickly, right-click the row number above which you want the new row inserted and choose **Insert**.

To insert multiple rows, drag over the same number of row headings as the number of rows you want to insert—for example, to insert three rows, drag over three row headings. Then, choose **Insert**, **Rows**. Excel inserts the new rows above the selected rows.

**FIGURE 5.8**

You can insert a row above the current row.

New row will be inserted above this row
Choose Insert, Rows

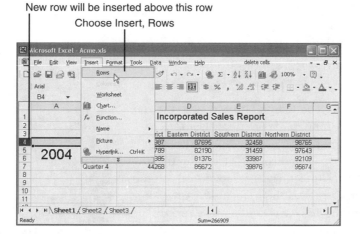

## Inserting Cells

As you enter data into a worksheet, you might skip an entry and end up typing all subsequent entries in the wrong cells. Fortunately, Excel enables you to insert blank cells right in the middle of a data area. Excel then shifts adjacent cells right or down to accommodate the new cells. To insert cells, here's what you do:

1. Click a cell or drag over a block of cells where you want the new cell(s) inserted. Excel inserts the same number of cells as the number you select.

2. Open the **Insert** menu and choose **Cells**. The Insert dialog box appears, as shown in Figure 5.9, asking which direction you want adjacent cells shifted.

3. Choose one of the following options:

**Shift cells right** moves the selected cell(s) to the right to make room for the new cell(s).

**Shift cells down** moves the selected cell(s) down to make room for the new cell(s).

**Entire row** inserts entire row(s) above the currently selected row(s).

**Entire column** inserts entire column(s) to the left of the currently selected column(s).

4. Click **OK**. Excel inserts the number of blank cells that matches the number of selected cells and shifts adjacent cells in the specified direction.

**FIGURE 5.9**

Specify the direction in which you want cells to shift.

# Deleting Rows and Columns

In Chapter 4, you learned how to clear the contents, formatting, and comments from selected rows and columns. Clearing removes the contents of the rows and columns, leaving the rows and columns intact. Deleting rows and columns completely removes them, including anything they contain. To completely remove rows or columns, take these steps:

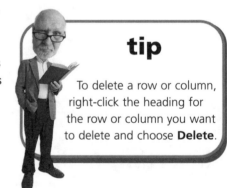

**tip**

To delete a row or column, right-click the heading for the row or column you want to delete and choose **Delete**.

1. Click the row or column heading for the row or column you want to delete. To select multiple rows or columns, drag over their headings.

2. Open the **Edit** menu and choose **Delete**. Excel immediately removes the selected rows or columns and shifts rows up (or columns left) to fill in the space left by the deleted rows or columns.

# Deleting Cells

As with rows and columns, you can choose to *clear* the contents, formatting, and/or comments from cells, leaving the cells intact, or you can *delete* the cells, removing them and everything they contain.

In Chapter 4, you learned how to clear cells. To completely remove cells, take the following steps:

1. Select the cells you want to delete.

2. Open the **Edit** menu and choose **Delete**. The Delete dialog box appears, as shown in Figure 5.10, asking you to specify where you want the adjacent cells shifted.

3. Choose one of the following options:

    **Shift cells left** shifts cells on the right to the left to fill in the space.

    **Shift cells up** moves cells up from below the deleted cells to fill in the space.

    **Entire row** shifts entire rows up from below the deleted cells.

    **Entire column** shifts entire columns on the right to the left.

4. Click **OK**. Excel shifts the adjacent cells, rows, or columns as directed.

note

Pressing the **Del** key clears the contents of the selected cells. It does not remove the cells themselves.

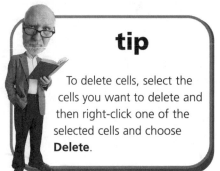

tip

To delete cells, select the cells you want to delete and then right-click one of the selected cells and choose **Delete**.

**FIGURE 5.10**

Specify the direction in which you want adjacent cells shifted.

# The Absolute Minimum

The lockstep structure of a worksheet might well be its most useful feature, but this rigid row-and-column format can often seem inflexible. Fortunately, now that you have completed this chapter, you have full control over the worksheet's structure. You now know how to

Widen columns to give cells more room for data entries.

Make rows taller and shorter.

Wrap long text entries inside cells.

Merge two or more cells to create a single cell.

Freeze column and row labels so they remain onscreen as you scroll.

Insert and delete rows, columns, and cells.

With the skills you acquired in this chapter, you can completely restructure a worksheet and give your data all the room it needs. In the next chapter, you change your focus from the structure and layout of your worksheet to its functionality as we begin to use formulas and functions to perform mathematical calculations.

**6**

# AUTOMATING CALCULATIONS WITH FORMULAS AND FUNCTIONS

# Learning the Order of Operations

One of your grade school math teachers probably introduced you to the *order of operations*, which governs the order in which a series of mathematical equations are performed. Excel follows this standard order of operations, as well. In every formula, Excel performs the equations from left to right in the following order, which gives some operators *precedence* over others:

1st    All operations in parentheses

2nd   Exponential equations or operations

3rd    Multiplication and division

4th    Addition and subtraction

This is important to keep in mind when you are entering formulas because the order of operations determines the result. For example, if you wanted to determine the average of the values in cells A1, B1, and C1, and you entered =A1+B1+C1/3, Excel would probably generate the wrong answer. Rather than total the three values and then divide by three, as you might expect, Excel first divides the value in C1 by 3 and then adds that result to A1+B1. It calculates this way because division takes precedence over addition. So, how do you correctly determine this average? You must enclose in parentheses the operations you want performed first. In this example, you need to total A1–C1 first. To do that, enclose the cell addresses in parentheses: =(A1+B1+C1)/3. This tells Excel to total the values *first* and then divide the total by three.

# Entering Formulas

As you learned in Chapter 1, "Understanding Excel Worksheets," every formula begins with an equal sign (=) and can include cell references, mathematical symbols (such as + and –), and actual numbers. You enter a formula in the cells in which you want the formula's *results* displayed. Excel gives you two options for entering formulas: you can type formulas or use the point-and-click technique. These techniques are described in the following sections.

## Using Point-and-Click Entry

The easiest and most foolproof way to enter a formula is to use the point-and-click approach. You simply start your formula with an equal sign, click cells to add their addresses to the equation, and type the required mathematical symbols. The following instructions lead you step by step through the process:

1. Select the cell in which you want the formula's result to appear.

2. Type the equal sign (=).

3. Click the cell whose address you want to appear first in the formula. The cell address appears in the Formula bar.

4. Type a mathematical operator after the value to indicate the next operation you want to perform. For example, type **+** to add the next entry, **–** to subtract, **\*** to multiply, or **/** to divide by.

5. Continue clicking cells and typing operators until you finish entering the formula, as shown in Figure 6.1. (Remember to group operations using parentheses, if necessary, to control the order of operations.)

6. When you finish, press **Enter** to accept the formula.

### caution

If an error message appears in the cell in which you typed a formula, make sure you did not enter a formula that told Excel to do one of the following: divide by 0 or a blank cell, use a value from a blank cell, delete a cell being used in a formula, or use a range name when a single cell address was expected. For more about formula error messages, see "Troubleshooting Errors in Formulas," later in this chapter.

**FIGURE 6.1**

The easiest way to compose formulas is to point and click.

Click a cell to insert its address          Start with an equal sign

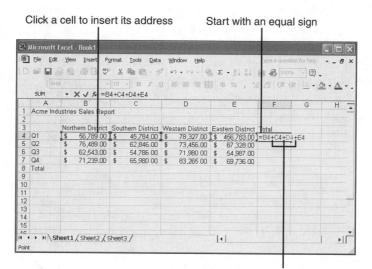

Type mathematical operators between cell addresses

## Typing Formulas Manually

Though point-and-click formula entry is the best error-free method of constructing formulas, typing is typically faster. To type a formula, click the cell in which you want the formula's result to appear, and then type the formula, starting with an equal sign, and press **Enter**. To use a value from another cell in your formula, type the cell's address. For example, if cell H3 contains your monthly income and you want to insert your annual income in cell H4, you would type =H3*12. This tells Excel to multiply the value in cell H3 by 12 and display the result.

## Displaying Formulas

When you enter a formula, Excel displays the result of that formula in the cell. When you're checking your worksheet for errors, however, you may want to view the formulas rather than their results. In such cases, you can switch to formula-display mode by pressing Ctrl+` (hold down the Ctrl key while pressing the grave accent key). Excel displays not only the formula, but also highlights the cells referenced in the formula, as shown in Figure 6.2. Press Ctrl+` to switch back to displaying the results. (For more information on viewing and troubleshooting formulas, see "Troubleshooting Errors in Formulas," later in this chapter.)

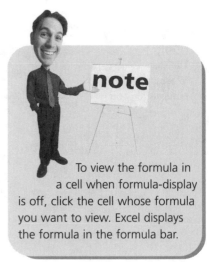

**tip**

Name the cells you want to refer to in your formula. You can then use the cell names in your formulas rather than using cryptic cell references. For example, if your worksheet has a cell named Income that displays your total income and another cell named Expenses that contains your total expenses, you can enter the formula =Income–Expenses to determine your net profit.

**note**

To view the formula in a cell when formula-display is off, click the cell whose formula you want to view. Excel displays the formula in the formula bar.

**FIGURE 6.2**

In formula-display mode, Excel displays formulas, rather than their results, in cells.

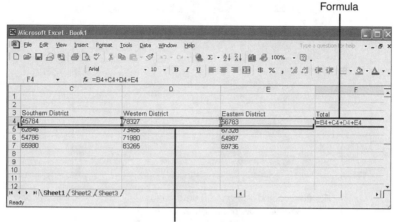

Formula

Cells referenced in the formula

# Editing Formulas

If you make a mistake while entering a formula, backspace over it and enter your correction as you would with any other cell entry. If you already accepted the entry (by pressing **Enter** or clicking the check mark button), take one of the following steps to edit the entry:

- Double-click the cell to enter Edit mode, and then edit the formula as you would edit any entry.
- Select the cell that contains the formula, click in the formula bar, and edit the formula as you would edit any entry.
- Select the cell that contains the formula, press **F2**, and then edit the formula right inside the cell.

# Copying and Pasting Formulas

You can copy and paste formulas just as easily as you copy and paste data entries. When you paste a formula, however, Excel adjusts the cell references in the formula to reflect their new positions in the worksheet. Figure 6.3 illustrates how Excel treats cell references when you paste a formula. Cell B8 contains the formula =B4+B5+B6+B7, which determines the total sales revenue for the Northern District. If you copy that formula to cell C9 (to determine the total sales revenue for the Southern District), Excel automatically changes the formula to =C4+C5+C6+C7. This is usually what you want Excel to do when you copy or move formulas.

**FIGURE 6.3**

Excel adjusts cell
references when
you copy
formulas.

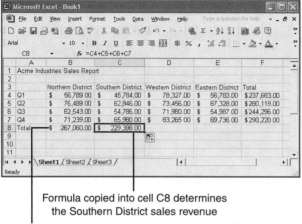

Formula copied into cell C8 determines
the Southern District sales revenue

Formula in cell B8 calculates the Northern
District's total sales revenue

Figure 6.3 shows a formula in which the cell references are *relative:* Excel changes
the cell addresses relative to the position of the formula. In this example, the formula was moved one cell to the right, so all the addresses in the formula are also
adjusted one cell to the right.

Sometimes, however, you might not want Excel to adjust a cell reference. Say, for
instance, that your worksheet has a formula that includes a reference to a cell that
contains the state sales tax percentage. You want that cell reference to remain
unchanged no matter where you move that formula or paste a copy of it. In such a
case, you can mark the cell address in the formula as an *absolute reference* to prevent
Excel from changing the address when you copy or move the formula to another
cell.

To mark a reference as an absolute, press the **F4** key immediately after typing the
reference or move the insertion point inside the cell reference and press **F4**. This
places a dollar sign before the column letter and the row number, as shown in
Figure 6.4. You can type the dollar signs yourself, but it's usually easier to let Excel
do it.

You also can mark the column letter *or* the row number (but not both) as absolute.
This enables the column letter or row number to change when you copy or move the
formula. Keep pressing **F4** until you have the desired combination of dollar signs.

**FIGURE 6.4**

To prevent a cell reference in a formula from changing, mark it as an absolute cell reference.

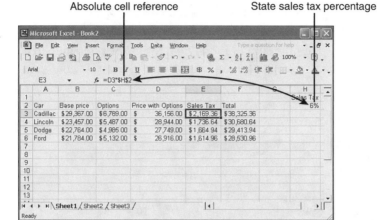

# Changing the Recalculation Setting

As you enter formulas, you might notice that Excel immediately performs the calculation and displays the result. If you change a value in a cell that the formula uses, Excel instantly recalculates the entire worksheet! If you have a slow computer and a long worksheet with a lot of formulas, this can slow down Excel significantly. To prevent Excel from bogging down, you can turn the Auto Calculation feature off. Here's what you do:

1. Open the **Tools** menu and choose **Options**. The Options dialog box appears.
2. Click the **Calculation** tab. The Calculation options appear, as shown in Figure 6.5.
3. Select **Manual** and click **OK**.

From now on, when you want to recalculate the worksheet, press **F9**.

**FIGURE 6.5**

You can choose manual recalculation to boost Excel's performance.

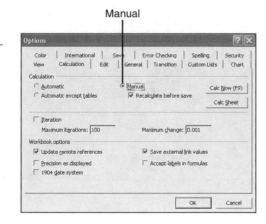

# Using the Auto Calculate Feature

Few Excel users notice that when they select a range of cells that contain values, the status bar displays the sum of those values, as shown in Figure 6.6. This provides you with a quick total of any values in the worksheet without your having to use a calculator.

Selected cells

**FIGURE 6.6**

Excel displays
the sum of
selected values.

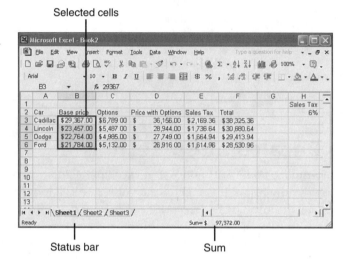

Status bar                           Sum

Even fewer Excel users realize that they can change the mathematical operation Excel performs on those values. Right-click the sum to display a context menu of available operations, as shown in Figure 6.7, and then click the desired operation.

Click the desired operation

**FIGURE 6.7**

You can change
the operation
Excel performs
on the values.

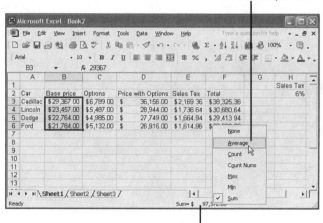

Right-click the sum

# Doing Higher Math with Functions

*Functions* are ready-made formulas you can use to perform a series of operations using two or more values or a range of values. For example, to determine the sum of a series of values in cells A5–G5, you can enter the function =SUM(A5:G5) rather than =A5+B5+C5+D5+E5+F5+G5. Other functions can perform more complex operations, such as determining the monthly payment on a loan when you supply the values for the principal, interest rate, and number of payment periods.

Every function must have the following three elements:

- **The equal sign (=)**: Indicates that what follows is a formula or function and not a label, value, or date.
- **The function name**: Indicates the type of operation you want Excel to perform—for example, SUM.
- **The argument**: Indicates the cell addresses of the values on which the function acts—for example, A3:F11. The argument is often a range of cells, but it can be much more complex.

A function can be part of another formula. For example, =SUM(A3:A9)+B43 uses the SUM function along with the addition operator to add the value in cell B43 to the total of the values in cells A3–A9.

## Using the AutoSum Tool

One of the tasks you perform most often is totaling a row or column of values. To simplify the process, Excel provides a tool devoted to determining totals—*AutoSum*.

To quickly determine the total of a row or column of values, first click an empty cell to the right of the row or just below the column of values. Then click the **AutoSum** button in the Standard toolbar, as shown in Figure 6.8. AutoSum assumes you want to add the values in the cells to the left of or above the currently selected cell, so it displays a marching ants box (called a *marquee*) around those cells. If AutoSum selects an incorrect range of cells, you can edit the selection by dragging over the cells whose values you want to total. When the AutoSum formula is correct, press **Enter** or click another cell.

If your worksheet contains two or more cells that contain subtotals, you also can use AutoSum to determine the grand total. Click the cell in which you want to insert the grand total and then click the **AutoSum** button. Click the first subtotal and then **Ctrl+click** any additional subtotals you want to include in the grand total. Press **Enter**.

Click the Enter button      Click AutoSum

**FIGURE 6.8**

**FIGURE 6.8**

With a click of a
button, AutoSum
determines the
total.

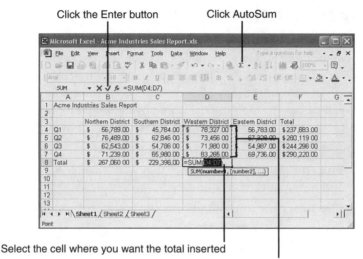

Select the cell where you want the total inserted

If you want different cells, drag over the cells that contain the desired values

Note that the AutoSum button doubles as a drop-down list. Click the arrow to the right of the button to access these additional functions:

- **Average** totals the values in the selected cells and divides by the number of values totaled to determine the average value.

- **Count** tallies the number of selected cells to determine the number of entries.

- **Max** compares all values in the selected cells and displays the highest value.

- **Min** compares all values in the selected cells and displays the lowest value.

- **More Functions** runs the Function Wizard, which leads you through the process of selecting a function and constructing the required argument. See the following section, "Entering Functions with the Insert Function Dialog Box."

## Entering Functions with the Insert Function Dialog Box

The SUM and AVERAGE functions are fairly easy to enter, because their arguments consist merely of a string of numbers. Some of the other functions, however—such as the financial function that determines the payment on a loan—contain several values and require you to enter those values in the proper *syntax* (order). To type the function, you must remember its name and know the required syntax, which can be quite difficult. The *Insert Function* dialog box can simplify the process greatly.

To use the Insert Function dialog box to paste a function into a cell, follow these steps:

1. Select the cell in which you want to insert the function.

2. 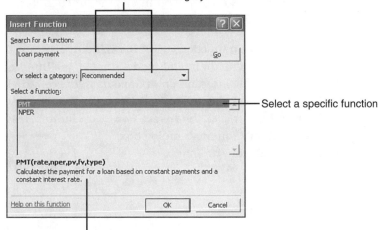 Open the **Insert** menu and select **Function**, or click the arrow to the right of the AutoSum button and click **More Functions**, or click the **fx** button in the formula bar. The Insert Function dialog box appears, as shown in Figure 6.9, displaying a list of available functions.

Type a description of what you want the function
to do, or select a function category

**FIGURE 6.9**

The Insert
Function dialog
box enables you
to select the
function rather
than type it.

Select a specific function

A description of the function appears here

3. Perform one of the following steps:

   In the **Search for a Function** box, type a description of what you want the function to do and then click the **Go** button or press **Enter**.

   Open the **Or Select a Category** list and select the type of function you want to insert. If you're not sure, select **All** to display the names of all the functions. They are listed alphabetically.

4. Select the function you want to insert from the **Select a Function** list and click **OK**. The **Function Arguments** dialog box appears, as shown in Figure 6.10, prompting you to type the argument. You can type

**note**

When you select a function in the Select a Function list, Excel displays a description of the function. Read this description to learn the purpose of the function.

values or cell addresses in the various text boxes. Alternatively, you can click the button to the right of the text box and then click the cell that contains the specified value.

5. Enter the values or cell ranges for the argument. You can type a value or an argument, or click the cells that contain the required values. (Some arguments, such as those that start with "If," are optional. Excel must "decide" which action to perform based on entries in your worksheet.)

6. Click **OK** or press **Enter**. Excel inserts the function and argument in the selected cell and displays the result.

When you need to edit a function, select the cell that contains the function you want to edit. (Make sure you're not in Edit mode—that is, the insertion point should not appear in the cell. If the insertion point appears in the cell, click a different cell and then click this cell again.) Open the **Insert** menu and select **Function**, or click the **Insert Function** button. This displays the Function Arguments dialog box, which helps you edit your argument.

## caution

If you click a button for one of the items in the Function Arguments dialog box, Excel tucks the dialog box out of the way, displaying the address of the currently selected cell and a button for bringing the dialog box back into view. After you select the desired cell, click the button to the right of the cell address to redisplay the dialog box.

Click the cell that contains the specified value

Click one of these buttons to hide the dialog box

**FIGURE 6.10**

Enter the values and cell references that make up the argument.

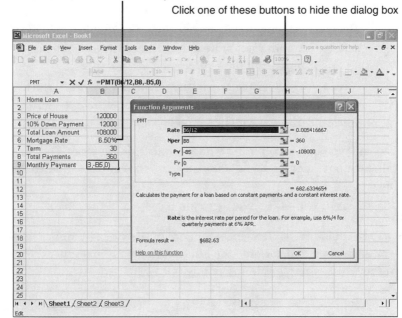

## Seeing a Loan Function in Action

To get some hands-on experience with functions, let's take a look at the PMT (*payment*) function. This function determines the monthly payment on a loan based on the loan amount, rate, and payment periods. Here's how the function and its argument appear:

### =PMT(rate,nper,pv,fv,type)

Let's break this down:

**=** An essential element in the function statement, as explained earlier.

**PMT** The function name, which stands for "payment."

**rate** The percentage rate of the loan per period. In other words, if you take out a 30-year mortgage at 6.5% and plan to make payments every month, the rate is 6.5%/12 or .541666%.

**nper** The number of payment periods. For example, on a 30-year mortgage, 12 payments are due per year, so the total number of payment periods would be 360.

**pv**  Stands for "present value," is the total amount you plan to borrow. This must be entered as a negative value. For example, if you're taking out a $120,000 loan, you would enter -**120000**.

**fv**  Stands for "future value," is zero—that is, the amount the loan will be worth after you pay the last payment.

**type**  Specifies the day in the payment period on which you are required to submit the payment—0 (or omit the type entry) for the last day of the payment period or 1 for the first day.

You can type a function using values in place of the codes. For example, to determine the payment on a $120,000, 30-year loan, at 6.5%, you could type the following:

**=PMT(.065/12,360,-120000,0,0)**

Or, you could use cell references in place of the values. Figure 6.11 shows a sample worksheet used to determine the future value of an investment. Note that each value in the typed example is in a separate cell.

**FIGURE 6.11**

Use cell references instead of values.

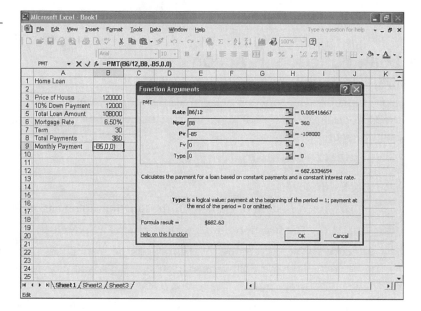

# Troubleshooting Errors in Formulas

When you enter a formula or function correctly, the cell that contains the formula or function displays the correct result of the equation. If the result is incorrect or the cell displays one of the error messages described in Table 6.1, the formula or function has a problem.

**TABLE 6.1** Formula and Function Error Messages

| Error Message | Indicates |
| --- | --- |
| ##### | Cell is too narrow to display the result. |
| #VALUE! | The wrong type of function, argument, or operand is in use. |
| #DIV/0! | The formula or function calls on Excel to divide a value by zero. In math, you are never allowed to divide a number by zero. |
| #NAME? | Excel does not recognize a cell reference or other text in the formula or function. Usually caused by a typo. |
| #N/A | A particular value inside the formula or function is unavailable to it. |
| #REF! | The formula or function contains an invalid cell reference. |
| #NUM! | A numerical value inside the formula or function is invalid. |
| #NULL! | The formula or function references an intersection of two ranges that do not intersect. Usually indicates that the formula has a space between two cell references instead of an operator or comma. |

In many cases, you can spot the cause of the problem by taking a quick glance at the formula or function. You may have mistyped an operator or cell reference or selected the wrong cell. To spot errors in more complex formulas and functions, however, you might need help. Fortunately, Excel features three of its very own *worksheet auditors* that can help you track down the causes of most errors. Following is a list of the worksheet auditors with a brief description of each:

- **Trace precedents** highlights the cells that supply values to the formulas, as shown in Figure 6.12. You can then verify the cell references in the formula and check to make sure the cells contain the correct values.

- **Trace dependents** highlights cells containing formulas that reference the currently selected cell.

- **Trace error** highlights any likely causes of a particular error message that appears in a cell that contains a formula or function. Trace error checks for syntax errors, wrong operands (mathematical symbols), and other possible causes.

**FIGURE 6.12**

Trace precedents highlights the cells that supply values to the formula.

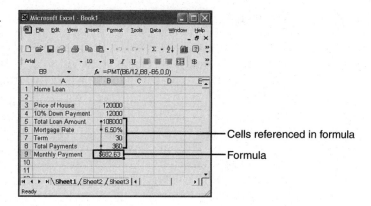

To run any one of these worksheet auditors, take the following steps:

1. Click the cell that contains the function or formula that is not working properly (or the cell that is referenced by a problem formula or function).

2. Open the **Tools** menu, point to **Formula Auditing**, and select the desired auditing tool: **Trace Precedents**, **Trace Dependents**, or **Trace Error**. The auditing tool displays arrows that point to the referenced cells or highlights errors. Figure 6.13 shows a worksheet analyzed by Trace Error.

4. Examine the contents of the cells that supply values to the formula and examine the formula for any faulty cell references, wrong mathematical operators, and typos.

5. To remove the auditor's highlighting and arrows, open the **Tools** menu, point to **Formula Auditing**, and click **Remove All Arrows**.

**FIGURE 6.13**

Trace Error can help you inspect a formula for common errors.

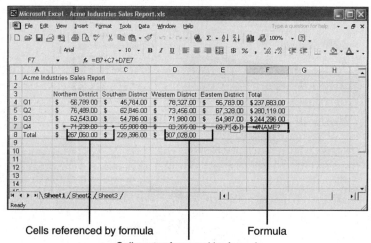

# Playing "What If?" with Scenarios

Say you're purchasing a home and need some idea of how much your monthly mortgage payment is going to be for various loan amounts. You have successfully created a worksheet that determines the monthly payment for a $120,000 house at 6.5%, but you want to know what the payment would be for a $110,000, a $130,000, and a $140,000 home. You also want to see the effects of other loan rates. You could create a bunch of separate worksheets, but a better solution is to create several scenarios for the same worksheet. A *scenario* is simply a set of values you plug into variables in the worksheet.

Excel offers a tool that enables you to plug various sets of values into your formulas to determine the effects of different values on the outcome. The following sections show you how to create and manage your own scenarios.

## Naming and Saving Different Scenarios

Making a scenario is fairly simple. You name the scenario, tell Excel which cells have the values you want to play with, and then type the replacement values you want Excel to use for the scenario. The following step-by-step instructions walk you through the process:

1. Display the worksheet for which you want to create a scenario.

2. Open the **Tools** menu and choose **Scenarios**. The Scenario Manager appears, indicating that this worksheet has no current scenarios.

3. Click the **Add** button. The Add Scenario dialog box appears.

4. Type a name for the scenario that describes the specific changes you're going to make. For example, if you were creating this scenario to determine payments for a $130,000 house at 6.75%, you might type **130K @ 6.75%**.

5. Click the **Changing Cells** text box and click the cell that contains the value you want to change in your scenario, as shown in Figure 6.14. To change values in other cells, hold down the **Ctrl** key and click them. (This inserts the addresses of the changing cells, separating them with commas.)

6. Click **OK**. The Scenario Values dialog box displays the current values in the cells you want to change.

7. Type the values you want to use for this scenario, as shown in Figure 6.15, and click **OK**. The Scenario Manager displays the name of the new Scenario.

Cells whose values
will be replaced    Cell references

**FIGURE 6.14**
Choose the cells
that contain the
values you want
to play with.

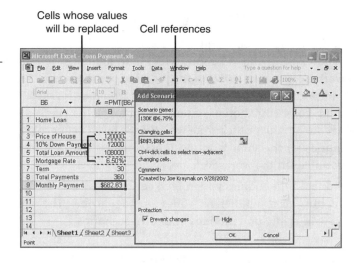

This entry replaces the price of the house in cell B3

**FIGURE 6.15**
To make a sce-
nario, enter dif-
ferent values for
the variables.

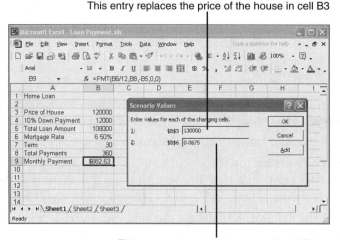

This entry replaces the loan rate in cell B6

8. To view a scenario, click its name and click the **Show** button. Excel replaces the values in the changing cells with the values you entered for the scenario.

## Viewing the Results of Different Scenarios

Whenever you want to play with the various scenarios you've created, open the **Tools** menu and choose **Scenarios**. This displays the Scenario Manager, introduced in the previous section. The Scenario Manager offers the following buttons for managing and displaying your scenarios:

- **Show**: Displays the results of the selected scenario right inside the worksheet.
- **Add**: Enables you to add another scenario.
- **Delete**: Removes the selected scenario.
- **Edit**: Enables you to select different cells used for the scenario and insert different values for the variables.
- **Merge**: Takes scenarios from various worksheets and places them on a single worksheet.
- **Summary**: Displays the results of the various worksheets on a single worksheet, as explained in the next section, "Creating a Summary Report."

**caution**

When working with scenarios, make sure the Auto Calculate feature is on, as explained earlier in this chapter. If the Calculation option is set to Manual, whenever you choose a scenario in the Scenario Manager and click Show, Excel does *not* recalculate the result with the scenario's values. To see the results, you must then close the Scenario Manager and then press F9 to calculate the results.

To play "What If?" with various scenarios, take the following steps to shift from one scenario to another:

1. Open the **Tools** menu and choose **Scenarios**. The Scenario Manager appears.
2. Click the name of the scenario you want to view.
3. Click the **Show** button. Excel replaces the values in the changing cells with the values from the scenario and shows the results. See Figure 6.16.
4. Repeat Steps 2 and 3 for any other scenarios you want to view.
5. When you've finished examining scenarios, click the **Close** button.

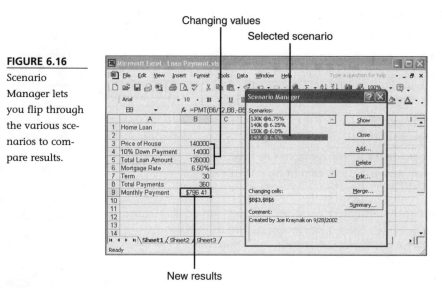

Changing values

Selected scenario

**FIGURE 6.16**

Scenario Manager lets you flip through the various scenarios to compare results.

New results

## Creating a Summary Report

Flipping through scenarios is an excellent way to see how the various scenarios affect the bottom line, but for a more thorough approach, consider creating a *scenario report*. A scenario report is a new, separate worksheet that displays the results of all your scenarios on a single page. And best of all, scenario reports are easy to create. Take the following steps:

1. Open the workbook that contains the desired scenarios.

2. Open the **Tools** menu and choose **Scenarios**. The Scenario Manager appears.

3. Click the **Summary** button. The Scenario Summary dialog box appears, prompting you to choose a report type and specify the cell in which the result appears.

4. Make sure Scenario Summary is selected and that the cell in which the scenario's result is displayed is selected.

5. Click **OK**. Excel creates a scenario report and displays a new worksheet tab for it, called Scenario Summary, as shown in Figure 6.17.

6. When you're finished with the report, simply click the tab for a different worksheet.

To get rid of the scenario report altogether, right-click the **Scenario Summary** tab and select **Delete**.

**FIGURE 6.17**

The Scenario Summary Report displays the results for all your scenarios on a single worksheet.

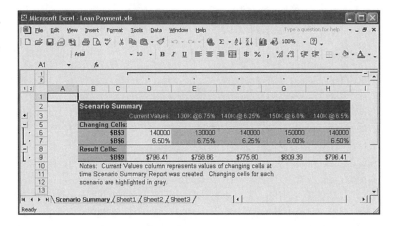

# THE ABSOLUTE MINIMUM

The most powerful features of any worksheet are the formulas and functions it contains. You can now create custom accounting sheets, complete with their very own built-in calculators. Specifically, you learned how to

Control the order in which Excel carries out its mathematical operations.

Enter formulas by typing them or using the point-and-click technique.

Copy and paste formulas and control cell references in formulas by marking them as absolute or relative.

Insert functions for performing more complex mathematical operations.

Track down the cause of many of the most common formula errors.

Play "What If?" by creating scenarios that substitute one set of key values for another set of key values in a worksheet.

With the skills you acquired in this chapter, you can create a dynamic worksheet capable of computing accurate results in a matter of seconds. In addition, you can safely experiment with other values without affecting the condition of your original worksheet. Now that you have a working worksheet, it's time to move on to the next part, "Formatting, Charting, and Printing Your Worksheet."

# PART III

# Formatting, Charting, and Printing Your Worksheet

7

# Formatting Your Worksheet

# Letting Excel Design Your Worksheet with AutoFormat

Although your worksheet's content is more important than its appearance, a little creative formatting can make your worksheet more attractive and readable. For example, you can add shading to rows and columns to make the spreadsheet easier to follow, add boxes around cells or lines between columns and rows, and change the type style for your column and row labels to make them stand out.

Excel offers a formatting feature called *AutoFormat* that applies a design scheme to selected cells. The design scheme controls everything from fonts and alignment to shading and borders. To use AutoFormat, take the following steps:

1. Select the cells you want to format.

2. Open the **Format** menu, and select **AutoFormat**. The AutoFormat dialog box appears, displaying the available design schemes, as shown in Figure 7.1.

3. Scroll down the list of designs to view additional designs.

4. Click the desired design.

5. Click **OK**.

Pick a design

Scroll down the list to view additional designs

**FIGURE 7.1**

Pick one of AutoFormat's design schemes for your worksheet.

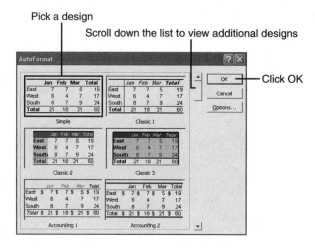

Click OK

Each design scheme contains settings that control the number format, borders, patterns (shading), font, alignment, row height, and column width of the selected area. You can disable some of the settings to tweak a design. When applying an AutoFormat design scheme, click the **Options** button to view a list of attributes the design scheme controls, as shown in Figure 7.2. Click an attribute to disable it (remove the check mark from its box). AutoFormat instantly redraws the design schemes to show how the design schemes look with the attribute disabled.

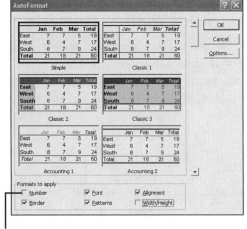

**FIGURE 7.2**
You can disable any of the attributes that the AutoFormat design scheme applies to your worksheet.

Click an attribute to turn it on or off

You need not accept everything AutoFormat does to the appearance of your worksheet. You can further customize the design by applying various formats to your worksheet manually, as instructed in the remainder of this chapter. You can also adjust column widths and row heights, as explained in Chapter 5, "Controlling Rows, Columns, and Cells."

# Changing the Appearance of Entries

Each data entry you type in a cell appears very generic—everything is displayed in Arial, 10-point type. Text entries are aligned on the left, and values are lined up on the right. If you want your worksheet to be merely functional, you can leave the entries as is. In many cases, however, you can make your worksheet more readable by making column and row labels larger, using a different typestyle, or applying text attributes, such as bold and italic. You might also want to change the way Excel aligns entries

**note**

AutoFormat does not change any formatting you applied to the worksheet yourself. If you have all your values displayed in Currency Style, and you choose a design that displays values as plain numbers, the values in your worksheet remain in Currency Style.

in cells or change a value's number format. The following sections provide instructions on how to take full control over the appearance of data entries in your worksheet.

## Changing Text Attributes with the Toolbar Buttons

The most convenient way to change the appearance of data entries in a worksheet is to use Excel's Formatting toolbar, shown in Figure 7.3. This toolbar contains buttons that provide single-click access to the most common text attributes. With it, you can change fonts, increase or decrease the type size, align text in cells, change the text color, add borders, and more.

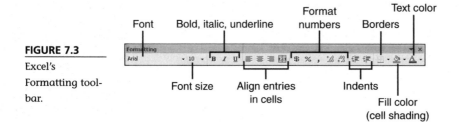

**FIGURE 7.3**
Excel's
Formatting tool-
bar.

To apply formatting with the Formatting toolbar, take the following steps:

1. Select the cells that contain the entries you want to format.

2. Do one of the following:

   Open the drop-down list for the attribute you want to change and then click the desired setting. For example, to change the text color, click the arrow to the right of the **Font Color** button, and then click the desired color.

   Click the button for the desired attribute. For example, to make the entries bold, click the **Bold** button.

**note**

Don't forget about the Undo button. If you apply an attribute, and the entries take on an undesirable appearance, click the **Undo** button to return the entries to their previous appearance.

Be aware that some of the buttons that open as drop-down lists retain the selected attribute. If you open the Font Color list, for example, and choose a color, the Font Color button retains the selected color. To apply the same color to other entries, select the cells that contain the entries, and then click the Font Color button.

## Using the Format Cells Dialog Box

The Formatting toolbar provides a quick way to apply common formats, but it does not give you access to all options. For that, you need to turn to the Format Cells dialog box. To apply formatting with this dialog box, select the cells you want to format, and then open the **Format** menu and select **Cells**. The Format Cells dialog box appears, as shown in Figure 7.4.

**FIGURE 7.4**

Each tab displays a set of related formatting options.

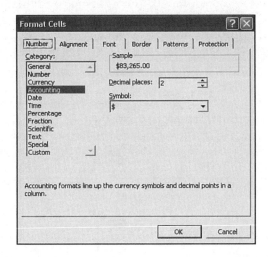

You can easily change many of the formatting features for your data by clicking the appropriate tabs in this dialog box and selecting the desired options. Following is a list of tabs in the Format Cells dialog box, along with a brief description of each tab:

- **Number**—Provides various formats to control the appearance of values, including currency, percentages, dates, and times. Select the desired category and then click the specific format you want to use, as explained in Chapter 4, "Entering and Editing Labels and Values," in the section "Adjusting Number Formats."

- **Alignment**—Enables you to control the way labels and values are positioned inside cells. You can even rotate text to display it on an angle inside a cell. See the following section, "Changing the Alignment of Entries in a Cell," for details.

- **Font**—Enables you to select a typeface and size for your text and to add enhancements, such as bold, italic, and color.

- **Border**—Provides options for adding lines between and around cells. (The light gray *gridlines* that Excel uses to mark cell boundaries do not print.) See "Adding Cell Borders," later in this chapter, for details.

- **Patterns**—Enables you to shade the selected cells. See "Adding Shading to Cells," later in this chapter, for details.

- **Protection**—Provides options for hiding the cell's contents or locking the cell (to prevent someone from editing it). This option does nothing, however, unless you choose to protect the worksheet. This is covered in Chapter 10, "Printing and Protecting Your Workbook, Worksheets, and Charts."

---

**CHANGING THE DEFAULT FONT**

To use any font as the normal font for all your worksheets, you can change the default font. Open the **Tools** menu, choose **Options**, and click the **General** tab. Open the **Standard Font** drop-down list and click the desired font. Open the **Size** drop-down list and click the font size you want. Then click **OK**. The change doesn't take effect until you restart Excel.

---

# Changing the Alignment of Entries in a Cell

When you enter data in an Excel worksheet, Excel automatically aligns the data entries within each cell. Text entries are pushed to the left side of the cells, and values are pushed to the right. All entries are aligned near the bottoms of the cells, and Excel adds a little space inside each cell border to prevent entries from overlapping. To change the way Excel aligns data entries in cells, take the following steps:

1. Select the cell or range you want to align. To center a title or other text over a range, select the entire range of cells in which you want the text centered, including the cell that contains the entry.

2. Open the **Format** menu and choose **Cells**. The Format Cells dialog box appears.

3. Click the **Alignment** tab. The alignment options appear, as shown in Figure 7.5.

4. Choose from the following options and option groups to set the alignment:

   **Horizontal** lets you specify left/right alignment in the cell(s). (The Center Across Selection option enables you to center a title or other text across a range of cells.)

   **Vertical** lets you specify how you want the text aligned in relation to the top and bottom of the cell(s).

**Text Control** contains three options: **Wrap text**, **Shrink to fit**, and **Merge cells**. **Wrap text** allows text to move from one line to the next within a cell; with wrap text off, all text within a cell appears on a single line. **Shrink to fit** reduces the font size of the text to make it fit in the cell on a single line. **Merge cells** combines the selected cells to make one big cell.

**Orientation** lets you tilt the entry within the cell from its normal 0° up to 90° or down to –90°. You can enter a setting in the Degrees text box or drag inside the half-clock area to set the desired tilt.

**Right-to-Left** is available only if you change the orientation of the entry. This setting enables you to have tilted text arranged according to its context, from left to right, or from right to left.

5. After you have set the options as desired, click **OK**.

**FIGURE 7.5**

Set the text alignment within a cell.

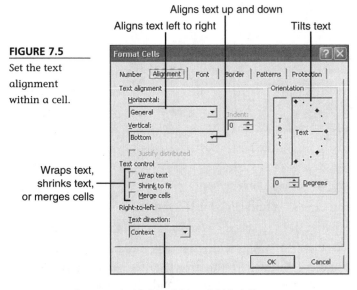

Aligns text up and down

Aligns text left to right

Tilts text

Wraps text, shrinks text, or merges cells

Arranges text left to right or right to left

# Adding Cell Borders

One of the most common attributes added to a worksheet are cell borders—lines that divide rows, columns, and cells. Borders provide a visual break and help the reader follow a line of data across a row or down a column. To add borders to your worksheet, take the following steps:

1. Select the row, column, cell, or range to which you want to add borders. (To add borders around all cells in the data area, drag over all cells that contain data entries.)

2. Open the **Format** menu and choose **Cells**. The Format Cells dialog box appears.

3. Click the **Border** tab. The border options appear, as shown in Figure 7.6.

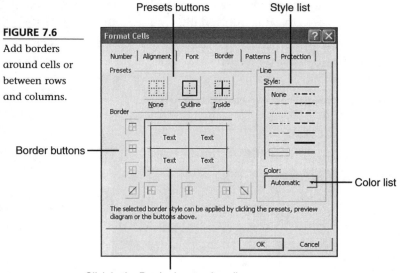

Presets buttons        Style list

**FIGURE 7.6**

Add borders around cells or between rows and columns.

Border buttons

Color list

Click in the Border box to place lines

4. In the **Style** list, click the desired line style.

5. Open the **Color** drop-down list and click the desired color for the borders.

6. Take one of the following steps to specify where you want the lines placed:

   Click one of the three Presets buttons: **None** removes any borders, **Outline** places a border around the perimeter of the selected area, and **Inside** adds lines between all the cells. You can click Outline and then Inside to place a border around each selected cell.

   Click the desired **Border** button to add a line between rows, between columns, at the top or bottom of the selected cell(s), or on the left or right side of the selected cell(s).

   Inside the large Border box (which has the word "Text" in it one or more times), click the area(s) where you want line(s) to appear. (You can click a line to remove it.)

7. Click **OK**.

Excel 2002 offers a Draw Border feature, which makes the process of adding borders much more intuitive. Click the arrow to the right of the **Borders** button in the Formatting toolbar and click **Draw Borders**, or right-click any toolbar and click **Borders** to display the Borders toolbar, as shown in Figure 7.7.

To draw borders with the Draw Borders toolbar, take the following steps:

1. 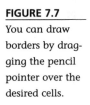 Click the **Line Color** button and click the desired color for your borders.

2. [line style selector] Open the **Line Style** list and click the desired line thickness and style.

3. [Draw Border button] Click the **Draw Border** button and select one of the following options:

**Draw Border** to draw a line along one of the gridlines or a box around the perimeter of a cell block.

**Draw Border Grid** to draw a line around a cell or lines around and between cells in a cell block.

**tip**

Use the Borders button in the Formatting toolbar to add borders. First select the cells, rows, or columns where you want to add borders. Click the arrow next to the **Borders** button and select the desired placement.

Pencil pointer                          Draw Borders toolbar

**FIGURE 7.7**

You can draw borders by dragging the pencil pointer over the desired cells.

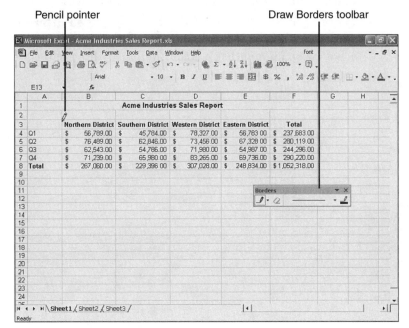

4. Drag over the gridline where you want a line placed or drag over the cell block you want to box in or add a grid to.

5. 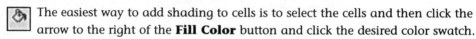 To erase a border, click the **Erase Border** button and take one of the following steps:

    Click a line segment to remove it.

    Drag over the cells where you want the borders removed.

# Adding Shading to Cells

To enhance your worksheet with a simple, dramatic effect, add shading to cells, rows, or columns. Like borders, shading not only helps you follow a row or column of entries, but it also enhances your worksheet's appearance.

The easiest way to add shading to cells is to select the cells and then click the arrow to the right of the **Fill Color** button and click the desired color swatch.

For more color and shading options, you can shade the cells using the Format Cells dialog box, as instructed in the following steps:

1. Select the row, column, cell, or range to which you want to add shading.

2. Open the **Format** menu and choose **Cells**. The Format Cells dialog box appears.

3. Click the **Patterns** tab.

4. Under **Color**, click the main color you want to use for the cell shading.

5. To overlay a pattern of a different color, open the **Pattern** drop-down list and click a pattern, as shown in Figure 7.8. Then open the **Pattern** drop-down list again and click a color (from the bottom of the list).

6. Click **OK**.

Click a pattern

**FIGURE 7.8**

Excel can create
a two-color pat-
tern for shading
the cells.

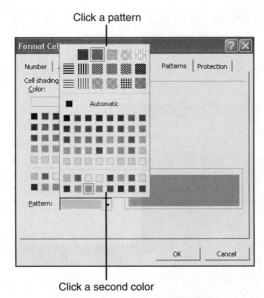

Click a second color

# Using Conditional Formatting to Flag Entries

You can apply *conditional formatting* to a cell to make Excel display a value in a
unique way if the value falls within a certain range. For example, you can apply a
conditional format telling Excel that if this value falls below 0, it should shade the
cell red and place a big, thick border around it to alert you. To apply conditional formatting, take the following steps:

1. Select the cell(s) that contains the formula(s) or value(s) you want to format.

2. Open the **Format** menu and choose **Conditional Formatting**. The
   Conditional Formatting dialog box appears, as shown in Figure 7.9. In steps
   3-5, you use the dialog box to create a condition that triggers Excel to apply
   the formatting; for example, you might construct a condition such as **Cell
   Value Is between 100,000 and 150,000**.

3. Open the drop-down list (on the far left) and choose the desired type of conditional formatting:

   **Cell Value Is** to base the conditional format on a value inside the cell. The
   value can be the result of a formula.

   **Formula Is** to base the conditional format on a TRUE or FALSE entry in the
   cell. Rather than produce a value as a result, some formulas and functions
   generate the result TRUE or FALSE.

4. Open the operator list, and choose the desired operator, such as **between** or **greater than**.

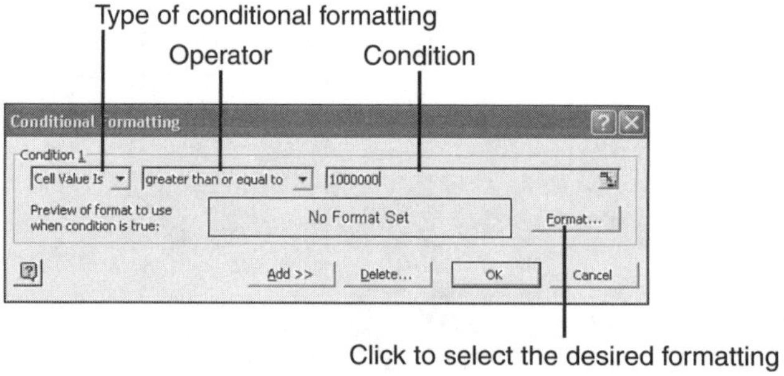

Type of conditional formatting

Operator          Condition

**FIGURE 7.9**

Have Excel
apply formatting
to a cell based
on the value in
that cell.

Click to select the desired formatting

5. In the text box(es) on the right, type the value or values that trigger Excel to apply the format.

6. If you need to specify another condition, click the **Add>>** button and repeat steps 3-5 to specify another condition.

7. Click the **Format** button. A streamlined version of the Format Cells dialog box appears, providing you with options for specifying font, border, and shading formats.

8. Use the Format Cells dialog box to select the desired formatting that Excel will apply to the cells if the specified condition is met.

9. Click **OK** to return to the Conditional Formatting dialog box.

10. Click **OK** to apply the conditional formatting and return to your worksheet.

# Copying Formatting with the Format Painter

 You can copy the formatting from one cell or a block of cells to other cells by using the Format Painter. Select the cell that contains the formatting you want to copy and click the **Format Painter** button (in the Standard toolbar). Drag your pointer (which now has a paintbrush icon next to it) over the cells you want to paint. Format Painter applies the formatting!

**tip**

To paint the format in multiple locations, double-click the **Format Painter** button to lock it in the "on" position. Then paint away. When you're finished, click the **Format Painter** button again to turn it off.

# Formatting with Styles

You can spend hours formatting a worksheet, applying multiple formats to various cells and tweaking the appearance of entries until your worksheet looks just right. Fortunately, Excel provides a feature that enables you to apply several formatting attributes with a single command or keystroke: *styles*.

A style is a group of cell formatting options that you can apply to a cell or cell block. If you change the style's definition later, that change affects the formatting of all cells formatted with that style. Each style contains specifications for one or more of the following options:

- **Number Format** controls the appearance of values, such as dollar values and dates.

- **Font** specifies the type style, type size, and any attributes for text contained in the cell.

- **Alignment** aligns entries in relation to the left, right, top, and bottom borders inside the cell.

- **Border** specifies the border placement and line style options for the cell.

- **Pattern** adds specified shading to the cell.

- **Protection** allows you to protect or unprotect a cell. See Chapter 10, "Printing and Protecting Your Workbook, Worksheets, and Charts," for details about protecting cells.

Excel provides the following six default styles:

**Normal:** The default style. Number is set to 0, Font to Arial, Size to 10 point, Alignment of numbers is right, and Alignment of text is left, No Border, No Pattern, and Protection is set to locked.

**Comma:** Number is set to #,##0.00.

**Comma [0]:** Number is set to #,##0.

**Currency:** Number is set to $#,##0.00_); (Red) ($#,##0.00).

**Currency [0]:** Number is set to $#,##0); (Red) ($#,##0).

**Percent:** Number is set to 0%.

The following sections show you how to apply these styles to selected cells, create your own styles, and save styles in a worksheet template.

## Applying Existing Styles

You can apply most of Excel's default styles by selecting the cell or cell range and then clicking on the appropriate button in the Formatting toolbar. For example, to apply the Currency format, select the cells, and then click the **Currency Style** button (the button with the dollar sign on it).

To apply an Excel style that does not have a button or to apply a style that you will create in the next section, perform the following steps:

1. Select the cell or range to which you want to apply the style.

2. Open the **Format** menu and choose **Style**. The Style dialog box appears, as shown in Figure 7.10.

3. Click the down arrow to the right of the **Style name** drop-down list and click the desired style. Excel applies the style to the selected cell or range.

Select a style

**FIGURE 7.10**

Use the Style dialog box to apply styles.

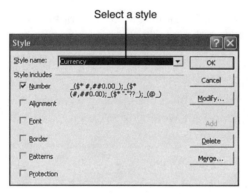

If you make much use of styles, consider placing the Styles drop-down list on the Formatting toolbar. Here's what you do:

1. Open the **Tools** menu and choose **Customize**. The Customize dialog box appears.

2. Click the **Commands** tab.

3. In the **Categories** list, click **Format**. The Format options appear in the Commands list.

4. Scroll down the **Commands** list and click the **Style** entry that has a drop-down list next to it. See Figure 7.11.

5. Drag the **Style** entry you just selected up to a blank area on the Formatting toolbar and release the mouse button to drop it in place. The Style drop-down list appears on the toolbar.

Now, whenever you want to apply a style to a cell or range, simply select the cell or range, open the Style list, and click the desired style.

Drag Style drop-down list to the Formatting toolbar

**FIGURE 7.11**

You can add a Style drop-down list to any toolbar.

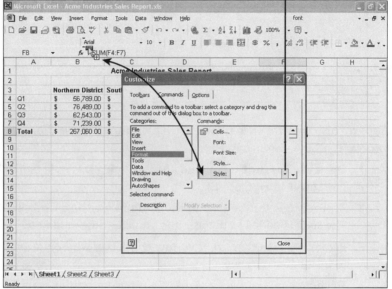

## Creating Your Own Styles

Because Excel features such a limited number of styles, you probably will want to create your own styles. The easiest way to create a style is by example—you format a cell or range to suit your tastes, and then create a style that saves the formatting applied to the cell(s). To create a new style by example, take the following steps:

1. Select a cell whose formatting you want to use.

2. Open the **Format** menu and choose **Style**. The Style dialog box appears, as shown in Figure 7.12.

3. Type a name for the style in the **Style Name** box.

4. Click the **Add** button. The named style is added to the Style Name box.

**tip**

If you added the Style drop-down list to the Formatting toolbar, as explained in the previous section, creating a style by example is even easier. Simply select the cell that has the desired formatting and then click in the Style box, type a name for the style, and press **Enter**.

Type a name for the style

**FIGURE 7.12**

Type a name for
the style and
click Add.

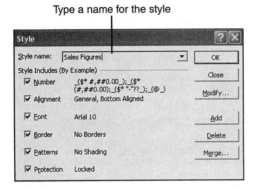

You can also create a style from scratch by using the Style dialog box, though the
process is a little step-heavy:

1. Open the **Format** menu and choose **Style**. The Style dialog box appears, as
   you saw it in Figure 7.12.

2. Type a name for the style in the **Style Name** box, and click the **Add** button.
   The style is added to the list, and you can now modify it.

3. Remove the check mark from any check box whose attribute you do not want
   to include in the style.

4. To change any of the format settings for the attributes in the list, click on the
   **Modify** button. Excel displays the Format Cells dialog box.

5. Use the **Format Cells** dialog box, as explained earlier in this chapter, to
   enter your formatting preferences for this style.

6. Click on **OK** or press **Enter**. You are returned to the Style dialog box.

7. Click on **OK** or press **Enter**. The style is created and saved.

## Editing Styles

If you apply a style to one or more cells and then modify the style later, any changes
you enter are immediately applied to all cells you formatted with that style. You
don't need to reapply the style to the cells you formatted with that style.

To edit a style, simply select the style in the **Style** dialog box, click the **Modify** button, and use the Format Cells dialog box to enter your preferences. Click **OK** to close
the Format Cells dialog box, and then click **OK** to save your changes.

## Saving Styles in a Template

Whenever you save a workbook, the styles you created while formatting that work-book stay with the workbook. You can also save the workbook as a template. When you create a new workbook, you can then choose one of the **New from Template** options to open a new workbook that contains the styles in that template. To learn how to save a workbook as a template, see Chapter 3, "Working with Workbook Files," in the section named "Saving a Workbook as a Template."

## Copying Styles from Another Workbook

If you already created a workbook and want to use styles you created in a different workbook, you can copy the styles from one workbook to the other. To copy styles, take the following steps:

1.  Open both workbooks.
2.  Switch to the workbook that will be receiving the styles.
3.  Open the **Format** menu and choose **Style**. The Style dialog box appears.
4.  Click the **Merge** button. The Merge Styles dialog box appears, as shown in Figure 7.13.
5.  Select the name of the worksheet to copy from.
6.  Click **OK** or press **Enter** to close the Merge dialog box.
7.  Click **OK** or press **Enter**.

Name of worksheet from which to copy styles

**FIGURE 7.13**

You can copy the styles from one workbook to another.

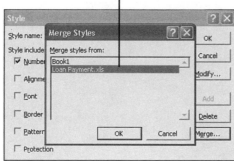

# THE ABSOLUTE MINIMUM

A worksheet without formatting is a dreary sight, but now that you have completed this chapter, you know everything you need to know to enhance your worksheets with color, lines, and better-looking text. Now you're able to

Give your worksheets a major overhaul with AutoFormat.

Change the most common text attributes by clicking a button in the Formatting toolbar.

Use the Format Cells dialog box to change number formats, control the way entries align in cells, and add borders and shading.

Make Excel flag data entries when they meet certain specified conditions.

Use the Format Painter to copy formatting from one cell and apply it to other cells.

Use styles to apply several formats to a cell or range with a single command.

With the skills you acquired in this chapter, you can liven up the most dreary worksheet and save loads of time by using styles. In the next chapter, we go beyond the mere appearance of numbers by transforming the numbers into something more meaningful: charts (graphs).

# 8

# CHARTING (GRAPHING). THE WORKSHEET DATA

# Understanding Charting Terminology

Graphs or *charts*, as Excel likes to call them, present data in a more meaningful, visual format. Instead of displaying a block of meaningless values, charts can help you compare annual sales figures, see which portions of a budget are devoted to various programs, analyze the growth of a portfolio, and much more.

In this chapter, you learn how to create various types of charts in Excel and enhance those charts to achieve the desired effect. But before you get started, you need to understand some key charting terminology, as defined in Table 8.1.

**TABLE 8.1**   Charting Terminology

| Charting Term | Definition |
| --- | --- |
| Chart | A diagram that shows the relationship between various values or sets of values. |
| Data series | A collection of related data, such as the monthly sales for a particular division. A data series is typically a single row or column of data. |
| Axis | An edge of a chart. A two-dimensional chart is comprised of an X-axis (horizontal line) and a Y-axis (vertical line). Charts that have a Z-axis display a third dimension, where the Z-axis adds the front-to-back dimension. |
| Legend | A color key that shows what each data series represents. Legends typically display several colors along with the name of the data series each color represents. |

# Creating a Chart

Charting data in Excel does not require you to return to the days of graph paper and rulers. You don't need to draw axes, plot points, or even connect the dots. Excel provides advanced tools that transform your data into any chart type you can imagine. You simply drag over the data you want to chart, run the Chart Wizard, pick a chart type, and enter any additional preferences. (See "Making Data Graphical with Charts," in Chapter 1, for descriptions of the most common chart types.)

The following sections show you how to create charts with Excel's Chart Wizard and how to use the Chart toolbar to modify the chart and enhance its appearance.

## Making a Chart with the Chart Wizard

Excel's Chart Wizard can whip up a chart in a matter of minutes, and best of all, the Chart Wizard leads you step-by-step through the process. To use the Chart Wizard, take the following steps:

1. Select the data you want to chart. If you typed names or other labels (Qtr 1, Qtr 2, and so on) and you want them included in the chart (as labels), include them in the selection.

2. Click the **Chart Wizard** button in the Standard toolbar. The Chart Wizard Step 1 of 4 dialog box appears, asking you to select the desired chart type. (Ignore the Custom Types tab for now.)

3. Make sure the **Standard Types** tab is up front, and then click the desired chart type in the **Chart Type** list, as shown in Figure 8.1. The Chart Sub-type list displays various renditions of the selected chart type.

4. In the **Chart Sub-type** list, click the chart design you want to use. (To see how this chart type appears when it charts your data, point to **Press and Hold to View Sample** and hold down the mouse button.)

Pick a chart type

**FIGURE 8.1**

The Chart Wizard leads you through the process of charting your data.

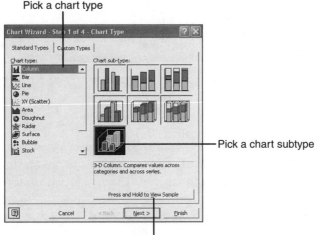

Pick a chart subtype

Point and hold down the mouse button to see how your data looks with the selected chart type

5. Click the **Next** button. The Chart Wizard Step 2 of 4 dialog box appears, asking you to specify the worksheet data you want to chart, which you have done already.

6. If the data you want to graph is already selected, go to Step 7. If the Chart Wizard is highlighting the wrong data, drag over the correct data in your worksheet, as shown in Figure 8.2. (You can move the Chart Wizard dialog box out of the way by clicking the **Collapse Dialog Box** button just to the right of the Data Range text box.)

Drag over the data you want to chart

**FIGURE 8.2**

If you selected
the wrong data,
you get a second
chance to
change it.

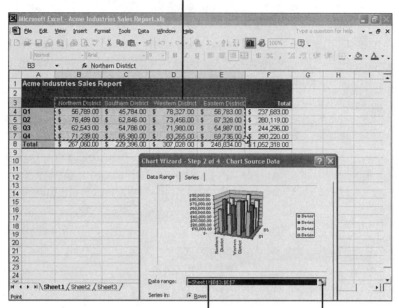

The range of the selected data appears here

The Collapse Dialog Box button

7. Under Series In, click **Rows** or **Columns** to specify how you want the data graphed. Your selection tells Excel which labels to use for the category axis and which ones to use for the legend. This is a tough choice that is best done by trial and error.

8. Click the **Next** button. The Chart Wizard Step 3 of 4 dialog box appears, prompting you to enter additional preferences for your chart.

9. Enter your preferences on the various tabs to give your chart a title, name the X and Y axes, turn on additional gridlines, move the legend, enter data labels, and more.

10. Click the **Next** button. The Chart Wizard Step 4 of 4 dialog box appears, asking whether you want to insert the chart on the current worksheet or on a new worksheet.

11. If you want the chart to appear alongside your data, select **As Object In** and choose the worksheet on which you want the chart to appear. To have the chart appear on a worksheet of its own, select **As New Sheet** and type a name for the sheet.

12. Click **Finish**. Excel makes the chart and adds it to your worksheet or as a separate worksheet.

To change any of the settings you entered for your chart, click the chart and then run the Chart Wizard again. Step through the Chart Wizard's four dialog boxes, and change any settings, as desired.

## Moving and Resizing a Chart

If your chart has only two or three data types to graph, it probably looks okay. If you choose to graph several columns or rows, chances are that all of your data labels are scrunched up, your legend is chopped in half, and your chart contains several other eyesores. Fortunately, you can fix most of these problems by resizing the chart.

If you inserted the chart as an object, you can move and resize the chart. First click the chart's background to select it. (If you haven't clicked outside the chart since creating it, it is already selected and the Chart toolbar is displayed.) Make sure you click the chart's background and not an object on the chart itself. When you click a chart's background, the entire chart should be selected, and tiny squares called *handles* appear around its perimeter, as shown in Figure 8.3. If you click an object, such as the data area or an axis, that object is selected, and handles appear around the selected object, not around the entire chart. This can be a bit tricky at first.

To resize the chart, drag one of its handles. To move the chart, position the mouse pointer over the chart (not on a handle), and drag the chart to the desired location. To delete the chart and start over, select the chart and press the **Delete** key. If the chart is on a separate worksheet, delete the worksheet.

**tip**

A chart blends in with the worksheet, acting like a clip art image "pasted" to the page. If you prefer to have the chart displayed in its own window, right-click the chart and choose **Chart Window**. To return to displaying the chart on its worksheet, right-click the chart and choose **Chart Window** to turn off the window view.

**note**

When resizing a chart, you can hold down the **Ctrl** key and drag to expand or shrink the chart from the center. Hold down the **Shift** key and drag to ensure that the chart retains its relative dimensions (that the horizontal and vertical axes become proportionally larger or smaller).

**FIGURE 8.3**

When the chart is selected, handles appear around its perimeter.

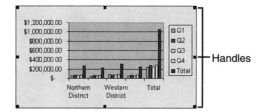

Handles

## Using the Chart Toolbar

One of the best tools for tweaking the chart design is the Chart toolbar. To display it, right-click any toolbar and click **Chart**. The Chart toolbar offers several chart formatting tools, as listed and described in Table 8.2. (If a button you want to use is not on the toolbar, click the **Toolbar Options** button, on the right end of the toolbar, point to **Add or Remove Buttons**, point to **Chart**, and then click the desired button.)

**TABLE 8.2** Chart Toolbar Tools

| Tool | Tool Name | Purpose |
|---|---|---|
| Chart Area ▾ | **Chart Objects** | Displays a list of the elements inside the chart. Select the item you want to format from this list, and then click the **Format Chart Object** button, listed next (where *Chart Object* is the type of object currently selected). |
|  | **Format *Chart Object*** | Displays a dialog box that contains formatting options for only the specified chart object. (The button's name varies depending on the object. If you selected the legend, the button's name is Format Legend.) |
|  | **Chart Type** | Enables you to change the chart type (bar, line, pie, and so on). |
|  | **Legend** | Turns the legend on or off. |

| Tool | Tool Name | Purpose |
|------|-----------|---------|
| ⊞ | **Data Table** | Turns the data table on or off. A data table displays the charted data in a table right next to (or on top of) the chart, so you can see the data and chart next to each other. |
| ▤ | **Series in Rows** | Charts selected data by row. (If the chart looks wrong, click Series in Columns.) |
| ▥ | **Series in Columns** | Charts selected data by column. (If the chart looks wrong, click Series in Rows.) |
| ⅋ | **Angle Clockwise** | Enables you to angle text entries so they slant down from left to right. Angled text is a nice effect, but it's also great for fitting text in a box when room is tight. |
| ⅋ | **Angle Counterclockwise** | Enables you to angle data labels so they slant up from left to right. |

The tools in Table 8.2 function differently, depending on the tool, but the following steps provide overall instructions on how to use the tools to format the various elements that make up the chart:

1. Open the **Chart Objects** list and choose the object you want to format.

2. Click the **Format *Chart Object*** button (where *Chart Object* is the type of object you selected in Step 1). The Format dialog box for the selected object appears. Figure 8.4 shows the Format Chart Area dialog box, which appears when you choose to format the chart area.

3. Enter your preferences and click **OK**.

**tip**

Right-click the chart or one of its objects to view a context menu that lists commands for formatting the selected object. Click the desired command and enter your preferences.

**FIGURE 8.4**

The Format
Chart Area dia-
log box.

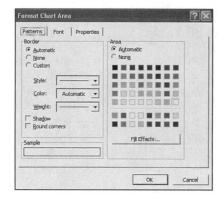

## Using the Chart Menu

Another way to access the options for formatting your charts is to use the Chart menu. This menu contains options for changing the chart type, selecting different data to chart, adding data, and even moving the chart to its own page. The Chart menu remains hidden when the worksheet is selected, but it pops into view on Excel's menu bar whenever you select a chart. Simply click **Chart** on Excel's menu bar, as shown in Figure 8.5, and then choose the desired option. If a dialog box pops up, enter your preferences and click **OK**.

For most formatting options, open the **Chart** menu and click **Chart Options**. The Chart Options dialog box appears, providing tabs for changing the chart and axes titles, configuring the axes, adding gridlines, positioning the legend, adding data labels, and turning the data table on or off. Enter your preferences and click **OK**. The following sections provide additional details for formatting specific design elements that make up the chart.

**FIGURE 8.5**

You can use the Chart menu to customize and format your chart.

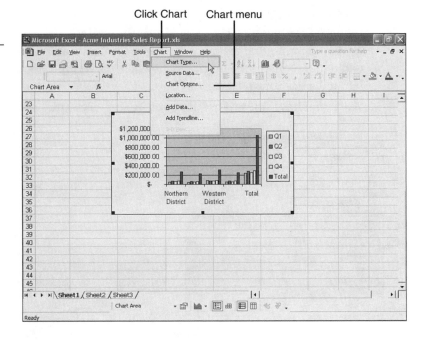

# Formatting Text on a Chart

Though charts are primarily graphic objects, every chart contains plenty of text in the form of a chart title, axis labels, and a legend. Even though the chart obtains its raw data (including text) from the worksheet, the chart itself controls the appearance of this text, and you can change the text appearance without affecting the appearance of your worksheet data.

Before formatting text on a chart, be aware that all entries that appear within an object on the chart use the same text formatting. For example, if you change the font for the legend, all entries in the legend appear in the same font. You can't change one legend entry without changing all of them.

To change the appearance of text on a chart, take the following steps:

1. Double-click the text whose appearance you want to change. You can change the appearance of the chart title, axis labels, or legend. The Format dialog box for the selected object appears.

2. Click the **Font** tab. The font options appear, as shown in Figure 8.6.

3. Use the font options to specify the desired font, text size, color, enhancements (such as bold and italic), and other text attributes.

4. If you are formatting text for axis labels, you can lean the text to provide additional room for the labels (so they don't overlap). Click the **Alignment** tab and enter your preferences.

5. When you have finished entering preferences, click **OK**.

**FIGURE 8.6**

The Font options.

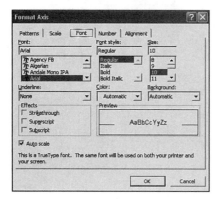

# Formatting the Chart Axes

Bar, column, line, area, and stock charts all have two axes (X and Y); 3D versions of these chart types include a third axis (Z). In addition to being able to change the fonts and alignment used for the axis labels, you can specify the line type and color of the axes, add tick marks, change the scale (value increments), and specify a number format.

To change the appearance of any axis of a chart, take the following steps:

1. Take one of the following steps to display the Format Axis dialog box for the desired axis, as shown in Figure 8.7.

   Right-click on the axis you want to format and choose **Format Axis**.

   In the Chart toolbar, open the **Chart Objects** list and click **Value Axis** or **Category Axis**, depending on which axis you want to format. Click the **Format Axis** button.

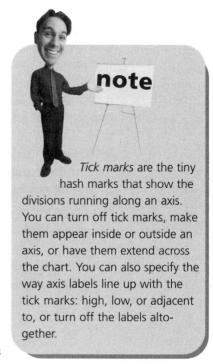

*Tick marks* are the tiny hash marks that show the divisions running along an axis. You can turn off tick marks, make them appear inside or outside an axis, or have them extend across the chart. You can also specify the way axis labels line up with the tick marks: high, low, or adjacent to, or turn off the labels altogether.

**FIGURE 8.7**

The Format Axis
dialog box lets
you change the
look of the axis
and its text.

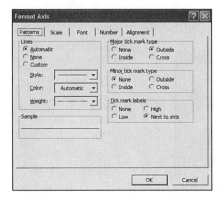

2. On the **Patterns** tab, select the desired line style, color, and weight for the
   axis, and enter any tick mark preferences.

3. Click the **Scale** tab and enter your preferences to specify how you want values or labels to appear along the axis. For example, if values run along the
   axis, you can specify the minimum value, the maximum value, and how you
   want values broken down between the minimum and maximum.

4. If values appear along the axis, click the **Number** tab and enter your preferences for the number format—Currency, Percentage, and so on.

5. Enter any additional preferences and then click **OK** or press **Enter**.

# Enhancing the Chart Frame

Up to this point, you have been micromanaging your chart, adding and removing
objects from the chart and formatting text, axes, and data series. For a more global
change, you can modify the overall appearance of a chart by adding a border or
shading. To change a chart's border and its background shading (or color), take the
following steps:

1. Select the chart. Handles appear around the entire chart.

2. In the Chart toolbar, open the **Chart Objects** list and click **Chart Area** and
   then click the **Format Chart Area** button, or right-click on the chart and
   choose **Format Chart Area**. The Format Chart Area dialog box appears, as
   shown in Figure 8.8.

Background color and shading

Border settings

**FIGURE 8.8**

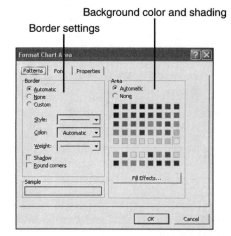

**FIGURE 8.8**

You can add a border and background to your chart.

3. Click the **Patterns** tab, if needed, to bring it to the front.

4. Under **Border**, enter the preferences for the line style, weight, and color of the line that surrounds the chart. You can also choose to add a drop shadow to the border and/or have the corners rounded.

5. Under **Area**, choose the desired color for the chart's background.

6. Click **OK** to save your changes and have the specified formatting applied to your chart.

# Changing the Appearance of 3D Charts

Most charts are flat, two-dimensional graphics that are slightly more visually appealing than the data they represent. To create a truly dramatic effect, consider using one of the three-dimensional charts. The third dimension can create a dramatic effect, lifting your data right off the page. With a third dimension, bar charts begin to look like high-rise buildings and pie charts look like actual pies.

The third dimension also enables you to rotate and tilt the chart to accentuate its three-dimensional appearance. To rotate or tilt the chart, take the following steps:

1. Click the chart to select it.

2. Open the **Chart** menu and choose **3-D View**, or right-click the chart and choose **3-D View**. The 3-D View dialog box appears, as shown in Figure 8.9. As you make changes, they are reflected in the wire-frame picture in the middle of the 3-D View dialog box.

Tilt controls                    Perspective controls

**FIGURE 8.9**

You can tilt and rotate a three-dimensional chart.

Rotation controls

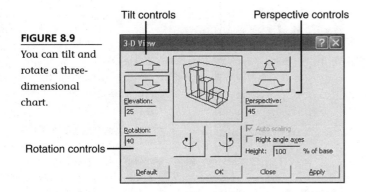

3. To change the elevation (or tilt), click the up or down elevation control, or type a number in the **Elevation** box.

4. To change the rotation (rotation around the z-axis), click the left or right rotation controls, or type the desired degrees of rotation in the **Rotation** box.

5. Take one of the following steps:

   To increase or decrease the chart depth (the ratio of the front of the chart to the back of the chart, expressed as a percentage between 0 and 100), click the back or forward **Perspective** control, or type a number in the **Perspective** box.

   To change the height of the chart in respect to its base, click in the **Height: ___ of Base** box and type the desired percentage. For example, to make the chart twice as tall as it is wide, type **200**.

6. To see the proposed changes applied to the actual chart, click the **Apply** button.

7. When you finish making changes, click **Close** or press **Enter**.

## caution

Some changes in the 3-D View dialog box can cause the Perspective controls to disappear. For example, turning on the Right Angle Axes option disables your ability to change the perspective. To redisplay the Perspective controls, click the **Default** button.

# THE ABSOLUTE MINIMUM

Charting is one of the most exciting aspects of creating worksheets. With a few clicks of the mouse, you can now transform even the dreariest collection of data into a dynamic graphic that illustrates just how the numbers stack up. To review, you now know how to

Create a chart with the Chart Wizard and use the Chart toolbar to make quick changes.

Move and resize the chart on a worksheet.

Use the Chart menu for entering commands that apply only to charts.

Change the type style, size, and color of any text that appears on a chart and change other text attributes.

Modify the lines that make up the chart axes and configure the tick marks that run along the axes.

Change the overall appearance of a chart by formatting its border and background.

Tilt and rotate 3D charts to accentuate their third dimension.

With the skills you acquired in this chapter, you can transform existing worksheet data into a chart in a matter of minutes, change the chart type, add a border and shading to the chart, change the chart type, and format every object that composes the chart. In the next chapter, you will pick up additional skills for working with the more graphical aspects of Excel worksheets.

9

# INSERTING CLIP ART AND OTHER GRAPHICS

# Working with Graphic Objects

Excel comes with several tools that enable you to add pictures to your workbooks and charts. You can add a picture created in another program, you can add clip art (included with Excel), or you can use the Drawing toolbar to draw your own pictures. The following list describes the various objects you can add to your worksheets and charts to make them more engaging and visually appealing:

■ **Clip art:** Excel includes a collection of professionally created images, called *clip art*, that includes images related to business, sports, education, animals, family, art, architecture, communication, government, and much more. See the next section, "Inserting Clip Art and Other Graphics," for details.

■ **Pictures:** If you find an image on the Web (and obtain permission to use it) or if you have images created in other programs, such as the Windows Paint program, you can add these images to your worksheets with the **Insert**, **Picture**, **From File** command. See "Inserting Other Pictures" for details.

■ **Images from scanners and digital cameras:** If you have a digital camera or scanner connected to your computer, you can use the **Insert**, **Picture**, **From Scanner or Camera** command to bring an image from the scanner or camera into your worksheet.

■ **WordArt:** To add fancier text to your worksheets and charts, you can insert WordArt objects. WordArt is text with a more graphic flair—WordArt text can curve up or down, rise along a slope, or even appear three-dimensional. For details, see "Inserting WordArt Objects," later in this chapter.

■ **Lines and arrows:** Excel provides tools for drawing lines and arrows to point out interesting facts and figures and enhance your charts. See "Drawing Your Own Pictures from Scratch," later in this chapter, for details.

> **note**
>
> A *graphic object* is any picture, diagram, or illustration that does not act like data entries inside cells. Graphic objects include objects you can draw (such as ovals and rectangles), text boxes, charts, and clip art. These items are not added to the worksheet itself, but "float above" the worksheet on an imaginary layer.

■ **AutoShapes:** A complete collection of circles, boxes, block arrows, stars, starbursts, cartoon bubbles, and other AutoShapes are just a click away. See "Drawing Your Own Pictures from Scratch," later in this chapter, for details.

■ **Text boxes:** To add text outside a cell, you can create a text box that floats above your worksheet or chart. You can then type anything you like in the text box. See "Adding Text Outside a Cell," later in this chapter, for details.

■ **Organization charts:** If you work in a corporation and need a way to show the line of command, consider creating a custom organization chart. The Organization Chart tool manages the structure for you; all you need to do is type in positions and names. See "Creating an Organization Chart," near the end of this chapter, for detailed instructions.

# Inserting Clip Art and Other Graphics

Excel includes its own clip art gallery that you can access via the Insert Clip Art task pane. This task pane provides the tools you need to search the clip art gallery by keyword or browse the gallery's collection by category.

To search the gallery for an image and insert the desired image, take the following steps:

1. Display the area on the worksheet or chart where you want the image inserted.

2. Open the **Insert** menu, point to **Picture**, and click **Clip Art**.

   The first time you choose to insert clip art, the Add Clips to Gallery dialog box appears, explaining that you can import images from your hard disk into the gallery now or later.

3. If asked whether you want to add clips to the gallery, click **Later** so you can move on. The Insert Clip Art task pane appears.

## caution

The initial Microsoft Excel or Microsoft Office installation typically installs only a limited number of clip art images. To expand the collection, you may need to insert the Office or Excel Media CD and install additional media on your computer.

4. Click in the **Search Text** text box, type a brief description of the desired image (for instance, "teacher"), and click **Search**. As shown in Figure 9.1, the Insert Clip Art task pane displays thumbnail versions of all the images that match your search instructions.

Click the desired clip to
add it to your document

**FIGURE 9.1**

The Insert Clip
Art task pane
helps you track
down images in
the vast clip art
gallery.

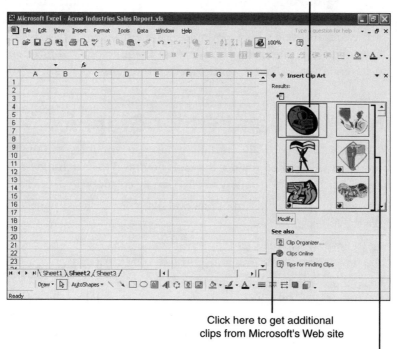

Click here to get additional
clips from Microsoft's Web site

Images that match your
search instructions

5. To modify the search or start a new search, click the **Modify** button below the thumbnails, enter your changes, and click **Search**.

6. Scroll down the list of thumbnails and click the desired image. Excel inserts the image. (The Picture toolbar appears next to the image. See "Touching Up Images with the Picture Toolbar," later in this chapter, for instructions on how to use it.)

## Browsing Through the Clip Art Galleries

To browse through the clip art collection and other media files, rather than search for a particular image, click the **Clip Organizer** link near the bottom of the Insert Clip Art task pane. The Microsoft Clip Organizer appears, as shown in Figure 9.2, which is a Windows Explorer–like window that lists the folders in which the various media files are stored.

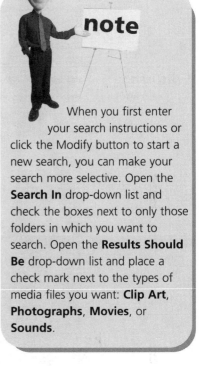

**note**

When you first enter your search instructions or click the Modify button to start a new search, you can make your search more selective. Open the **Search In** drop-down list and check the boxes next to only those folders in which you want to search. Open the **Results Should Be** drop-down list and place a check mark next to the types of media files you want: **Clip Art**, **Photographs**, **Movies**, or **Sounds**.

**FIGURE 9.2**

Use the Microsoft Clip Organizer to browse through the clip art collection.

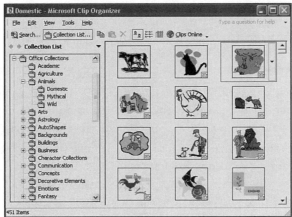

To expand a folder and view the subfolders it contains, click the plus sign next to the folder. If you click the plus sign next to the Office Collections folder, for instance, the list expands to show a subfolder for each clip art category—Academic, Business, Food, Government, and so on. Click a subfolder to view its contents in the pane on the right—the clip art images stored in the folder.

To insert an image from the Clip Organizer, you copy and paste the image. Move the mouse pointer over the desired image to display a drop-down list bar to the right of the image, as shown in Figure 9.3. Click the drop-down list bar and click **Copy**. Change to the area of the worksheet or chart where you want the image pasted, and then open the **Edit** menu and click **Paste** (or press **Ctrl+V** or click the **Paste** button in the Standard toolbar). This inserts the image on your worksheet or chart.

**FIGURE 9.3**

Copy the image from the Clip Organizer and then paste it in place.

## Inserting Other Pictures

Excel's clip art gallery is not the only source of graphic images. You can purchase separate libraries of clip art, obtain digitized photos using a digital camera, draw your own images, obtain images someone else has created and sent you, or copy images from the Web.

Digitized images are stored in a variety of *file formats*. For digitized images, the file format is computer code that a program uses to render a particular image onscreen and in print. Not all programs can translate all file formats, but Excel supports numerous common and uncommon graphic file formats, including WMF (Windows

Meta File), TIFF (Tagged Image File Format), GIF (Graphics Interchange Format), PCX (PC Paintbrush), and BMP (Bitmapped), to name a few.

Though you can obtain images from numerous sources, the process for inserting an image in Excel is always the same:

1. Change to the worksheet or display the graph on which you want the picture inserted.

2. Open the **Insert** menu, point to **Picture**, and click **From File**.

3. The Insert Picture dialog box appears, as shown in Figure 9.4. This dialog box initially displays the contents of the My Pictures folder on your computer.

4. If the picture you want is stored on a different disk drive or in a folder other then My Pictures, open the **Look In** list and click the drive or folder where the picture is stored.

5. If necessary, in the folder/file list (the big area that shows the contents of the currently selected disk drive or folder), double-click the folder where the picture is stored.

**note**

You can tell a particular file's format by looking at its filename extension—the three characters tacked on to the end of a filename, after the period. Excel's clip art images, for instance, are stored as WMF files or Windows Meta Files. Your computer may be set up to hide filename extensions, but if you right-click a file or thumbnail and click **Properties** or **Preview/Properties**, you can see the complete filename, including its extension.

**FIGURE 9.4**

The Insert Picture dialog box.

Look in list

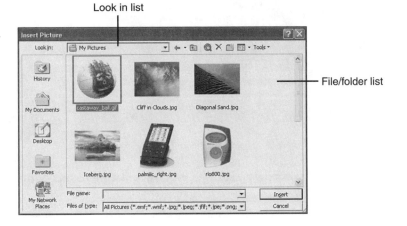

File/folder list

6. If necessary, repeat step 4 until the file/folder list displays the contents of the disk or folder where the picture is stored.

7. If necessary, scroll down the file/folder list to bring the desired picture into view.

8. To insert the picture, double-click its name or click it and click the **Insert** button. Excel inserts the picture on the current worksheet.

**tip**

Store all your images in the My Pictures folder or a subfolder of it to make them more easily accessible.

# Resizing and Reshaping Your Pictures

Pictures rarely fit where they're first placed. Either they're so large that they take over the entire worksheet, or they're too small to make any impression at all. Changing the size of an image is a fairly standard operation. When you click the picture, squares or circles (called *handles*) surround it, as shown in Figure 9.5.

Drag a handle to resize or reshape an image

**FIGURE 9.5**

You can quickly resize and reshape an image.

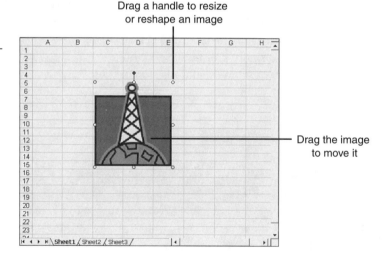

Drag the image to move it

You can drag the handles to change the size and dimensions of the image as follows:

- Drag a top or bottom handle (not in the corner) to make the picture taller or shorter.

- Drag a side handle (not in the corner) to make the picture thinner or wider.

- Drag a corner handle to change both the height and width proportionally.

- If the image has a green circle handle floating above it, drag the green handle to spin the image around its center point.

- Hold down the **Ctrl** key while dragging to increase or decrease the size from the center out. If you hold down the Ctrl key while dragging a handle on the right side out, for example, the picture gets wider on both the left and right sides. (If you hold down the Ctrl key while dragging the image itself, instead of one of its handles, you create a copy of the image rather than resize it.)

For more control over the size and dimensions of an image, right-click the image, click **Format Picture** (or **Format *Object***, where *Object* is the name of the selected object), and click the **Size** tab. This page of options enables you to enter specific measurements for your picture. (The Size tab also has an option called Lock Aspect Ratio, which is on by default. This ensures that when you change the height or width of a picture, the corresponding dimension is resized proportionally.)

# Touching Up Images with the Picture Toolbar

Excel features the Picture toolbar, which provides several tools you can use to adjust the picture's brightness and contrast, crop the image (to use only a portion of it), transform a color picture into grayscale or black-and-white, and add a border around the picture. To access these tools, display the Picture toolbar by right-clicking any toolbar and choosing **Picture**. To use a tool, select the image and then click the button for the desired effect. Table 9.1 lists the buttons in the Picture toolbar and describes the function of each button.

**TABLE 9.1** Picture Toolbar Buttons

| Button | Name | Function |
| --- | --- | --- |
| | **Insert Picture** | Enables you to insert a graphic file from disk. |
| | **Color** | Displays a menu that enables you to transform a color image into grayscale, black-and-white, or washout (a ghost image that can lie on top of text without hiding it—a watermark). |
| | **More Contrast** | Is similar to a TV control that increases the contrast of the image. |
| | **Less Contrast** | Decreases the contrast of an image. |
| | **More Brightness** | Makes the image brighter. |

**TABLE 9.1** (continued)

| Button | Name | Function |
|---|---|---|
| | **Less Brightness** | Makes the image darker. |
| | **Crop** | Turns the mouse pointer into a cropping tool. Move the pointer over one of the handles and drag it to chop off a portion of the picture. You can use the cropping tool to un-crop a cropped picture, as well. |
| | **Rotate Left** | Rotates the image 90° counterclockwise around its center point. |
| | **Line Style** | Enables you to add a border around the picture. |
| | **Compress Pictures** | Automatically reduces the file size of pictures in your document, so they take up less disk space and download and print more quickly. |
| | **Format Picture** | Displays the Format Picture dialog box, which offers plenty of options for changing the appearance and layout of the image. |
| | **Set Transparent Color** | Makes the selected color in a picture transparent so that the background of the page (paper) or screen shows through. Click this button, and then click the color you want to make transparent. (This button is available for most bitmapped images, but for only some clip art images.) |
| | **Reset Picture** | Changes the options back to their original settings in case you make a mistake while entering changes. |

# Inserting WordArt Objects

With WordArt, you can create 3D text objects that curve, angle up or down, or even lean back. To insert a WordArt object on a worksheet or chart, take the following steps:

1. Click a cell near the place where you want the WordArt object inserted, or display the chart on which you want the WordArt object inserted.

2. Open the **Insert** menu, point to **Picture**, and choose **WordArt**. The WordArt Gallery appears, as shown in Figure 9.6, displaying several designs from which you can choose.

**FIGURE 9.6**

The WordArt gallery.

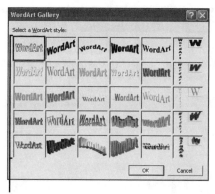

Pick a design

3. Click the desired style and click **OK**. The Edit WordArt Text dialog box appears, as shown in Figure 9.7.

**FIGURE 9.7**

Edit and style the WordArt text.

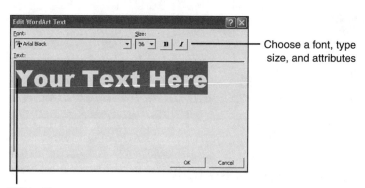

Choose a font, type size, and attributes

Edit text here

4. In the Edit WordArt Text dialog box, type your text and select the desired font, font size, and attributes (bold or italic).

5. Click **OK**. Excel creates the object and places it on the page along with the WordArt toolbar, as shown in Figure 9.8.

A WordArt object is essentially a graphic object. When it first appears and whenever you click it, small circles called *handles* appear around it. You can drag a handle to change the size of the object. If you move the mouse pointer over the object, the pointer appears as a four-headed arrow. You can drag the object to move it. The little green handle above the object enables you to pivot the object around its center point—drag the handle in the direction you want the object to lean. The yellow diamond handle enables you squish the WordArt object or make it taller. Drag the handle up or down to set the desired dimensions.

In addition to changing the object's size and position, you can use buttons on the WordArt toolbar to modify the object, as explained in Table 9.2.

**FIGURE 9.8**

The WordArt toolbar appears alongside the WordArt object.

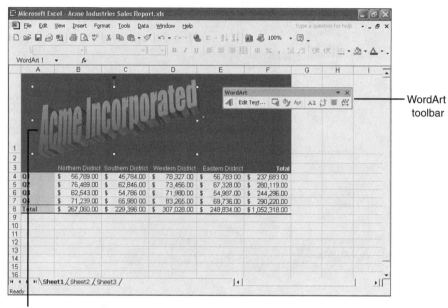

WordArt object

**TABLE 9.2**    WordArt Toolbar Buttons

| Button | Name | Function |
|---|---|---|
| | **Insert WordArt** | Inserts another WordArt object on the page. |
| Edit Text... | **Edit Text** | Enables you to edit the text used in the WordArt object. |
| | **WordArt Gallery** | Enables you to select a different style for this WordArt object from the WordArt Gallery. |
| | **Format WordArt** | Displays a dialog box that enables you to change the WordArt object's size and position, change the object's color, and specify how the WordArt object moves with surrounding cells. |

**TABLE 9.2**   (continued)

| Button | Name | Function |
|---|---|---|
| Abc | **WordArt Shape** | Enables you to pick a different shape for the object. |
| Aa | **WordArt Same Letter Heights** | Displays all the characters in the object (uppercase or lowercase) at the same height. |
| Ab<br>b | **WordArt Vertical Text** | Displays characters running from top to bottom, rather than left to right. |
| ≣ | **WordArt Alignment** | With two or more lines of text, this button enables you to align the text left, right, or center, or to justify it (so that it spreads out to touch both sides of the imaginary WordArt box). |
| AV | **WordArt Character Spacing** | Enables you to change the space between characters in the WordArt object. |

# Adding Text Outside a Cell

Most of the text you type in a worksheet is contained in individual cells. However, Excel does enable you to add text outside the cells in separate text boxes. This is useful for adding text to charts or adding notes to worksheets. And, because the text in a text box is independent of the cells, you can place a text box anywhere on a worksheet or chart. To create a text box, take the following steps:

1. Display the area on the worksheet or chart where you want the text box placed.

2. If the Drawing toolbar is not displayed, right-click any toolbar or Excel's menu bar and click **Drawing**. The Drawing toolbar appears.

3. Click the **Text Box** button. When you move the mouse pointer over the worksheet area, it appears as a crosshair pointer.

4. Position the pointer where you want one corner of the text box to appear, and then drag the pointer to the opposite corner to define the box size and dimensions. Excel inserts the text box, as shown in Figure 9.9.

5. Type your text in the text box, and use the **Formatting** toolbar to style the text. As with WordArt, the text box is surrounded by handles you can drag to change the size or dimensions of the box. Drag the box's border to move it.

**FIGURE 9.9**

Excel inserts the
text box.

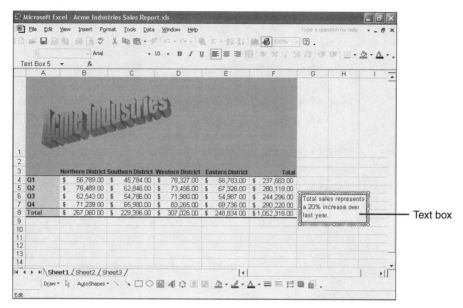

Text box

You can change the appearance of the text box itself
by using the following buttons on the Drawing toolbar:

 **Fill Color** adds the selected color
inside the box as a background.

 **Line Color** controls the color of the
line that defines the outline of the
box.

 **Font Color** controls the color of the
text inside the box.

 **Line Style** controls the thickness
and design of the line that defines
the outline of the box.

 **Dash Style** transforms the line that
defines the outline of the box into a
dashed line.

 **Shadow Style** adds a drop shadow
to the box.

 **3-D Style** turns the box into a three-
dimensional box.

note

You can change the
appearance of the text box
and the text it contains by using
the Format Text Box dialog box. To
display this dialog box, right-click
the text box's border and then
click **Format Text Box**. Use the
options and settings in this text
box to change the font and text
size, the appearance of the border
that defines the box, the text
alignment inside the box, and the
way the text box moves or stays
fixed when surrounding cells
move.

# Drawing Your Own Pictures from Scratch

If you don't have a drawing program, or you don't want to use it to create a separate illustration, you can use Excel's Drawing toolbar to create a simple illustration or to add lines, arrows, and basic shapes to a chart or worksheet. To turn on the Drawing toolbar, right-click any toolbar or Excel's menu bar and click **Drawing**.

To draw an object, select the tool for the line or shape you want to use and then drag the shape on the screen. Following is the step-by-step procedure:

1. Take one of the following steps:

   Click the button for the desired line, arrow, or shape on the Drawing Toolbar. Your mouse changes into a crosshair pointer.

   Click **AutoShapes** on the Drawing toolbar, point to the desired shape category, and click the desired shape. Your mouse changes into a crosshair pointer.

2. Move the crosshair pointer to the point where you want one corner or one end of the object to appear.

3. Hold down the mouse button and drag the pointer away from the starting point in the desired direction until the object is the size and shape you want, as shown in Figure 9.10.

4. Release the mouse button.

**FIGURE 9.10**

You can drag a line, arrow, or shape into existence.

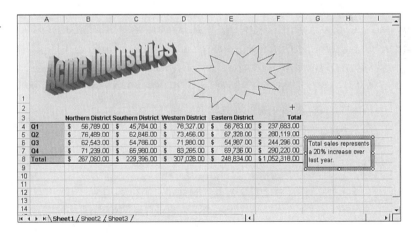

To save yourself some time and reduce the frustration when drawing objects, read through the following list of drawing tips:

- To draw several objects of the same shape, double-click the desired button and then use the mouse to create as many of those shapes as you like.
- To draw a uniform object (a perfect circle or square), hold down the **Shift** key while dragging.
- Hold down the **Ctrl** key while dragging to draw the object out from an imaginary center point. Without the Ctrl key, you drag the object out from its corner or starting point.
- Hold down **Ctrl+Shift** while dragging to draw the object out from its center point and create a uniform shape.
- To select an object, click it.
- To delete an object, select it, and press **Del**.
- To move an object, select it and drag one of its lines.
- To resize or reshape an object, select it and drag one of its handles. (If you used the Free-form tool to draw an irregularly shaped object, you must open the **Draw** menu and click **Edit Points** to reshape the object.)
- To copy an object, hold down the **Ctrl** key while dragging it.
- To quickly change the appearance of an object, right-click on it and select the desired option from the shortcut menu.

After you have an object on the page, you can use some of the other buttons in the Drawing toolbar to change qualities of the object, such as its fill color and the color and width of the line that defines it. First, select the shape whose qualities you want to change. Then use the buttons listed in Table 9.3 to change the object's qualities.

**TABLE 9.3**   Drawing Toolbar Buttons for Altering a Drawn Object

| Button | Name | Function |
|---|---|---|
| Draw ▾ | **Draw** | Provides options for turning on a grid (for more precise positioning), changing the order of layered objects (as explained in the following section, "Working with Layers of Objects"), grouping objects, flipping objects, and wrapping text. |
| ▷ | **Select Objects** | Turns the mouse pointer into a selection tool, so you can use it to select objects rather than draw them. |
| ▨ | **Fill Color** | Colors inside the lines (as you would in a coloring book). Click the button to fill the object with the color shown. To change the fill color, click the arrow next to this button and select the color from the menu. |

**TABLE 9.3**   (continued)

| Button | Name | Function |
|---|---|---|
| | **Line Color** | Changes the color of the line that defines the shape. Click the button to use the color shown. To change the color, click the arrow next to this button and select the color from the menu. |
| | **Font Color** | For text boxes only. Drag over the text inside the box, open Font Color, and select the desired color. |
| | **Line Style** | Displays a menu from which you can choose the line thickness and style you want to use for the line that defines the shape. |
| | **Dash Style** | Enables you to use dashed lines rather than solid lines. |
| | **Arrow Style** | Works only for arrows you have drawn. Select the arrow, and then use this menu to select the type of arrow you want to use or to change the end on which the arrowhead appears. |
| | **Shadow Style** | Works only for ovals, rectangles, AutoShapes, and other two-dimensional objects (including text boxes). This menu contains various drop-shadow styles you can apply to objects. |
| | **3-D Style** | Works for ovals, rectangles, AutoShapes, and text boxes. It turns rectangles into blocks and ovals into cylinders. |

# Working with Layers of Objects

When you place two or more objects on a worksheet or chart, they may overlap—the top object may block the object beneath it and prevent you from seeing it. Sometimes, you want various objects to overlap; for instance, you might want to draw an arrow on top of a chart. However, you must also be able to change the positions of various overlapping objects in relation to one another, and sometimes the object you want to move is at the bottom of the stack. Fortunately, Excel offers a couple of drawing tools that can help you flip through the stack and group two or

**tip**

You can add some interesting special effects to a document by combining text with AutoShapes. For sales brochures or announcements, for example, you might consider placing small bits of text inside a starburst. Just lay a text box on top of the starburst and format the text box to give it a transparent background and no border.

more objects so they act as one, which makes manipulating them much easier. The following sections provide details on how to select, change the order of, and group drawn objects.

## Selecting Objects

Selecting an object is fairly simple, assuming the object is at the top of the stack or has an edge that's visible. To select an object, click its line. (You can select most two- and three-dimensional objects by clicking anywhere on the object, unless the object has no fill.)

## Moving an Object Up or Down in the Stack

When stacked objects overlap, selecting an object that's buried deep in the stack can seem impossible. To access the object, you must bring it to the front of the stack or move the objects that are obscuring it to the bottom of the stack. You can send an object that's up front back one layer or all the way to the bottom of the stack, or you can bring an object from the back to the front. First, select the object you want to move (if possible). If you cannot select the object you want to move, select the object in front of it, so you can move the in-the-way object down in the stack.

After selecting the object you want to move, right-click it, point to **Order**, and select the desired movement: **Bring to Front**, **Send to Back**, **Bring Forward**, **Send Backward**, **Bring in Front of Text**, or **Send Behind Text**, as shown in Figure 9.11. These options are also available in the Drawing toolbar—click **Draw** on the Drawing toolbar and then click the desired movement.

**tip**

To make an object transparent, except for its border, remove the object's fill (or shading). Right-click the object and click **Format Object** (where *Object* specifies the type of object). In the Format *Object* dialog box, click the **Colors and Lines** tab, open the **Fill Color** list, and click **No Fill**. (When a two- or three-dimensional object has no fill, you must click the object's border to select it; clicking inside the shape selects whatever is *behind* the object.)

**FIGURE 9.11**

You can move
an object up or
down in a stack
of objects.

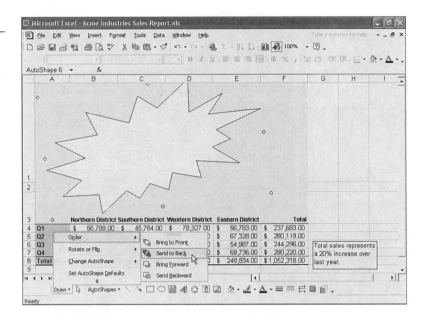

## Grouping and Ungrouping Objects

Moving a collection of shapes or resizing them as a whole becomes difficult. If you
drag one object, you ruin its relative position to the other objects. Similarly, if you
need to shrink or enlarge the drawing, you should not need to resize each object separately. And you don't have to. Excel enables you to group two or
more objects so you can move and resize them as if they were a
single object. To group two or more objects, take
the following steps:

1. Click the **Select Objects** button in
   the Drawing toolbar.

2. Move the mouse pointer somewhere outside the imaginary square in which the
   objects are contained.

3. Hold down the left mouse button and
   drag a selection box around all the objects
   you want to include in the group. Handles
   appear around each of the selected
   objects.

**caution**

When selecting objects,
you must drag a selec-
tion box around all the
objects. Make sure the
box completely surrounds
all objects you want included in the
group; if a portion of an object is
outside the box, the object will not
be selected.

4. Right-click one of the selected objects, point to **Grouping**, and click **Group** (or open the **Draw** menu in the Drawing toolbar and choose **Group**). The handles around each individual object disappear, and a single set of handles appears around the group, as shown in Figure 9.12. You can now drag a handle to resize all the objects in the group, or you can drag any object in the group to move the group.

Drag this handle
to rotate the image

**FIGURE 9.12**

You can group
two or more
objects and treat
them as a single
object.

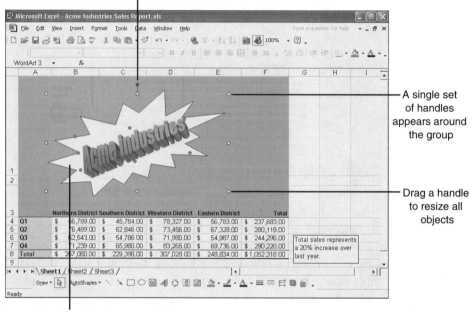

A single set
of handles
appears around
the group

Drag a handle
to resize all
objects

Drag any object
in the group to move
all the objects

To turn off grouping so you can work with an individual object, open the **Draw** menu again and click **Ungroup**. After you're finished working with the individual object, you can regroup the objects by opening the **Draw** menu and selecting **Regroup**.

**tip**

If you insert a picture from your hard disk using Insert, Picture, From File, you might be able to select the image, ungroup its component parts, and edit the image. Unfortunately, this doesn't work with Excel clip art.

# Changing an Object's Appearance

Objects typically are made up of a thin black line with white or gray fill inside it. If you want to add color to an object, or change its line thickness or color, you must format the object. There are three ways to display the Format dialog box for an object:

- Right-click the object and choose **Format** *Object* (where *Object* is the type of graphic object).
- Click the object, open the **Format** menu and choose *Object*, or press **Ctrl+1**.
- Double-click the object.

Any way you do it, the Format Object dialog box appears, as shown in Figure 9.13. The available options vary depending on the selected object. Enter your preferences and then click **OK**.

**FIGURE 9.13**

The Format Object dialog box.

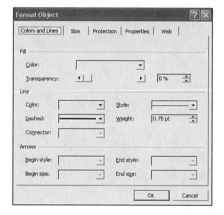

# Creating an Organization Chart

Suppose you've landed a job in the personnel department of a major corporation, and it's your job to explain the company's organizational structure to new employees. You could type up a list of the managers' names from the top down into individual cells, but there's a better way: create an organization chart. Excel provides a tool that enables you to draw an organization chart, complete with boxes and lines, into which you can type the names and positions of each person on the corporate ladder. To create an organization chart, take the following steps:

1. Open the **Insert** menu, point to **Picture**, and choose **Organization chart**. A basic organization chart appears in its own frame along with the Organization Chart toolbar, as shown in Figure 9.14.

**FIGURE 9.14**

Excel provides the tools you need to create a professional-looking organization chart.

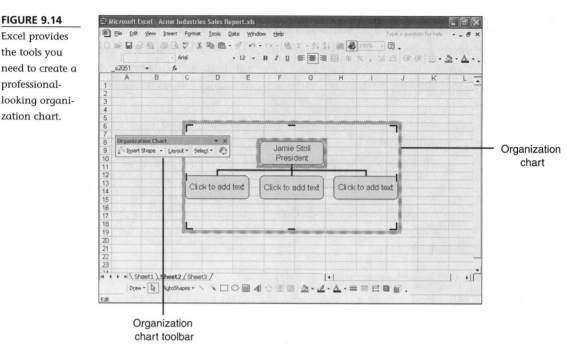

Organization chart

Organization chart toolbar

2. To add a person to the chart, click in the desired box, type the person's name, press **Enter**, and then type the person's position.

3. **Insert Shape ▾** To add a box to the chart, click the box to which or next to which you want to attach the new box, and then click the arrow next to **Insert Shape** in the Organization Chart toolbar and click the desired box type:

   **Subordinate** inserts a box below the current box with a line connecting the two boxes.

   **Coworker** inserts a box to the right of the current box with a line connecting the new box to the level above it.

   **Assistant** inserts a box below the current box with an L-shaped line attaching the two boxes.

4. **Layout ▾** To change the overall layout of the organization chart, click the box for the person who sits above the level you want to restructure, click **Layout**, and click one of the following layouts:

   **Standard** displays subordinates below superiors in a similar fashion to a family tree.

**Both Hanging** displays subordinates below and to the left and right of superiors.

 **Left Hanging** displays subordinates to the left of superiors.

 **Right Hanging** displays subordinates to the right of superiors.

5. To change the overall appearance of the organization chart, click the **Autoformat** button in the Organization Chart toolbar. The Organization Chart Style Gallery appears, as shown in Figure 9.15.

6. Click the desired style and click **Apply**. Excel applies the selected style to your organization chart.

FIGURE 9.15

The Organization Chart Style Gallery.

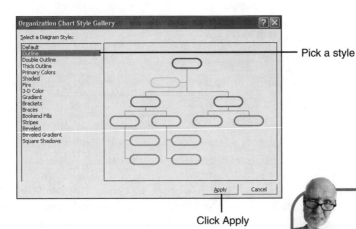

Pick a style

Click Apply

## tip

For more diagram options, open the **Insert** menu and choose **Diagram**. Excel displays six diagrams commonly used in business, including an organization chart, a pyramid, and a target diagram. Select the desired diagram type, click **OK**, and follow the onscreen directives to customize your diagram.

# THE ABSOLUTE MINIMUM

Though your data and charts are the most important and integral components of your worksheets, graphics can bring your worksheets to life and actually make you and others want to look at them. Now that you have completed this chapter, you know exactly how to add various graphic objects to your worksheets and charts and how to manipulate the various objects. You now know how to:

- Insert Excel clip art objects and import pictures from a wide variety of other sources.

- Resize and reshape graphic images without distorting their relative dimensions.

- Touch up pictures by adjusting their brightness and contrast or by transforming color images into grayscale.

- Insert graphical text objects called WordArt, and change the overall appearance of a WordArt object.

- Insert text boxes to add text outside worksheet cells and charts.

- Draw lines, circles, squares, and more complex shapes and combine the shapes to create illustrations.

- Create your own organization charts to illustrate the corporate or hierarchical structure of your business or organization.

With the skills you acquired in this chapter, you can completely revamp the appearance of your worksheet and transform bland worksheets into graphically illustrated reports. After you have whipped your worksheets and graphs into shape with some fancy formatting and graphics, you're well primed to move on to the next chapter and learn how to print and protect your creations.

# In This Chapter

- Previewing your worksheets to see how Excel plans to print them.

- Formatting tricks to make your worksheet fit on one page.

- Repeating column headings on every page.

- Hiding inessential or confidential columns and rows.

- Printing only the most essential blocks of data with print areas.

- Preventing unauthorized changes to your worksheets and charts.

**10**

# Printing and Protecting Your Workbook, Worksheets, and Charts

# Previewing Your Worksheets Before Printing

Worksheets are typically too wide for standard 8.5-by-11-inch paper and often too wide for legal paper, even if you print them sideways on a page. Fortunately, Excel offers several features that can help, as you will see throughout this chapter.

Before you start tweaking the worksheet layout and adjusting print settings to make a worksheet fit on 8.5-by-11-inch pages, check your page setup to determine how Excel is prepared to print your worksheet(s). Frequently, Excel inserts awkward page breaks, omits titles and column headings from some of the pages, and uses additional settings that result in an unacceptable printout.

To check your worksheet before printing, click the **Print Preview** button (or select **File**, **Print Preview**). This displays your worksheet in Print Preview mode, as shown in Figure 10.1.

**FIGURE 10.1**

Excel's Print Preview lets you see how a worksheet will print before you print it.

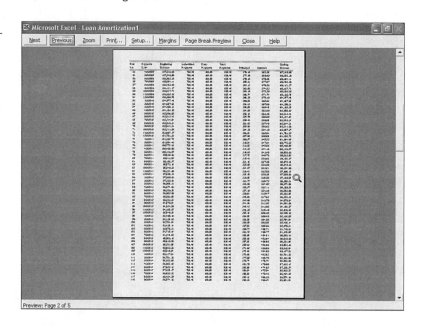

Along the top of the preview area are several buttons that enable you to flip pages, zoom in and zoom out on the page, and change some common print settings. Table 10.1 lists and describes these buttons in greater detail.

**TABLE 10.1** Print Preview Buttons

| Button | Button Name | Purpose |
|--------|-------------|---------|
| Next | **Next** | Displays the next page of the printout, assuming the worksheet requires more than one page. |
| Previous | **Previous** | Displays the previous page of the printout, if you flipped to the next page. |

**TABLE 10.1** (continued)

| Button | Button Name | Purpose |
|---|---|---|
| Zoom | **Zoom** | Zooms in on a page or, if you zoomed in, zooms out. |
| Print... | **Print** | Starts printing the worksheet. |
| Setup... | **Setup** | Displays the Page Setup dialog box, which enables you to set the page size and orientation, adjust margins, add a header or footer, and adjust the way Excel determines page breaks. See the next section, "Changing the Page Setup," for details. |
| Margins | **Margins** | Displays margin and column markers around the page's perimeter. You can drag the markers to change the margin or column widths. |
| Page Break Preview | **Page Break Preview** | Displays an image of where Excel will break pages. You can change the page breaks by dragging the page break lines. See "Checking and Adjusting Page Breaks," later in this chapter, for details. |
| Close | **Close** | Closes Print Preview and returns to the normal view of your worksheet. |
| Help | **Help** | Displays additional help specifically about how to view and manipulate worksheets in Print Preview. |

One of the best features offered in Print Preview is the ability it gives you to change margins without having to guess what the effects will be. When you click the **Margins** button, margin and column markers appear, as shown in Figure 10.2. To change the margins or column widths, simply drag a marker. Instantly, Print Preview redraws the screen to show the effects of the change on your worksheet.

When you are finished previewing your pages, click the **Close** button to return to the main Excel screen.

## caution

Most printers cannot print all the way to the edge of a page. If you drag a margin marker too close to an edge, part of your worksheet might fall into the *unprintable* region of the page and may appear chopped off. Zoom in on any text that's near the edge of a page to determine whether it will be chopped off during printing.

Margin markers

**FIGURE 10.2**

You can drag a margin marker to change margin settings.

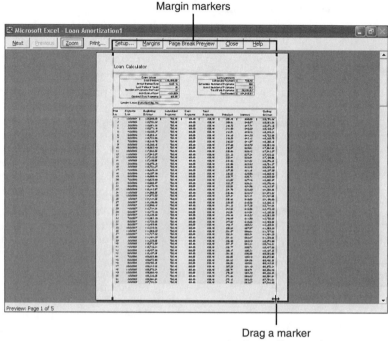

Drag a marker
to change the margin

# Changing the Page Setup

If your worksheet is close to fitting on a single page, you usually can adjust the left and right margins to pull another column or two onto the page. If the worksheet still doesn't fit, you may need to adjust the page setup, via the Page Setup dialog box. To display the Page Setup dialog box, open the **File** menu and click **Page Setup**, or click the **Setup** button on the Print Preview screen. The Page Setup dialog box appears, as shown in Figure 10.3, featuring four tabs: Page, Margins, Header/Footer, Sheet. The following sections explain the available settings in detail.

## Changing the Page Settings

The leftmost tab in the Page Setup dialog box, **Page**, contains options for specifying the page orientation, the paper size, print quality, and at the number at which Excel starts numbering the pages. (See Figure 10.3.) This tab also offers an interesting feature that can shrink your worksheet to fit on one or more pages. The following list explains your options in greater detail:

**Orientation** gives you two choices: Portrait or Landscape. With portrait orientation, the page is longer than it is wide. With landscape orientation, the page is wider than it is long. You don't need to feed paper into your printer sideways if you choose landscape orientation; Excel rotates the print 90°, so rows run along the long edge of the page.

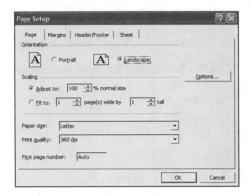

**Scaling** enables you to shrink your worksheet by a specified percentage or have Excel automatically shrink the worksheet to make it fit on a fixed number of pages. If you have a worksheet that almost, but not quite, fits on a single page, you can have Excel shrink the entire worksheet to make it fit. (If the worksheet is too long or wide, Excel might not be able to shrink it down enough to fit on the specified number of pages, in which case you must spread the worksheet out over more pages.)

**Paper size** enables you to specify the dimensions of the paper on which you intend to print your worksheet. You can choose *Letter* (to print on 8.5-by-11-inch paper), *Legal* (to print on 8.5-by-14-inch paper), *Executive* (7.5-by-10-inch paper), *A3* (297-by-420-millimeters paper), or whatever paper size your printer supports.

**Print quality** determines the print quality in *dpi* (dots per inch). The higher the setting, the higher the print quality and the slower the printout.

**First page number** determines the number Excel uses to start numbering the pages of your printout. You might, for instance, want to start numbering the pages at 3 if you're printing a report, and the first two pages of the report already are numbered 1 and 2.

## Adjusting the Page Margins

The most intuitive way to adjust page margins is to drag the margin markers in Print Preview, as instructed earlier in this chapter. For more precise control over margins, display the Page Setup dialog box and click the **Margins** tab. The Margins tab contains spin boxes for setting the top, bottom, left, and right margins and for specifying the distance between the top edge of the page and the header and the distance between the bottom edge of the page and the footer, as shown in Figure 10.4.

Margin, header,
and footer settings

**FIGURE 10.4**

The Page Setup
Margins settings.

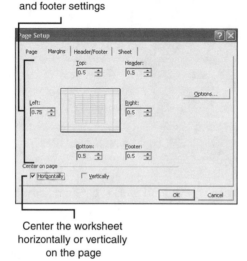

Center the worksheet
horizontally or vertically
on the page

Click the up arrow next to a spin box to increase the setting in increments of .25 inch, or click the down arrow to decrease the setting. You can also click inside a spin box and type the desired setting.

Near the bottom of the Margins tab are two options that enable you to have Excel center the worksheet vertically and/or horizontally on a page. Click the check box next to Horizontally to position the worksheet at an equal distance from the left and right edges of the page. Click the check box next to Vertically to position the worksheet at an equal distance from the top and bottom edges of the page.

## Adding a Header and Footer

Excel can print a footer (on the bottom of each page) or a header (at the top of each page) that automatically numbers the worksheet pages for you and prints the file's name, the worksheet title, the date and time, and any other information you want to include. To add headers and footers to your worksheets, take the following steps:

1. Do one of the following:

   Display the **Page Setup** dialog box and click the **Header/Footer** tab.

   Open the **View** menu and select **Header and Footer**. The Page Setup dialog box appears with the Header/Footer tab in front. See Figure 10.5.

2. To use a header, open the **Header** drop-down list and click the desired header.

3. To use a footer, open the **Footer** drop-down list and click the desired footer.

4. Click **OK**.

**FIGURE 10.5**

The Page Setup dialog box's Header/Footer tab.

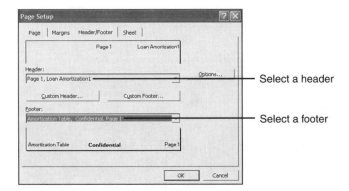

Select a header

Select a footer

To create a custom header or footer (for example, to include your name or company's name), click one of the **Custom** buttons on the Header/Footer tab. This displays the Header or Footer dialog box, as shown in Figure 10.6, which enables you to create a header or footer consisting of three sections. Type the desired text in each section, and use the dialog box buttons to format the text and insert codes for the date, time, filename, worksheet name, and page numbers. To insert "Page 1 of 5," "Page 2 of 5," and so on, type **Page**, press the spacebar, click the **#** button, press the spacebar, and click the **++** button. # inserts the number of the current page, and ++ inserts the total number of pages.

## Changing the Worksheet Settings

If your worksheet is longer than one page, Excel inserts a *horizontal page break* to mark the end of one page and the beginning of the next. If your worksheet is wider than one page, Excel inserts a *vertical page break* along one of the column divisions.

Unless you specify otherwise, Excel prints pages from top to bottom, printing all pages to the left of the vertical page break and then pages to the right of the vertical page break. In most cases, this is

**note**

The Header and Footer features use some odd codes for inserting information. For example, the code for inserting the date is &[Date] and the code for inserting the number of pages is &[Pages].

how you want your pages printed, so you can easily read each column from top to bottom. If, however, you typically read the worksheet data from left to right, you want Excel to print the pages from left to right. To change the page order, open the **File** menu, select **Page Setup**, and click the **Sheet** tab, as shown in Figure 10.7. Under **Page Order**, select **Over, Then Down**, and then click **OK**.

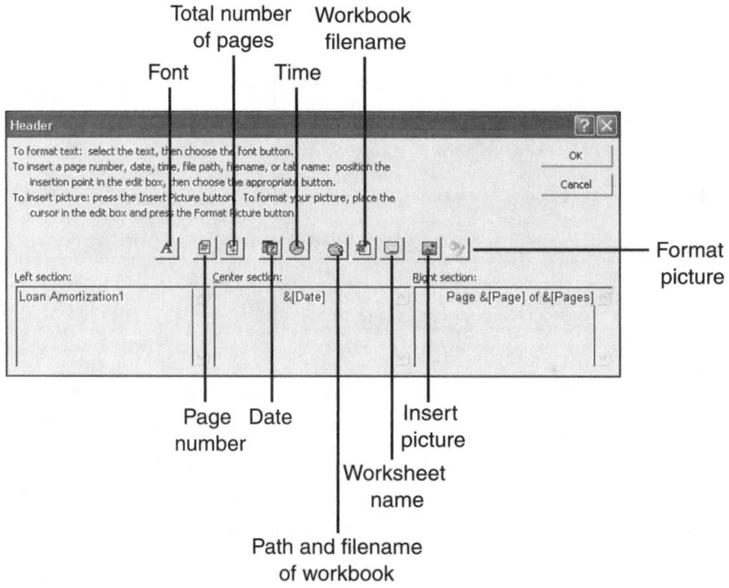

**FIGURE 10.6**

Create a custom header or footer consisting of three sections.

Total number of pages

Workbook filename

Font

Time

Format picture

Page number

Date

Insert picture

Worksheet name

Path and filename of workbook

**FIGURE 10.7**

If your work-sheet has both horizontal and vertical page breaks, select the desired page order.

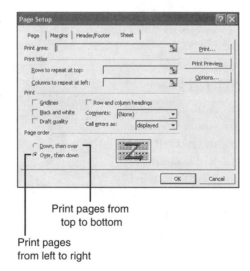

Print pages from top to bottom

Print pages from left to right

As you can see in Figure 10.7, the Sheet tab contains many more options for controlling the way Excel prints your worksheets. The following list explains those options:

 **Print Area** enables you to select a portion of the worksheet to print. Click the **Collapse Dialog Box** button that's next to the Print Area box, drag over the portion of the worksheet you want to print, and then click the **Collapse Dialog Box** button again to bring the Page Setup dialog box back into full view.

 **Rows to Repeat at Top** enables you to designate rows that you want printed at the top of each page of your worksheet. This is useful if you typed column headings at the top of each column. Click the **Collapse Dialog Box** button that's next to the Rows to Repeat at Top box, drag over the row(s) you want to repeat at the top of each page, and then click the **Collapse Dialog Box** button again to bring the Page Setup dialog box back into view.

 **Columns to Repeat at Left** enables you to designate columns that you want printed at the left of each page of your worksheet. If you typed row headings in a column along the left side of your worksheet, and Excel is inserting a vertical page break, this forces Excel to print the row headings along the left side of each page. Click the **Collapse Dialog Box** button that's next to the Columns to Repeat at Left box, drag over the column(s) you want to repeat at the left of each page, and then click the **Collapse Dialog Box** button again to bring the Page Setup dialog box back into view.

**Gridlines** tells Excel to print the gridlines that divide the cells. Typically, gridlines are displayed only to make it easier for you to determine each cell's boundaries, but if you turn on this option, Excel prints the gridlines.

**Black and White** tells Excel to print the worksheet in grayscale rather than color. If you're printing your worksheets using a black-and-white printer or want to save some money by conserving your printer's color ink, click the check box next to **Black and White**. This can reduce the print time, as well.

**Draft Quality** directs Excel to print a low-quality version of the worksheet. If you're using the worksheet for your own benefit, you might want to turn this on to save time printing and conserve ink.

**Row and Column Headings** tells Excel to print column letters (A, B, C, and so on) above the columns and print row headings (1, 2, 3, and so on) along the left side of the page. This option does not affect the row and column headings you may have typed in your worksheet or the row(s) and column(s) you chose to repeat at the top or left of every page.

**Comments** prints any comments (notes) you might have added to cells. (See the note under "Adjusting Number Formats," in Chapter 4, "Entering and Editing Labels and Values," for instructions on how to enter a comment.) You can choose **(None)** to have comments omitted, **At End of Sheet** to have all comments printed at the end the worksheet, or **As Displayed on Sheet** to have comments printed near the cell where you added them.

**Cell errors as** enables you to specify how you want Excel to print the contents of any cell whose result is an error. You can choose to have errors printed as **displayed** (as they appear in the worksheet), as **<blank>** (empty), as -- (dashes), or as **#N/A** (#N/A appears in the cell).

> **caution**
>
> If comments are not displayed, Excel will not print them, even if you choose to have them printed. To display comments on your worksheet, open the **View** menu and choose **Comments**. To display individual comments, right-click the cell that contains the comment and click **Show Comment**.

Enter your preferences and then click the **Print Preview** button to display the effects of any settings you entered.

## Checking and Adjusting Page Breaks

As you create your worksheet, Excel displays dotted lines to indicate where it is going to divide the pages. You can insert your own page breaks by using the **Insert, Page Break** command. However, Excel has a feature called Page Break Preview that displays page breaks more clearly and enables you to easily move page breaks by dragging them.

To turn on Page Break Preview, either open the **View** menu and select **Page Break Preview** or click the **Page Break Preview** button in Print Preview. Excel displays page breaks as thick blue lines and displays the page number in big gray type on each page. You can then drag the lines with your mouse to move them, as shown in Figure 10.8. Although this does not help you fit the worksheet on a page, it does give you control over how Excel divides the columns and rows that make up your worksheet. When you're finished, open the **View** menu and select **Normal**.

Page number

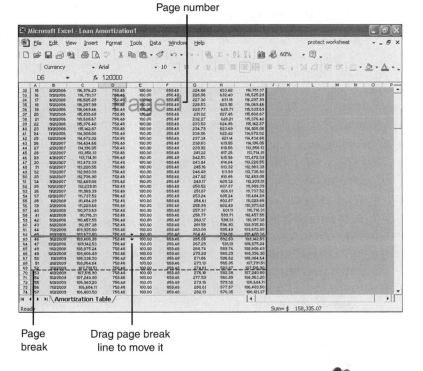

**FIGURE 10.8**

You can drag the blue lines in Page Break Preview to move the page breaks.

Page break

Drag page break line to move it

To insert a new page break, take the following steps:

1. Click the cell below and to the right of where you want the new page break inserted. Excel inserts a horizontal page break above the cell and a vertical page break to the left of the cell.

2. Open the **Insert** menu and choose **Page Break**. Excel inserts a horizontal page break above the selected cell and a vertical page break to the left of the cell. The page breaks appear as dotted lines.

To remove a page break that you inserted, right-click the cell below the horizontal page break or to the right of the vertical page break, open the **Insert** menu, and choose **Remove Page Break**.

**note**

To insert only a horizontal page break, click the cell in column A that's below the point where you want the page break inserted. To insert only a vertical page break, click the cell in row 1 that's to the right of where you want the page break inserted.

# Hiding Columns and Rows

If you're having trouble fitting your worksheet on the desired number of pages, or you want to prevent someone viewing the printout from seeing some confidential data, you can hide selected columns or rows. To hide columns or rows and prevent Excel from printing them, take the following steps:

1. Drag over the column or row headers for the columns or rows you want to hide.

2. Open the **Format** menu and select **Column**, **Hide** or **Row**, **Hide**. (Alternatively, right-click one of the selected columns or rows and select **Hide** from the context menu.) A dark line appears on the worksheet to indicate that rows or columns are hidden.

3. Click the **Print Preview** button. Excel displays the worksheet, omitting the hidden columns or rows.

**caution**

People viewing your worksheet in Excel can tell when columns are hidden by noticing that one or more column letters do not appear. They can then unhide the columns by performing the steps above. To prevent them from viewing hidden columns, you must password-protect your worksheet as explained later in this chapter, in the section called "Preventing Unauthorized Changes to a Workbook."

Bringing hidden rows or columns back into view isn't the most intuitive operation. First, drag over the column or row headings before and after the hidden columns and rows. If columns C, D, and E are hidden, for example, drag over column headings B and F to select them. Open the **Format** menu and select **Columns**, **Unhide** or **Rows**, **Unhide**.

# Printing Your Worksheets

When you're satisfied with the way your worksheet looks in Print Preview, you're ready to send it to your printer. The quickest way to print is to click the tab for the worksheet you want to print and then click the **Print** button. This sends the worksheet off to the printer, no questions asked. To print more than one worksheet or set additional printing preferences, take the following steps:

1. Click the tab for the worksheet you want to print. Ctrl+click tabs to print additional worksheets. (To print all the worksheets in the workbook, you can skip this step.)

2. Open the **File** menu and choose **Print** (or press **Ctrl+P**). The Print dialog box appears, as shown in Figure 10.9.

**FIGURE 10.9**

The Print dialog box.

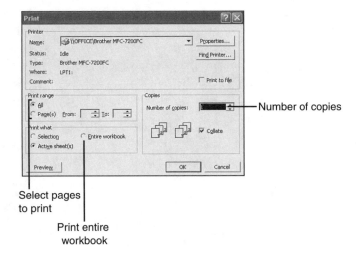

Number of copies

Select pages to print

Print entire workbook

3. To print all the worksheets in the workbook, select **Entire Workbook**. Excel prints all worksheets that contain entries.

4. To print one or more pages of the selected worksheets, select **Page(s)** under **Print Range** and enter the page numbers to specify the range.

5. To print more than one copy, specify the desired number of copies under **Copies**.

6. You can click the **Properties** button to enter additional printer settings, including the print quality. After entering the desired settings, click **OK** to return to the Print dialog box.

7. Click the **OK** button to start printing.

# Previewing and Printing Charts

When your chart is ready for the printer or when you think it's ready, click the chart and then click the **Print Preview** button (or select **File, Print Preview**) to check it out. This displays a full-page version of the chart, as shown in Figure 10.10. To print the worksheet data and the chart together on the same page, click outside the chart area, somewhere on the worksheet, to deselect the chart; then click **Print Preview**. If everything looks the way you want it to look, click the **Print** button to start printing.

**FIGURE 10.10**

If you select a
chart, Excel
assumes you
want a full-page
version of it.

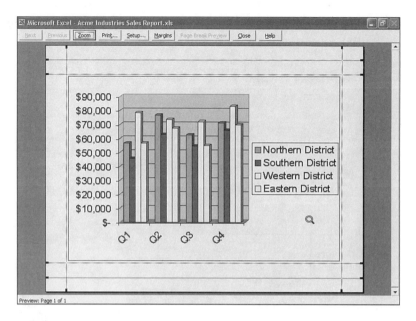

# Preventing Unauthorized Changes to a Workbook

In many businesses, one person or team is in charge of creating workbooks that many people in the business use. In some cases, the person who created the workbook doesn't want the people who are using the workbook to change it. In other cases, the creator wants users to be able to enter data but does not want users to change formatting or any of the formulas or functions that perform the calculations.

Whatever the case, you can password-protect a worksheet, as explained in the following steps. The steps might seem backward to you at first; you unlock certain cells to permit users to change them *before* you password-protect the worksheet. However, after you password-protect the worksheet, you cannot unlock cells, so you must mark the cells as unlocked *before* password-protecting the worksheet. Now that you know that, take the following steps to password-protect a worksheet:

1. Open the worksheet you want to protect.

2. Drag over any cells you want to unlock; that is, cells whose contents you want other users to be able to edit. (By default, all cells in a password-protected worksheet are locked, preventing other users from changing the cells or their contents. You must unlock any cells you want other users to be able to change.)

3. Open the **Format** menu and choose **Cells**. The Format Cells dialog box appears.

4. Click the **Protection** tab. The Protection options appear, as shown in Figure 10.11.

Remove checkmark
to unlock cells                    Protection tab

**FIGURE 10.11**

You must unlock
any cells that
you want to
enable other
users to change.

> **Format Cells**   ? ✕
>
> Number | Alignment | Font | Border | Patterns | Protection
>
> ☐ Locked
> ☐ Hidden
>
> Locking cells or hiding formulas has no effect unless the
> worksheet is protected. To protect the worksheet, choose
> Protection from the Tools menu, and then choose Protect
> Sheet. A password is optional.
>
> OK      Cancel

5. Click **Locked** to remove the check mark next to it.

6. Click **OK**.

7. To hide any formulas in the worksheet, select each cell that contains a formula you want to hide. (You can drag over a range of cells or Ctrl+click each cell to select multiple cells.)

8. Open the **Format** menu and choose **Cells**. The Format Cells dialog box appears.

9. Click **Hidden** to place a check mark in its box.

10. Click **OK**.

11. Open the **Tools** menu, point to **Protection**, and choose **Protect Sheet**. The Protect Sheet dialog box appears, as shown in Figure 10.12.

12. If no check mark appears in the box next to **Protect Worksheet and Contents of Locked Cells**, then click the option to add a checkmark.

13. Click in the **Password to Unprotect Sheet** text box and type a unique password that's easy for you to remember but difficult for anyone else to guess.

## caution

Write down the password you use and store it in a secure place. If you lose the password, you will be unable to edit the worksheet yourself.

Make sure this
option is checked

**FIGURE 10.12**

You can pass-
word-protect a
worksheet to
prevent unau-
thorized
changes.

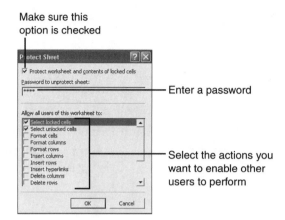

Enter a password

Select the actions you
want to enable other
users to perform

14. Under **Allow All Users of This Worksheet To**, click each action you want other users of this worksheet to be able to perform. (You can turn an action off; remove the check mark by clicking it again.)

15. Click **OK**. Excel prompts you to retype the password.

16. Type the password again, exactly as you typed it in Step 13, and click **OK**.

If you need to edit the worksheet later, you must unlock it. To unlock a worksheet, open it and then choose **Tools**, **Protection**, **Unprotect Sheet**. Type the required password (the password you assigned to the worksheet) and click **OK**.

# THE ABSOLUTE MINIMUM

Many users wrestle with worksheets, never satisfied with the way they print and never realizing that Excel features a host of tools for controlling the printouts. Fortunately, now that you have completed this chapter, those print control tools are right at your fingertips, and you now have complete control over how Excel lays out your worksheets in print. Specifically, you know how to

- Pull up the Print Preview screen, so you can see how Excel will print your worksheets before you actually print them.
- Print wide worksheets in landscape mode and/or have Excel shrink them to fit on a fixed number of pages.
- Adjust the margins in the Page Setup dialog box and in Print Preview.
- Add headers and footers that print at the top and bottom of every page.
- Print only a selected portion of a worksheet.
- Force Excel to print column headings at the top of each page or row headings along the left side of each page.
- Control the order in which Excel prints the pages.
- Adjust page breaks to control the way Excel distributes your worksheet data on two or more pages.
- Print a worksheet.
- Prevent unauthorized changes to your worksheet if you decide to share it with other people.

With the skills you acquired in this chapter, you have complete control over the appearance and structure of your worksheets as they appear in print. You also have complete control over who can make changes to the workbook and the types of changes they can make. At this point, you have mastered the techniques for creating, saving, enhancing, and printing your workbooks and worksheets, and are now prepared to go beyond the basics in Part 4.

# PART IV

# GOING BEYOND THE BASICS

# APPENDIXES

**11**

# MANAGING A DATABASE WITH EXCEL

# What Is a Database?

A *database* (or *data list*) is a collection of data. A phone book is a database. Your collection of cooking recipes is a database. Even your summer reading list can be considered a database.

A database is a collection of *records*, each of which consists of one or more *field entries*. In the case of a phone book, the field entries could be a person's first name, last name, home phone number, work phone number, mailing address, email address, and so on. All the information relating to a particular person composes a single record.

Excel's worksheets provide an ideal format for creating simple databases. Each cell in a worksheet can store a single field entry. The data entries in each row make up a single record, as shown in Figure 11.1.

**FIGURE 11.1**

In an Excel worksheet, each row contains a single record.

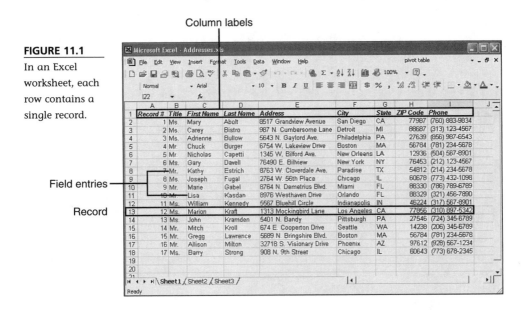

In this chapter, you learn how to create a simple database in Excel, sort and filter records, and even use pivot tables to compare data.

# Database Terminology

Before you create a database, you should familiarize yourself with some basic database terminology and concepts. Following is a list of database terms you will encounter throughout this chapter, along with a brief definition of each term:

- **Field**—On a fill-in-the-blanks form, fields are the blanks. You type a unique piece of data (such as last name, first name, or middle initial) into each field.

- **Record**—A completed form. Each record contains data for a specific person, place, or thing. In a recipe database, for example, each recipe is a record.

- **Form**—A fill-in-the-blanks document you use to type entries into your database. This is just like a form you would fill out to apply for a new credit card.

- **Sort**—To rearrange records in alphabetical or numerical order based on the entries in a particular field. For example, you might sort records in a phone/address database alphabetically by last name.

- **Filter**—To display a select group of records in a database. For example, you might filter out all records in a phone/address database except those records that have Chicago as the city entry.

- **Table**—A way of displaying records in a database other than by using forms. A table is laid out in a worksheet format, consisting of rows and columns that intersect to form cells. Each record is contained in its own row and consists of field entries, each of which is typed in its own cell.

- **Pivot Table**—A report that consolidates data in worksheets and databases and enables you to restructure the data to compare and analyze it.

# Creating Your Database

An Excel database is a fairly basic worksheet. You type field names or *column labels* (such as First Name, Last Name, Address, and Home Phone) in the top row, and then you enter records in the rows below it. When creating a database, keep the following rules in mind:

- You must enter column labels in the top row of the data area. (This may or may not be the top row of the worksheet, but all records must be entered in the rows directly below the row that contains the column labels.) Column labels describe and identify the contents of each field.

- Do NOT skip a row between the column labels row and the first record. If you skip a row, Excel loses track of the field entries in each column.

- If the worksheet that contains your database contains other unrelated data, leave a blank column or row between that area of the worksheet and the area that contains your database records.

- Type each record in a separate row, with no empty rows between records.

■ The cells in a given column must contain information of the same type. For example, if you have a ZIP CODE column, all cells in that column must contain a ZIP code.

■ Keep all records on one worksheet. A database that spans several worksheets is difficult to manage, and Excel may not be able to perform all available database functions, such as sorting records on data that's entered on separate worksheets.

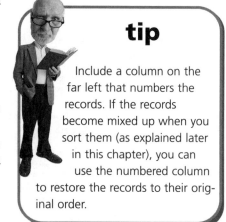

**tip**

Include a column on the far left that numbers the records. If the records become mixed up when you sort them (as explained later in this chapter), you can use the numbered column to restore the records to their original order.

## Entering Column Labels

The first step in creating a database is to type column labels (field names) in the top row of the worksheet. Excel uses these column labels to locate field entries, sort and filter records, and retrieve data. To format and enter column labels properly and avoid problems later, take the following steps:

1. Click the row heading (the "1") to the left of the top row to select the entire row.

2. Open the **Format** menu and choose **Cells**. The Format Cells dialog box appears.

3. Click the **Number** tab if it is not already up front and then, in the Category list, click **Text**, as shown in Figure 11.2. This ensures that Excel will treat all column labels as text entries rather than values.

**FIGURE 11.2**

Change the cell format for the topmost row to Text.

| Format Cells | ? X |
|---|---|

Number | Alignment | Font | Border | Patterns | Protection |

Category:
General
Number
Currency
Accounting
Date
Time
Percentage
Fraction
Scientific
Text
Special
Custom

Sample
Record #

Text format cells are treated as text even when a number is in the cell. The cell is displayed exactly as entered.

OK | Cancel

4. Apply any text and cell formatting as desired to designate the entries in this row as column labels. (I recommend making the entries bold and/or italic and adding a cell border to the bottom of the cells.) This helps Excel distinguish between the column labels and the records, and it gives you a visual indicator of where column labels end and records begin.

5. Click one of the cells in the top row and type column labels in the cells of the top row from left to right. Figure 11.3 shows a sample row of column label entries.

**FIGURE 11.3**

Type column labels in the top-most row.

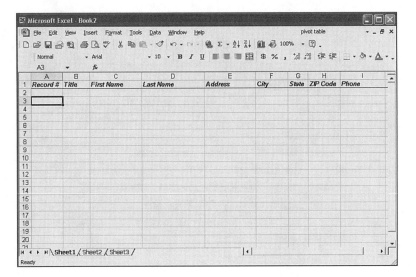

## Formatting Database Fields

In the preceding section, you formatted the column labels as Text. You can save some valuable data entry time by formatting the cells in each column—the cells in which you will type the data entries. For example, if you have cells that will contain phone numbers, you can apply a number format, such as (###) ###-####, which will format the phone number for you. When you begin to enter phone numbers, all you need to type are the 10 digits that make up the phone number, such as 1234567890, and Excel displays the number as (123) 456-7890.

**caution**

When typing column labels or any entry, do not type leading or trailing spaces (spaces before or after the entry). Spaces can cause problems later when you sort or filter your records.

To format the cells that will contain field entries, take the following steps:

1. Select three cells directly below the desired column label. If, for instance, you want to apply a phone number format to the cells in the Phone column, select the three cells below "Phone." DO NOT select the column label.

2. Open the **Format** menu and choose **Cells**. The Format Cells dialog box appears.

3. In the **Category** list, click the desired format category. If none of the categories contains a format you want to use, click **Custom** at the bottom of the list, as shown in Figure 11.4.

4. Click the desired format on the right side of the dialog box, or, if you chose Custom, highlight the entry in the Type text box and type a representation of the desired format. For example, to create your own phone number format, you might type (###) ###-#### or ###.###.####.

5. Press **Enter** or click **OK**.

**note**

Excel automatically extends formatting from one cell to the cell below it, as long as three of the previous five cells use the same formatting. So if you apply a format to the three cells directly below a column label, those three cells and any cells below them will use the same formatting. (To turn off this feature, open the **Tools** menu, choose **Options**, click the **Edit** tab, and clear the check box next to **Extend List Formats and Formulas**.)

**FIGURE 11.4**

Format the cells that will contain your data entries.

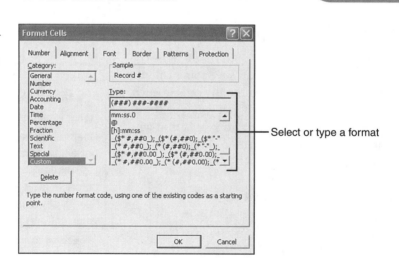

Select or type a format

# Using Data Forms to Enter, Edit, and Delete Data

After you have typed the column labels and formatted at least three cells in any columns that require special formatting, you can begin entering records into your database by using either of the following two methods:

- Type individual entries in cells, just as you add any entries to a worksheet.
- Display a fill-in-the-blanks form and type your entries into the text boxes to complete the form, as explained next.

Excel can identify the column labels you entered and formatted earlier in this chapter and use them to create the form you need to begin entering records. To display and use the form, take the following steps:

1. Click any cell that contains a column label.

2. Open the **Data** menu and choose **Form**. The Microsoft Excel dialog box appears, as shown in Figure 11.5, indicating that Excel cannot determine which row contains the column labels. Excel assumes you want to use the topmost row.

3. Click **OK**. The data entry form appears, as shown in Figure 11.6. The form's name matches the name of the worksheet tab. Note that the name of the text boxes (fields) match the column labels you entered.

*If your database already contains records and you want to insert additional records through the use of a form, click any cell in your database that contains a field entry and then open the **Data** menu and choose **Form**. Excel immediately displays the form.*

**FIGURE 11.5**

Excel cannot determine initially which row contains the column labels.

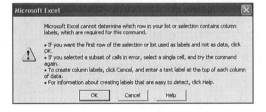

4. Type entries into the text boxes to complete the form. Press the **Tab** key after each entry to move to the next text box.

5. After you have completed the form, press **Enter** or click the **New** button to save the record and display a blank form for entering a new record. The information you entered on the form is transferred to the corresponding cells in the worksheet, as shown in Figure 11.7.

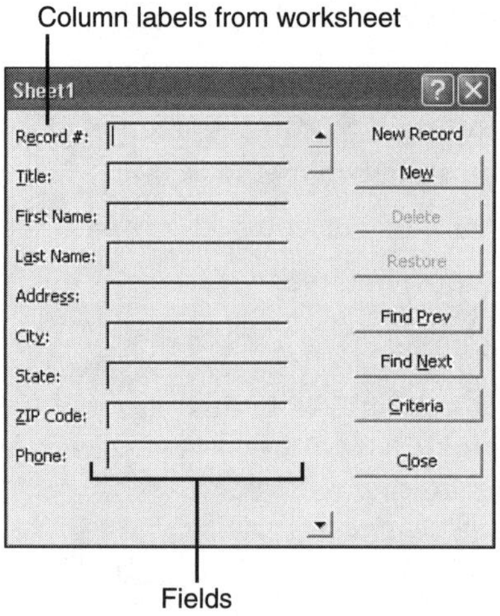

Column labels from worksheet

**FIGURE 11.6**

Enter records
with a form.

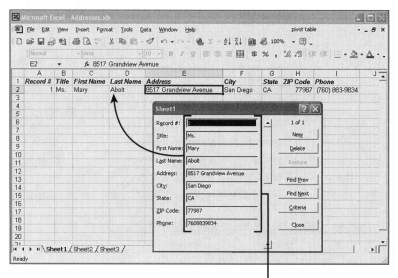

Fields

**FIGURE 11.7**

When you click
New or press
Enter, Excel
transfers the
form data to the
worksheet as a
record.

Data transferred to worksheet as a record

6. Repeat steps 4 and 5 until you have entered every record you need to enter.

7. Click the **Close** button.

If you choose to type field entries in cells, you might notice that as you type entries,
Excel automatically completes some entries for you. If, for instance, you select a cell
in the First Name column, and that column already contains the entry "Allison,"
when you type Al, Excel automatically inserts "Allison." To accept the entry, simply

press the Tab key to move to the next cell. To type a different entry, such as Albert, just keep typing to complete the entry and then press the Tab key.

# Finding Records in Your Database

Databases that contain only a handful of records are easy to search; you simply display the database and then scan through it to find the desired record. Some databases, however, can contain hundreds or even thousands of records, making it nearly impossible, not to mention tedious, to track down a specific record.

Fortunately, Excel provides a tool that can help you locate records in your database. To find a particular record, take the following steps:

note

You can use forms to edit records as well as enter them. Click any cell in the database and then open the **Data** menu and choose **Form**. Click the down arrow button at the bottom of the scroll bar until the record you want to edit is displayed. Enter your changes and then click the **New** button.

1. Click any cell in the database that contains an entry.

2. Open the **Data** menu and choose **Form**. The data form appears, displaying the first record in the database.

3. Click the **Criteria** button. Excel displays a blank Criteria form, which you can use to search for a record.

4. Click in the desired field (text box) and type an entry that is unique to the record you want to find, as shown in Figure 11.8. In a phone database, for example, you might click in the Last Name field and type the last name of the person whose record you want to find. (You need not type the entire entry; sometimes one to three characters are sufficient. You can also type entries in more than one field to narrow the search.)

5. Click the **Find Next** button. Excel displays the first record in the database that matches the search entry you typed, as shown in Figure 11.9.

6. To find the next record that matches your search entry, click **Find Next**. To find the previous record that matches your search entry, click **Find Prev**.

7. When you are finished searching for records, click the **Close** button.

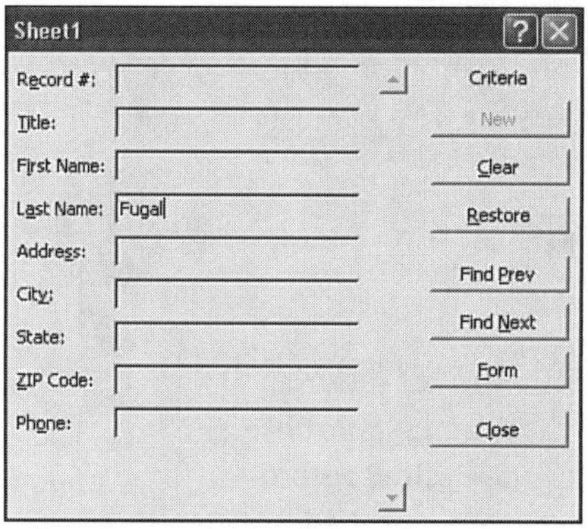

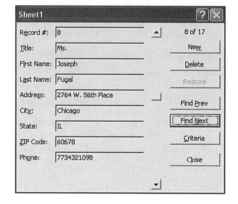

**FIGURE 11.8**

You can search for records using the Criteria form.

**FIGURE 11.9**

Excel displays the first record in the database that matches your search entry.

Excel also supports more general searches designed to turn up groups of records that match a range of criteria. For example, if you have a database of salespeople that includes each sales person's total annual sales figures, you might enter **>100000** (greater than 100,000) in the Sales field. The search would then return the records of all salespeople who had annual sales of more than $100,000. This type of criteria entry consists of a *comparison operator* (such as = or > or <), followed by a value or label entry. The Table 11.1 shows the comparison operators that Excel supports.

## Table 11.1    Excel's Comparison Operators

| Operator | Meaning |
| --- | --- |
| = | Equal to |
| > | Greater than |
| < | Less than |
| >= | Greater than or equal to |
| <= | Less than or equal to |
| <> | Not equal to |

You can also use the following wild cards when specifying criteria:

**?**   Represents a single character

**\***   Represents multiple characters

In the Name field, for instance, you might type **M\*** to find everyone whose name begins with an M. To find everyone whose three-digit department code has 10 as the last two digits, type **?10**.

# Sorting Your Records

Sometimes, sorting a database can help you locate specific records or arrange the records in a more logical order. You might sort the records by ZIP code, for example, to help group individuals who live in the same geographical area.

To sort a database, first decide which field to sort on. For example, an address database could be sorted by Name or by City—or it could be sorted by Name within City within State. Each of these sort fields is considered a *key*.

You can use up to three keys when sorting your database. The first key in the preceding example would be Name, then City, and then State. You can sort your database in *ascending order* (A, B, C... or 1, 2, 3...) or *descending order* (Z, Y, X... or 10, 9, 8...).

To sort the records in your database, take the following steps:

1. Select all the records in your database, but do not select the top row (the row with the column labels).

2. Open the **Data** menu and choose **Sort**. The Sort dialog box appears, as shown in Figure 11.10.

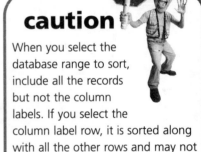

# caution

When you select the database range to sort, include all the records but not the column labels. If you select the column label row, it is sorted along with all the other rows and may not remain at the top.

**FIGURE 11.10**

Specify the sort criteria.

3. Open the **Sort By** drop-down list and click the first field you want to sort by.

4. Click **Ascending** or **Descending** to specify a sort order.

5. To sort on another field, open the top **Then By** drop-down list and click the second field you want to sort by.

6. Click **Ascending** or **Descending** to specify a sort order.

7. To make the sorting operation even more detailed, repeat steps 5 and 6 for the second **Then By** drop-down list.

8. Click **OK** or press **Enter**.

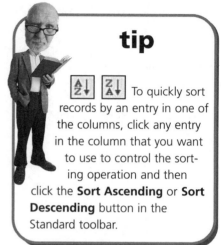

**tip**

To quickly sort records by an entry in one of the columns, click any entry in the column that you want to use to control the sorting operation and then click the **Sort Ascending** or **Sort Descending** button in the Standard toolbar.

# Narrowing Your List with AutoFilter

Excel offers a feature called AutoFilter that allows you to easily display only a select group of records in your database. For example, you can display the records for only those people who live in Boston. Here's how you use AutoFilter:

**caution**

If the sorting operation does not turn out as planned, you can undo the sort. Open the **Edit** menu and choose **Undo Sort** or press **Ctrl+Z**.

1. Select the entire database, including the row you used for column labels.

2. Open the **Data** menu, point to **Filter**, and choose **AutoFilter**. Excel displays drop-down list arrow buttons inside each cell that contains a column label.

3. Click the drop-down list button for the field you want to use to filter the list. For example, if you want to display records for those people living in Boston, click on the button in the City cell. A drop-down list appears, as shown in Figure 11.11. This list contains all the entries in the column.

4. Select the entry you want to use to narrow your list. You can use the arrow keys to scroll through the list, or type the first character in the entry's name to quickly move to it. Press **Enter**, or click the entry with your mouse. Excel filters the list.

Click the desired entry

**FIGURE 11.11**

You can use
AutoFilter to
narrow your list.

| Record ▼ | Titl ▼ | First Nam ▼ | Last Nam ▼ | Address | City ▼ | Stai ▼ | ZIP Coc ▼ | Phone ▼ |
|---|---|---|---|---|---|---|---|---|
| 1 Ms. | Mary | Abolt | 8517 Grandview Avenue | (All) | CA | 77987 | (760) 883-9834 |
| 2 Ms. | Carey | Bistro | 987 N. Cumbersome Lane | (Top 10...) | MI | 88687 | (313) 123-4567 |
| 3 Ms. | Adrienne | Bullow | 5643 N. Gaylord Ave. | (Custom...) | PA | 27639 | (856) 987-6543 |
| 4 Mr. | Chuck | Burger | 6754 W. Lakeview Drive | Boston / Chicago | MA | 56784 | (781) 234-5678 |
| 5 Mr. | Nicholas | Capetti | 1345 W. Bilford Ave. | Detroit | LA | 12936 | (504) 567-8901 |
| 6 Ms. | Gary | Davell | 76490 E. Billview | Indianapolis / Los Angeles | NY | 76453 | (212) 123-4567 |
| 7 Mr. | Kathy | Estrich | 8763 W. Cloverdale Ave. | Miami | TX | 54812 | (214) 234-5678 |
| 8 Mr. | Joseph | Fugal | 2764 W. 56th Place | New Orleans / New York | IL | 60678 | (773) 432-1098 |
| 9 Mr. | Marie | Gabel | 8764 N. Demetrius Blvd. | Orlando | FL | 88330 | (786) 789-6789 |
| 10 Mr. | Lisa | Kasdan | 8976 Westhaven Drive | Paradise | FL | 88329 | (321) 456-7890 |
| 11 Mr. | William | Kennedy | 5567 Bluehill Circle | Philadelphia / Phoenix | IN | 46224 | (317) 567-8901 |
| 12 Ms. | Marion | Kraft | 1313 Mockingbird Lane | Pittsburgh / San Diego | CA | 77856 | (310) 897-5342 |
| 13 Ms. | John | Kramden | 5401 N. Bandy | Seattle | PA | 27546 | (724) 345-6789 |
| 14 Mr. | Mitch | Kroll | 674 E. Cooperton Drive | | WA | 14238 | (206) 345-6789 |
| 15 Mr. | Gregg | Lawrence | 5689 N. Bringshire Blvd | Boston | MA | 56784 | (781) 234-5678 |
| 16 Mr. | Allison | Milton | 32718 S. Visionary Drive | Phoenix | AZ | 97612 | (928) 567-1234 |
| 17 Ms. | Barry | Strong | 908 N. 9th Street | Chicago | IL | 60643 | (773) 678-2345 |

To return to the full list, open the drop-down list again, and choose **(All)**. To turn off
AutoFilter, open the **Data** menu, point to **Filter**, and click **AutoFilter**.

# Summarizing and Comparing Data with Pivot Tables

Excel's Pivot Tables are reports that summarize
worksheet data and lay it out in a more meaningful format. For example, suppose you had a database which kept track of your monthly sales, by
product and salesperson. You could create a Pivot
Table that summarized the amount of each product
sold each month by each salesperson. You could
then quickly rearrange the table to analyze the
data in various ways. Figure 11.12 illustrates how a
pivot table works.

**note**

If this is your first
encounter with pivot
tables, expect to spend some time
working with them. After you
become accustomed to the data
buttons, the concept will seem
easy to you, but becoming accustomed to the data buttons takes
patience and practice.

Worksheet

**FIGURE 11.12**

A pivot table summarizes and organizes your data.

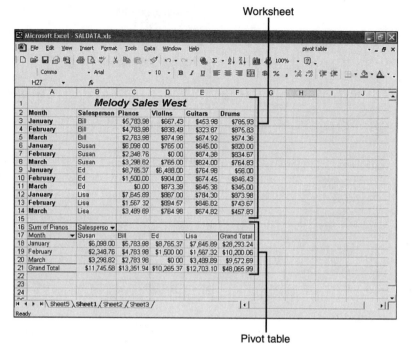

Pivot table

## Creating a Pivot Table Using the PivotTable Wizard

Fortunately, Excel provides a useful tool that can lead you step by step through the process of creating a pivot table: the Pivot Table Wizard. You simply run the Wizard and it prompts you to specify the following four elements:

**Pages** Pages enable you to create a drop-down list for one of the rows or columns in your worksheet. For example, you can use the Salesperson column to create a pages drop-down list that contains the names of all your salespeople. Select a salesperson from the list to see how much of each item that person is selling per month.

**Rows** Rows display row labels you may have entered along the left side of the worksheet.

**Columns** Columns display the column labels used in the worksheet. You can have up to eight columns.

**Data items** These are the values you want added to the pivot table for analysis. Typically, this consists of the data entries rather than row or column labels.

The procedure for creating a pivot table varies depending on whether you are selecting a single range of cells or multiple ranges. The following two sections cover both options in turn.

## Creating a Pivot Table from a Single Range

You create a pivot table by running Excel's Pivot Table Wizard, which leads you through the process with a series of dialog boxes. Here's how you use the PivotTable Wizard to create a pivot table from a single data range:

1.  Open the **Data** menu and choose **PivotTable and PivotChart Report**. Excel displays the PivotTable and PivotChart Wizard Step 1 of 3 dialog box.

2.  Make sure **Microsoft Excel List or Database** and **PivotTable** are selected, as shown in Figure 11.13, and then click the **Next** button. The PivotTable and PivotChart Wizard Step 2 of 3 dialog box appears, asking you to select the range of cells you want to transform into a pivot table. Excel shows a blinking dotted box that indicates what data it thinks you want to use.

**FIGURE 11.13**

The PivotTable and PivotChart Wizard.

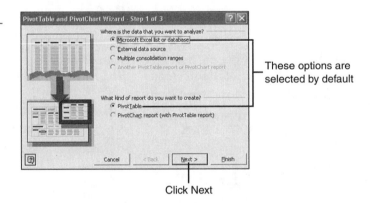

Click Next

3.  Type the cell addresses that define the range, or select the desired cells using your mouse, as shown in Figure 11.14.

4.  Click on the **Next** button. The PivotTable and PivotChart Wizard Step 3 of 3 dialog box appears asking whether you want to place the pivot table on the current worksheet or a new worksheet.

5.  Choose **New Worksheet** or **Existing Worksheet** to specify where you want the pivot table placed, and then click **Finish**. Excel displays a blank pivot table along with a PivotTable Field List box that lists the fields you can add to the pivot table.

**FIGURE 11.14**

Select the
desired range for
your pivot table.

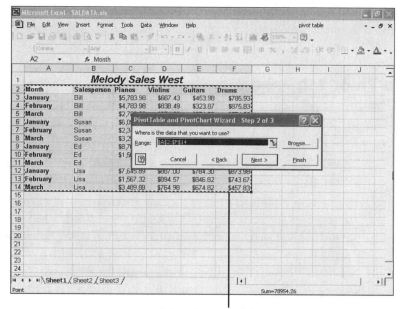

Select the desired data range

6. To add an item from the PivotTable Field List to your pivot
   table, drag the item from the list to the desired area on the
   pivot table, and then release the mouse
   button. Figure 11.15 illustrates the process.

7. Repeat step 6 to add any additional items
   to your pivot table.

## Creating a Pivot Table from Multiple Ranges

If you have data on several worksheets, or several
separate ranges on the same worksheet, you can
have Excel consolidate that data in a pivot table.
To do so, select Multiple Consolidation Ranges
from the PivotTable and PivotChart Wizard Step 1
of 3 dialog box. When it is time for you to specify
the ranges, you'll see the dialog box shown in Figure 11.16. Select the first range
and click on the **Add** button. Repeat the steps for subsequent ranges. The PivotTable
and PivotChart Wizard dialog box stays onscreen as you flip through your worksheets and select ranges.

**caution**

When the PivotTable
and PivotChart Wizard is
done, it creates a table
that may or may not be
exactly what you wanted.
Don't worry. Later in this chapter, in
the section called "Rearranging
Data in a Pivot Table," you will learn
how to drag data around for the
desired effect.

Drag fields from this list to the desired
location in the pivot table

**FIGURE 11.15**

Drag the field
entries to the
pivot table to
specify how you
want the data
arranged.

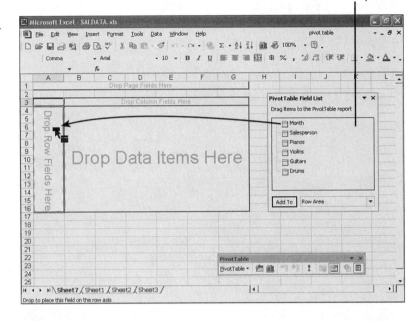

**FIGURE 11.16**

You can select
more than one
range from a
worksheet or
from separate
worksheets.

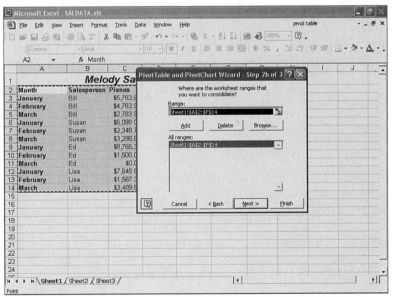

# Rearranging Data in a Pivot Table

Don't worry if your pivot table didn't turn out as you had envisioned it. You can rearrange the data simply by dragging the field buttons around onscreen, as shown in Figure 11.17.

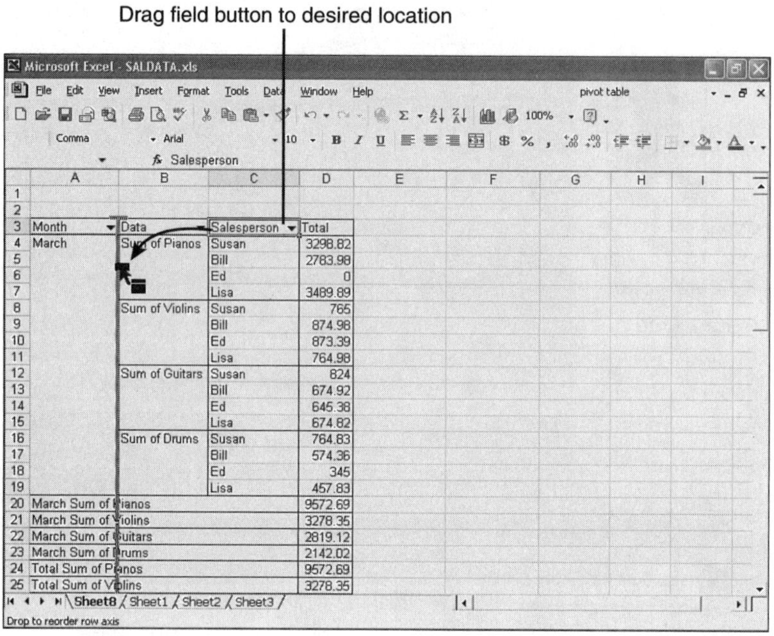

Drag field button to desired location

**FIGURE 11.17**

Drag the field buttons onscreen to rearrange your pivot table.

# THE ABSOLUTE MINIMUM

In this chapter, you learned that Excel provides not only one of the best automated calculators on the market, but it also acts as a database management tool, helping you store, manage, and analyze your records. Upon completing this chapter, you know exactly how to use Excel to create and manipulate a database. Specifically, you now know

- The essential database terminology and concepts required to understand databases.

- How to create a database by entering column labels and records and how to use a form to add records to your database.

- How to find specific records without having to search for them manually.

- How to sort your records alphabetically or numerically based on the entries in any field.

- How to bring up a select group of records by using AutoFilter.

- How to summarize, compare, and analyze data by using a pivot table.

With the skills you acquired in this chapter, you can create databases for storing contact lists, inventories, employee records, mailing lists, and even information about your video collection. The next chapter explores another slightly more advanced topic as you learn to customize Excel to enhance its performance and better suit the way you work.

## IN THIS CHAPTER

- Adding buttons to and removing buttons from Excel's toolbars.

- Creating your own custom toolbars.

- Rearranging items on Excel's menus.

- Changing Excel's default settings to a setting you use more commonly.

- Installing additional features from the Excel or Office installation CDs.

**12**

# CUSTOMIZING EXCEL

# Customizing Excel's Toolbars

Excel's toolbars provide quick access to the most commonly used commands, because they enable you to bypass the clunky menu system. Up to this point, you have used Excel's toolbars to open and save workbooks, format your worksheets, insert graphics, copy and paste selections, draw basic shapes, and much more. You even learned how to access more buttons via the Toolbar Options button.

Many users assume that the toolbars are fixed, unchangeable, and they use the toolbars, as they are, to work more efficiently. In fact, however, the toolbars are completely customizable. You can move and resize toolbars; rearrange, remove, and add buttons to any toolbar; and even create your own toolbars. The following sections provide instructions that show you how to customize Excel's existing toolbars and how to create your own toolbars.

## Changing the Toolbar Buttons

Excel features more than twenty toolbars, including the three toolbars you have used up to this point: the Standard, Formatting, and Drawing toolbars. Many of these toolbars contain buttons you might never use and omit buttons for commands you commonly enter. To make a toolbar conform to the way you work, you can remove buttons, add buttons, and rearrange the buttons on any toolbar. Take the following steps to customize a toolbar:

**note**

To review some basic toolbar skills, review Chapter 2, "Starting and Navigating Excel." This chapter contains two sections that explain how to move toolbars and how to turn Excel's toolbars on and off. In Chapter 2, review the sections "Taking Control of the Toolbars" and "Turning On Other Toolbars" to learn some very basic options for customizing the toolbars.

1. Open the **Tools** menu and choose **Customize**. The Customize dialog box appears.

2. Click the Toolbars tab to move it up front, as shown in Figure 12.1.

3. If the toolbar you want to customize is not displayed, click the check box next to the toolbar's name to place a check mark in its box. Excel displays the toolbar.

4. To remove a button you do not use, right-click the button and choose **Delete** or drag the button off the toolbar to a blank area of the screen, as shown in Figure 12.2.

**FIGURE 12.1**

The Customize dialog box is the key to reconfiguring toolbars.

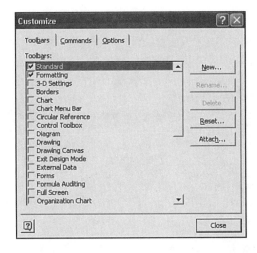

Drag a button off the toolbar

**FIGURE 12.2**

You can remove buttons you never use from a toolbar.

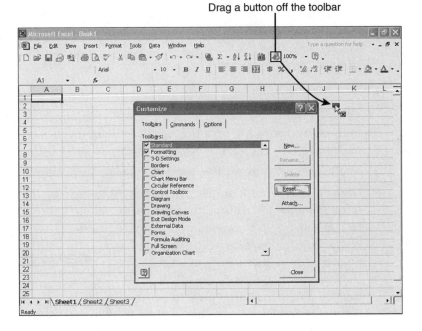

5. To change the name of a button (the name as it appears in the ScreenTip that pops up when the mouse point is over the button), right-click the button, highlight the entry in the **Name** text box, and type the desired button name, as shown in Figure 12.3.

Type a new name for the button

**FIGURE 12.3**

You can change
the name of a
button as it
appears in its
ScreenTip.

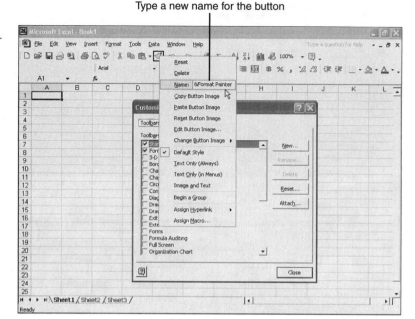

6. To add a command, as a button or list, to a toolbar, click the **Commands** tab and proceed to step 7.

7. In the **Categories** list, click the type of command you want to add to your toolbar, such as File, Edit, View, or Insert. See Figure 12.4.

8. Scroll down the **Commands** list to find the desired command.

9. Drag the command from the Commands list to the desired location on the toolbar and then release the mouse button. (When you drag a command over a toolbar, a plus sign appears next to the mouse pointer and an insertion point appears to show where the button or list will be inserted on the toolbar. If an X rather than a plus sign appears next to the pointer, Excel cannot place the button or list where the pointer is currently positioned.) When you release the mouse button, the selected command appears on the toolbar as a button or list.

**caution**

To return a toolbar to its original condition, open the **Tools** menu, choose **Customize**, click the **Toolbars** tab, click the name of the toolbar you want to restore, and click the **Reset** button.

Drag the desired command from here to the toolbar

**FIGURE 12.4**

You can drag commands from the Customize dialog box to a toolbar.

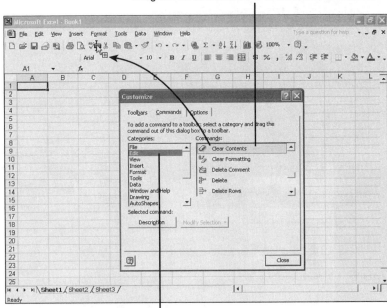

Click the desired command category

# Creating Your Own Toolbars

Although toolbars are great time-saving devices, they can take up a great deal of screen space, leaving less room for displaying your documents. One solution is to create your own toolbar containing only those buttons that you frequently use and then turn off the other toolbars. To create your own toolbar, take the following steps:

1. Open the **Tools** menu and choose **Customize** or right-click a toolbar and choose **Customize**.

2. Click the **Toolbars** tab, as shown in Figure 12.5.

3. Click the **New** button. The New Toolbar dialog box appears, as shown in Figure 12.6, prompting you to name the toolbar.

4. Type a name for your toolbar and click **OK**. The name of the new toolbar appears in the list of toolbars with a check mark next to it, indicating that it is on, and the toolbar appears onscreen, as shown in Figure 12.7. (Don't worry that it looks small; the toolbar expands as you add commands to it.)

**FIGURE 12.5**

You can create your own toolbar.

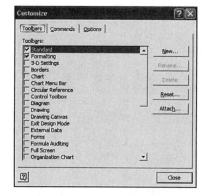

**FIGURE 12.6**

Excel prompts you to name the new toolbar.

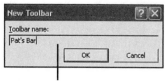

Type a more descriptive name

**FIGURE 12.7**

At first, the toolbar appears small.

New toolbar

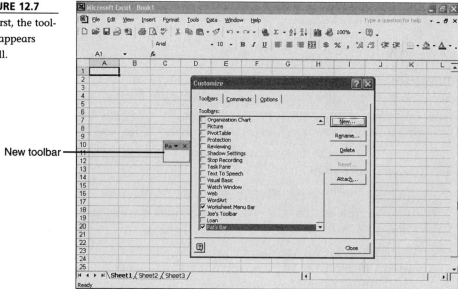

5. In the Customize dialog box, click the **Commands** tab.

6. In the **Categories** list, click the category for the command or button that you want to add to your toolbar.

7. Scroll down the **Commands** list to find the desired command.

8. Drag the desired command from the **Commands** list over your toolbar and release the mouse button, as shown in Figure 12.8. The command appears as a button or list on the toolbar, and your toolbar expands to accommodate it.

9. Repeat steps 6–8 to add more tools to your toolbar.

10. When your toolbar is complete, click the Customize dialog box's **Close** button.

**tip**

When the Customize dialog box is displayed, you can drag buttons from other toolbars and commands from pull-down menus to your toolbar. Simply display the toolbar button you want to copy to your toolbar or open a menu and display the desired command. Then hold down the **Ctrl** key while dragging the button or command over your toolbar. (Hold down the Ctrl key to copy rather than move the button or command.)

Drag the desired command over your toolbar

**FIGURE 12.8**

You can populate your toolbar with buttons and lists from the Commands list.

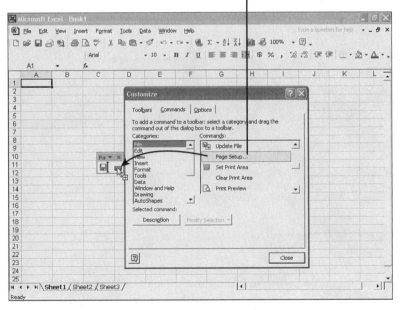

# Reconfiguring Excel's Menus

Excel's menus initially display only the most commonly used commands. If you leave a menu open for a few seconds or click the double-headed arrow at the bottom of a menu, Excel displays all the commands that the menu contains. In most cases, you want to leave the menus as they are; you don't want to remove commands, because you might need access to those commands later. However, you should know that Excel's menus are just as customizable as its toolbars. You can add or remove commands from the menus or rearrange commands according to your needs. Take the following steps to customize a menu:

> **tip**
>
> To move an item from one menu to another, drag the command you want to move over the name of the menu to which you want to move the command. The menu opens. Drag the command to the desired location on the destination menu, and then release the mouse button.

1. Open the **Tools** menu and choose **Customize**. The Customize dialog box appears, as you saw in Figure 12.1.

2. To move a menu command, open the menu that contains the command, drag the command to the desired position on the menu, as shown in Figure 12.9, and release the mouse button.

**FIGURE 12.9**

With the Customize dialog box open, you can move items on any menu.

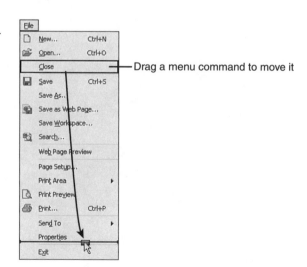

— Drag a menu command to move it

3. To add a command to a menu, click the **Commands** tab and proceed to step 4.

4. In the **Categories** list, click the category for the command you want to add to a menu.

5. Scroll down the **Commands** list to find the desired command.

6. Drag the desired command from the **Commands** list over the name of the desired menu in the menu bar. Without releasing the mouse button, let the mouse pointer rest on the menu name until the menu opens, and then drag the command to the desired location on the menu and release the mouse button.

7. To remove a command from a menu, right-click the command and choose **Delete**, or drag the command off the menu to a blank area in the worksheet.

8. When you are finished customizing Excel's menus, click the Customize dialog box's **Close** button.

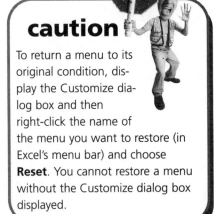

**caution**

To return a menu to its original condition, display the Customize dialog box and then right-click the name of the menu you want to restore (in Excel's menu bar) and choose **Reset**. You cannot restore a menu without the Customize dialog box displayed.

# Setting Toolbar and Menu Options

Up to this point, you have been micromanaging the menus and toolbars. Excel also features options that apply to all menus and toolbars. To check these options, open the **Tools** menu, choose **Customize**, and click the **Options** tab. The toolbar and menu options appear, as shown in Figure 12.10.

**FIGURE 12.10**

The toolbar and menu options.

Customize

Toolbars | Commands | Options

Personalized Menus and Toolbars

☑ Show Standard and Formatting toolbars on two rows

☐ Always show full menus

☑ Show full menus after a short delay

Reset my usage data

Other

☐ Large icons

☑ List font names in their font

☑ Show ScreenTips on toolbars

Menu animations: (System default) ▾

Close

The following list provides a brief explanation of each option:

**Show Standard and Formatting Toolbars on Two Rows** places the Standard and Formatting toolbars on two separate rows below Excel's menu bar. If you turn off this option (remove the check mark next to it), Excel places both toolbars in a single row, thus hiding many of the available buttons.

**Always Show Full Menus** displays all commands on the menu when you first open it. By default, Excel displays only the commands you most commonly use, thus hiding less commonly used commands.

**Show Full Menus After a Short Delay** tells Excel to display all menu items only after the menu has remained opened for several seconds or until you click the double-headed downward-pointing arrow at the bottom of the menu.

**Large Icons** enlarges the buttons in the toolbars. This makes the buttons huge and consumes a great deal of screen space but is a great feature for those who are visually impaired.

**List Font Names in Their Font** tells Excel to display fonts on menus and in any formatting dialog box in the typestyle that the font name represents. (See Figure 12.11.) This option is on by default, but you can turn it off to slightly improve Excel's performance. With this option off, you must imagine what a font looks like by viewing only its name.

**Show ScreenTips on Toolbars** tells Excel to display a ScreenTip (button or option name) when the mouse pointer is pointing to a button or command. You can turn off this option to slightly improve Excel's performance or if the ScreenTips become more annoying than helpful. When you're just starting to learn how to use Excel, keep the ScreenTips on.

**Menu Animations** controls the way menus make their entrance onscreen when you open them. Five options are available: *System default* (whatever your computer is set up to use), *Random* (uses a different type of animation each time you open a menu), *Unfold* (makes menus roll out from the upper left corner to the lower right corner), *Slide* (makes menus roll out from top to bottom), and *Fade* (causes menus to fade in from lower to higher intensity).

When you are finished entering your preferences, click the Customize dialog box's **Close** button to save the settings.

**FIGURE 12.11**

Excel can display font names in the typestyle they represent.

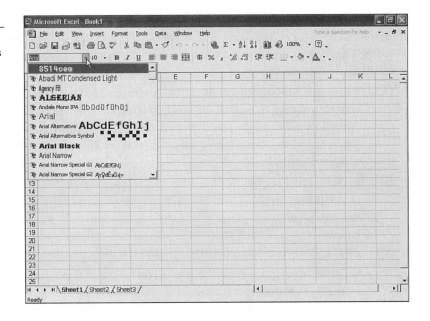

# Changing Excel's Default Settings

As you create and edit worksheets and charts, Excel performs various tasks in accordance with settings that most users rarely see. These settings work behind the scenes, and you rarely, if ever, need to change them. However, you should check out the settings to determine whether changing some of the settings would save you time and make Excel function more in accord with the way you work.

To check out the options that control Excel's performance and "work habits," open the **Tools** menu and choose **Options**. The Options dialog box appears, as shown in Figure 12.12.

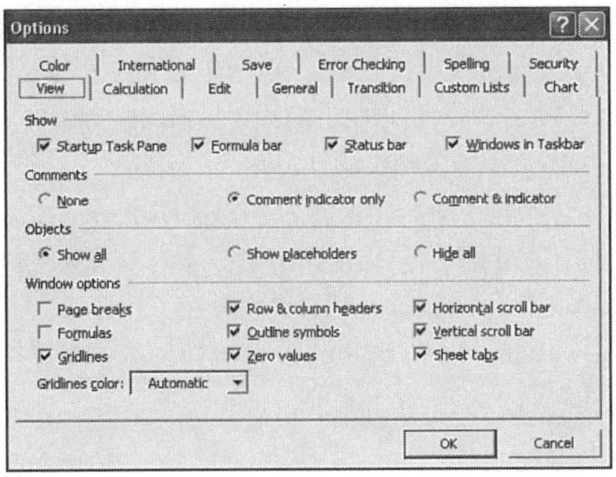

**FIGURE 12.12**

Use the Options dialog box to control the way Excel performs tasks.

The Options dialog box contains far too many options to be described individually in detail. For a detailed description of an option, right-click the option and choose **What's This?** The following list provides a brief overview of the types of options you will find on each tab:

**View** provides options that control the appearance of Excel and its worksheets. You can choose to display or hide the New Workbook task pane (which appears when you first start Excel), the status bar, comments, objects (such as charts and images), page breaks, scrollbars, sheet tabs, and other onscreen objects.

**Calculation** displays options for controlling the way Excel calculates and recalculates formulas and functions in a worksheet. The main option on this tab is the setting that tells Excel to automatically recalculate worksheets whenever you edit an entry or recalculate manually (only when you press F9 to initiate a recalculation).

**Edit** features options that control Excel's actions when you enter or edit worksheet entries. Using these options, you can control where the cell selector moves when you type an entry and press Enter, whether or not Excel allows you to drag and drop data in a worksheet, whether or not Excel uses AutoComplete when you're entering data, and whether or not Excel extends formatting from formatted cells to neighboring cells.

**General** provides a hodgepodge of settings for everything from specifying your username to enabling Excel to play sounds when you execute particular commands. You can specify the number of recently opened workbook file names Excel lists on the File menu, the number of worksheet tabs that appear in all new workbooks, the default font Excel uses for data entries in all new workbooks, and the folder Excel opens whenever you choose to save or open a workbook file.

**Transition** options are designed to help former Lotus 1-2-3 spreadsheet users make a smoother transition to Excel. Here, you can choose the default file format for saving Excel workbooks, specify a key to press to get help for Lotus 1-2-3 users, and set Sheet options that enable you to enter formulas and functions in Lotus 1-2-3 format.

**Custom Lists** displays the lists that Excel uses to AutoFill contents into two or more cells. You can use the features on this tab to create additional AutoFill lists. For more information, flip back to Chapter 4, "Entering and Editing Labels and Values" and review the section named "Entering Data Quickly with AutoFill."

**Chart** features a handful of options for controlling the way the currently selected chart is treated. You can turn off ScreenTips for various chart elements, have Excel ignore blank cells in the data area when it creates a chart, or plot only visible cells (if some cells in the data area are hidden).

**Color** enables you to modify the colors that appear on the color palette when you choose to change a font color, background color, or line color. Click a color you want to change and then click the **Modify** button to change it. Click the desired color or click the Custom tab and create the desired color. Then, click **OK** to return to the Options dialog box.

**International** provides options that help you create and edit worksheets that use settings that may be more appropriate for other countries. You can, for instance, choose to use a different character in place of a comma for the thousands separator, or have your worksheets set up to read from right to left rather than from left to right.

**Save** provides options that tell Excel to save AutoRecover information every specified number of minutes. With AutoRecover, if your computer crashes while you're creating or editing a worksheet, when you restart Excel, Excel displays a pane that allows you to recover your work. You can use the options on this tab to disable Auto Recover, but I highly recommend that you keep this feature enabled.

**Error Checking** features options that enable you to control Excel's error checking feature, which automatically checks your formulas and functions for common errors. You can disable background error checking or specify which errors you want Excel to look for.

**Spelling** options control the way Excel performs its spell checking. You can specify the spelling dictionary you want Excel to use, have Excel ignore some types of entries (such as entries that consist of numbers and letters or all UPPERCASE characters), and choose which custom dictionary you want Excel to add words to when you choose to add a word that Excel considers misspelled to a dictionary.

**Security** provides options for password-protecting a workbook file, protecting the workbook from unauthorized changes, removing any personal information from the file's properties when you save the workbook, and preventing Excel from running macros in a workbook you obtained from some other source. For more about macros, see Chapter 13, "Automating Tasks with Macros." To review workbook security options, return to Chapter 10, "Printing and Protecting Your Workbook, Worksheets, and Charts," and read the section named "Preventing Unauthorized Changes to a Workbook."

# Installing Optional Components

When you install Excel, using either the Excel installation CD or the Microsoft Office installation CD, the setup routine installs Excel's most common features and adds tools and features only when you choose to use them. Much of the available clip art and most international features, for example, are omitted from the installation. To manually install additional features and tools, perform the following steps:

1. Load the Excel or Office installation CD into your CD-ROM drive. (If you have more than one CD, you must run the installation routine for each CD.)

2. If the installation routine does not start automatically, double-click the **My Computer** icon (on the Windows desktop or on the **Start** menu), double-click the icon for your CD-ROM drive, and then double-click the **Setup** icon. The Microsoft Excel 2002 or Microsoft Office XP Setup dialog box appears.

3. Click the **Add or Remove Features** option and click **Next**. The Microsoft Excel 2002 or Microsoft Office XP Setup dialog box shows a list of programs and features included on the CD. Figure 12.13 shows the Microsoft Office XP Setup dialog box.

Click the plus sign
to expand the list

**FIGURE 12.13**

The Microsoft
Office XP Setup
dialog box.

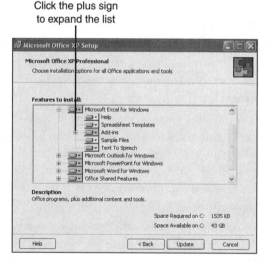

4. Click the plus sign next to a program or feature set to expand it.

5. Click the icon next to a feature and select one of the following options:

   **Run from My Computer** installs the feature on your computer's hard drive.

   **Run All from My Computer** installs the complete feature set on your computer's hard drive.

   **Installed on First Use** prompts you to install the feature or tool on your computer's hard drive the first time you select the command to use the feature or tool.

   **Not Available** removes the program or feature from your computer's hard drive and removes all commands that refer to the program or feature.

6. When you're finished entering your preferences, click **Update**. The installation routine installs the selected components as specified.

**tip**

If your computer is connected to the Internet, check for Excel program updates. To do this, open Excel's **Help** menu and choose **Excel on the Web** or **Office on the Web**. Click the link for your geographic location, click the link for Excel, and click the link for obtaining product updates. Follow the onscreen instructions to copy and install any program updates for Excel. If you see a link for the download center, click the link to find out whether any additional tools and templates are available.

# THE ABSOLUTE MINIMUM

Before working through this chapter, you were at the mercy of Excel, learning to use Excel to accomplish specific tasks. Now that you have completed this chapter, you know how to take control of Excel and make it conform to the way you work. Specifically, you know how to

- Add buttons to and remove buttons from Excel's toolbars.

- Create your own custom toolbars and populate them with the buttons and lists you use on a daily basis.

- Rearrange items on Excel's menus, remove options you never use, and add commands you want to enter via the menus.

- Adjust the settings Excel uses to control the appearance and behavior of all its toolbars and menus.

- Access the settings that control every aspect of Excel's appearance and performance and the way Excel performs various tasks.

- Run Excel's installation routine again to add components that were not installed initially and remove any tools you do not use.

Congratulations! You now have complete control over Excel's appearance, performance, and behavior. Well, you have *almost* complete control. In the next chapter, you learn another trick for working more efficiently in Excel: You learn how to create your very own macros, giving you the power to execute a complex sequence of commands by entering a single macro command, by pressing a specific key combination, or by clicking a button.

## IN THIS CHAPTER

- Using macros to automate step-heavy tasks you frequently perform.

- Recording a series of keystrokes and commands to create a macro.

- Running macros by pressing a key or clicking a button.

- Editing macro commands in Microsoft's Visual Basic Editor.

- Protecting Excel worksheets and your computer against macro viruses.

**13**

# AUTOMATING TASKS WITH MACROS

# What Is a Macro?

Excel is packed with tools to help you enter commands without winding through a series of menus and submenus. You can press Ctrl+S to save a workbook, click the Print button to print a worksheet, or press Ctrl+N to create a new workbook, just to name a few. By learning the dozens of toolbar buttons and shortcut keystrokes available in Excel, you can significantly reduce the amount of time you spend entering commands.

To become even more efficient, you can create your own *macros*. A macro is a recorded series of commands you can play back in Excel by selecting the macro's name from a list or by pressing a keystroke or clicking a button that's assigned to the macro. In this chapter, you learn how to record commands with the macro recorder, how to name and run your macros, and how to create toolbar buttons and keystrokes for convenient access to your macros.

note

Before creating your own macro to automate a task you commonly perform, check Excel's help system to determine whether Excel already offers a shortcut for that task. Also, ask yourself whether you can use an easier feature, such as AutoCorrect or AutoText, instead of a macro.

# Recording a Macro

The easiest way to create a macro is to use Excel's *macro recorder*. You simply turn on the recorder, type a name for the macro, perform the task you want to record, and then stop the recorder. The following instructions lead you step by step through the process of recording a macro:

1. Open the **Tools** menu, point to **Macro**, and choose **Record New Macro**. The Record Macro dialog box appears, as shown in Figure 13.1, prompting you to name the macro.

2. Type a unique, descriptive, and brief name for your macro, up to 64 characters (no spaces). The macro name must start with a letter—never a number. The macro recorder supplies a default name—Macro1, Macro2, and so on, as you keep recording macros—but nondescriptive names such as these are not very helpful when you're trying to determine the purpose of each macro.

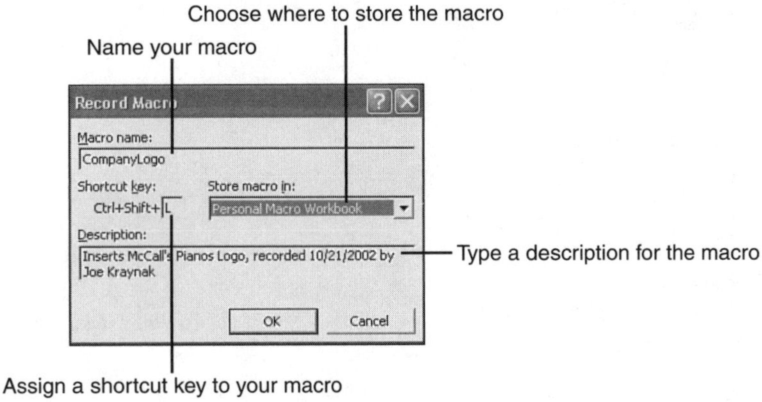

**FIGURE 13.1**

Excel's Record
Macro dialog
box.

Choose where to store the macro

Name your macro

Type a description for the macro

Assign a shortcut key to your macro

3. Open the **Store Macro In** drop-down list and choose one of the following options:

   ■ **Personal Macro Workbook** to make the macro available in all workbooks.

   ■ **New Workbook** to have Excel create a new workbook and store the macro in that workbook.

   ■ **This Workbook** to make the macro available only in the currently open workbook.

4. To assign a shortcut key to the macro, click in the **Shortcut key: Ctrl+** box and hold down the **Shift** key while pressing the letter key that you want to use in combination with the Ctrl key to launch your macro. This assigns the macro a **Ctrl+Shift+letter key** shortcut.

5. Click in the **Description** text box and type a brief description of the macro's function (the task it performs).

6. Click the **OK** button. The Stop Recording toolbar appears with buttons for stopping the recording and for switching between relative and absolute cell references, as shown in Figure 13.2. (If the toolbar does not appear, right-click any toolbar and click **Stop Recording**.)

## caution

When specifying a shortcut key, avoid using keys that Excel has already assigned to other tasks, such as Ctrl+C to copy or Ctrl+P to print. By holding down the Shift key when assigning a keystroke, you avoid most conflicts. For example, if you press Shift+P, Excel assigns the Ctrl+Shift+P shortcut to the macro. If you were to press P, Excel would assign the Ctrl+P keystroke to the macro, and whenever you pressed Ctrl+P, Excel would run the macro rather than printing a worksheet.

**FIGURE 13.2**

Excel's Stop
Recording tool-
bar.

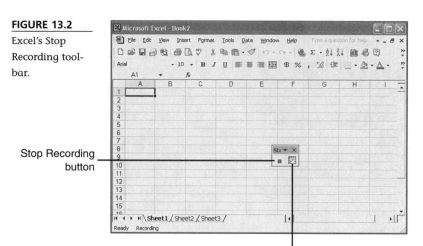

Stop Recording
button

Toggles between absolute and relative cell references

7. Perform the task whose steps you want to record. You can select menu commands, click toolbar buttons, and press keystrokes to enter commands. To select a cell, click it. To select a range of cells, drag over the cells. You can also type entries and select objects, such as charts and clip art.

8. When you are finished performing the steps, click the **Stop Recording** button or open the **Tools** menu, point to **Macro**, and click **Stop Recording**. Excel saves your macro with the name you entered in step 2.

# Running a Macro

When you record a macro, its name is added to the list of macros you have recorded. If you assigned a shortcut keystroke to the macro, the easiest way to run the macro is to press the keystroke. If you did not assign a keystroke to the macro, you must select the macro from a list, as explained in the following steps:

**note**

Excel macros automatically record any cell selections by using absolute references. If you want to use relative references, click the **Relative Reference** button on the **Stop Recording** toolbar. You can click this button repeatedly to switch back and forth from absolute to relative references. For an explanation of the difference between absolute and relative cell references, see Chapter 6, "Automating Calculations with Formulas and Functions."

1. Open the **Tools** menu, point to **Macro**, and choose **Macros**, (or press **Alt+F8**). A list of available macros appears, as shown in Figure 13.3.

2. Click the name of the macro you want to run.

3. Click the **Run** button.

Click the name of the
macro you want to run

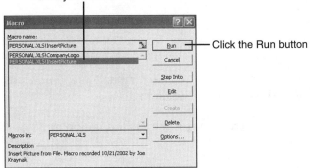

**FIGURE 13.3**

You can select the macro you want to run from a list of recorded macros.

Click the Run button

Although selecting a macro from a comprehensive macro list is a foolproof way to find and play the macro, it is hardly the most efficient. If you find yourself frequently playing back the macro, consider assigning a shortcut keystroke to the macro. To assign a keystroke to an existing macro, take the following steps:

1. Open the **Tools** menu, point to **Macro**, and choose **Macros** (or press **Alt+F8**). A list of available macros appears, as you saw in Figure 13.3.

2. Click the name of the macro to which you want to assign a keystroke.

3. Click the **Options** button. The Macro Options dialog box appears, as shown in Figure 13.4.

4. Click in the **Shortcut key: Ctrl+** box and hold down the Shift key while pressing the letter key you want to use in combination with the Ctrl key to launch your macro. This assigns the macro a **Ctrl+Shift+ letter key** shortcut.

## caution

Before running your macro for the first time, save your workbook. If the macro performs some actions that you do not approve, close the workbook without saving the changes. If, however, the macro includes a File, Save command, you might be out of luck. To stop a macro before it does too much damage, press **Ctrl+Break** to stop the macro and then use the **Undo** feature to try to recover from any damage the macro has caused.

**FIGURE 13.4**

The Macro
Options dialog
box.

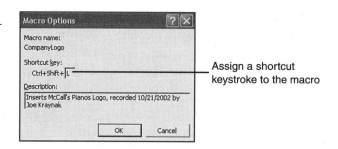

Assign a shortcut
keystroke to the macro

5. Click the **OK** button to close the Macro Options dialog box and return to the Macro dialog box.

6. Click the Macro dialog box's **Close** button. You can now use the shortcut keystroke you assigned to your macro to run it.

Another way to run a macro is to create a toolbar button for it, as explained in the following section.

# Creating a Toolbar Button for Your Macro

Excel's toolbars give you quick access to the most commonly used commands. Instead of having to flip through a series of menus and submenus, you simply click a button in one of the toolbars or select the desired option from one of the drop-down lists. These toolbars can give you quick access to your macros as well. To add a macro to one of Excel's toolbars, take the following steps:

1. Make sure the toolbar on which you want to place your macro button is displayed. (Select **View**, **Toolbars** to display a list of available toolbars.)

2. Open the **Tools** menu and choose **Customize**.

3. Click the **Commands** tab.

4. In the Categories list, click **Macros**, as shown in Figure 13.5.

5. Drag the **Custom Button** from the Commands list over the toolbar on which you want it to appear, drag it to the desired location (watch for a dark

**tip**

To learn how to create your own toolbars, flip back to Chapter 12, "Customizing Excel," and review the section named "Creating Your Own Toolbars."

I-beam pointer that shows where the button will appear), and release the mouse button. (See Figure 13.5.) The button appears on the toolbar. (Leave the Customize dialog box open to perform the next steps.)

**FIGURE 13.5**

You can add macro buttons to any toolbar.

Drag the Custom Button up to the toolbar

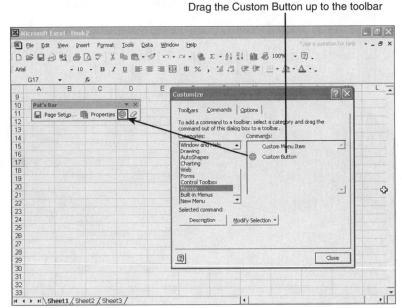

6. To change the name of the button, right-click it, drag over the entry in the **Name** text box, and type a new name for the button.

7. To add an image to the button, right-click the button, point to **Change Button Image** and click the desired image, as shown in Figure 13.6. If you want to display the image only, not the button name, right-click the button and select **Default Style**.

8. Right-click the button and choose **Assign Macro**. The Assign Macro dialog box appears, as shown in Figure 13.7.

9. Click the name of the desired macro and click **OK**.

10. When you are finished, click the Custom dialog box's **Close** button to close the dialog box.

**FIGURE 13.6**

You can pick a different image for your macro button.

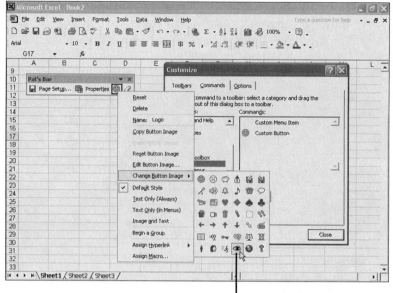

Click the desired image

Pick a macro to assign it to the button

**FIGURE 13.7**

Assign the desired macro to the button you created.

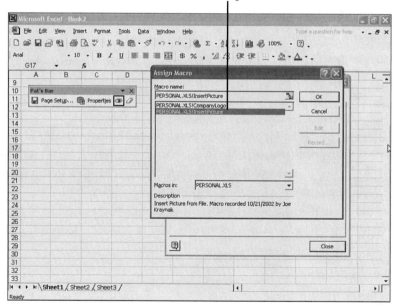

# Editing Macros in Visual Basic Editor

If you run a macro and it does not perform the desired task as you intended it to, you do not need to re-record the macro. Instead, you can modify the macro's recorded commands in Visual Basic Editor or delete commands you inadvertently recorded. To open a macro and edit it in the Visual Basic Editor, take the following steps:

1. If you saved the macro you want to edit in a particular workbook, open the workbook file in which you created and saved the macro.

2. Open the **Tools** menu, point to **Macro**, and choose **Macros**. The Macro dialog box appears, as shown in Figure 13.8.

Click the macro's name

**FIGURE 13.8**

You can edit
any recorded
macro.

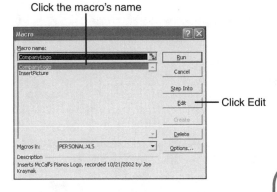

Click Edit

3. Click the name of the macro you want to edit.

4. Click the **Edit** button. Visual Basic Editor appears and displays the commands that compose the selected macro, as shown in Figure 13.9.

5. To delete a command or any text, drag over the command or text to highlight it and then press the **Del** key.

6. To add a command or text, type the command or text where you want it to "play" in the macro.

7. To save your macro, open the **File** menu and choose **Save** or press **Ctrl+S**.

## caution

If you try to edit a macro stored in the Personal Macro Workbook (Personal.xls), Excel displays a warning box indicating that you cannot edit a macro stored in a hidden workbook file. Click **OK** to close the warning box, and then click the Macro dialog box's **Cancel** button to close it. In Excel, open the **Window** menu and choose **Unhide**. Click **PERSONAL.XLS** and click **OK**. Repeat steps 1-3 to open the macro in Visual Basic Editor.

**FIGURE 13.9**

Use Visual Basic
Editor to edit
your macro.

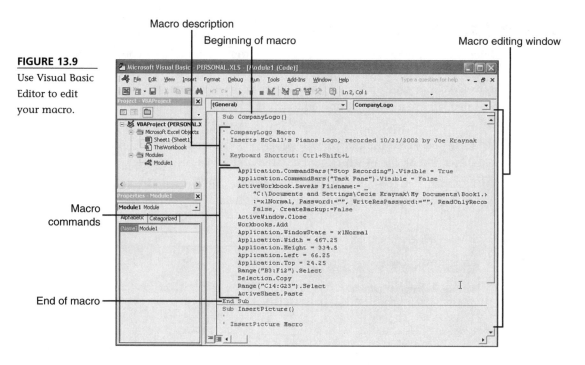

These steps make it sound as though typing macro commands is easy. You soon
realize, however, that you must know the command to type it. When you're getting
started with Visual Basic Editor, use it to delete
superfluous commands and edit any text entries
that are part of the macro. For example, if you
have a macro that inserts your company's logo
into a cell, the macro contains the location of
the logo's graphic file, as shown in the fourth
line of the following example:

```
Sub InsertLogo()
InsertLogo Macro
Macro recorded 11/21/2002 by Sally Rogers
ActiveSheet.Pictures.Insert("C:
➥\AcmeInc\logo.gif").Select
End Sub
```

If you move the graphic file, you can open the
macro in Visual Basic Editor and edit the path to
the file rather than record a new macro.

**note**

When you're ready to
do more with Visual Basic
Editor, purchase a book that's
devoted to it, such as *The
Complete Idiot's Guide to Visual
Basic 6.*

# Protecting Your System Against Macro Viruses

Excel's macros are powerful programs that can enter a complex series of commands with a mere keystroke, but this power comes with some risks. Just imagine the damage a macro could do if it were designed to highlight a worksheet, delete everything on it, and then save the blank worksheet to disk.

To prevent macros from running on your system without your permission, you can tighten Excel's macro security settings. These settings can warn you whenever you open a workbook that contains macros, so you can decide whether or not you want the workbook's macros to run.

To change the macro security setting in Excel, take the following steps:

1. Open the **Tools** menu, point to **Macro**, and click **Security**. The Security dialog box appears, as shown in Figure 13.10.

2. Click the desired macro security level:

   **High** to run only digitally signed macros from trusted sources.

   **Medium** to have Excel display a warning dialog box before opening a workbook file that contains macros. (You can then choose to disable macros for this workbook.)

   **Low** to have Excel open all workbooks without warning you about macro viruses. Choose this option only if you never open workbooks from outside sources or if you have a good anti-virus program that can identify macro viruses.

3. Click **OK** to save the security setting and close the Security dialog box.

**note**

If you don't share workbooks or open workbooks from the Web, you don't need to worry about macro viruses. However, if you open workbooks you receive from friends, relatives, colleagues, or unknown sources, your system is at risk, even if you trust the person who sent you the workbook.

**tip**

Macro security warnings are annoying. Install a good anti-virus utility, such as Norton or McAfee AntiVirus, and choose the Low macro security level in Excel.

**FIGURE 13.10**

Excel's macro
security settings.

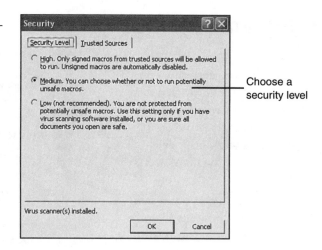

**FIGURE 13.10**

Excel's macro
security settings.

Choose a
security level

# THE ABSOLUTE MINIMUM

When you find yourself frequently entering the same series of commands to perform the same task in Excel, that's a good sign that you need a macro. The next time you perform the task, record the steps, save the recording as a macro, and assign the macro to a keystroke or toolbar button. To play back the macro, simply press its keystroke or click its button. As you work with macros, keep the following in mind:

- To start recording a macro, open the **Tools** menu, point to **Macro**, and choose **Record New Macro**.

- When assigning a keystroke to a macro, hold down the **Shift** key while pressing one of the letter keys.

- You can play a macro by pressing its keystroke, clicking the button you created for it, or by selecting it from a list of macros.

- To edit a macro, open the **Tools** menu, point to **Macro**, and click **Macros**. Click the name of the macro you want to edit and click the **Edit** button.

- Macros can contain both commands and text.

- To prevent macro viruses from damaging your files and infecting your computer, set the macro security level to **Medium** or **High** or install a good anti-virus program.

With the skills you acquired in this chapter, you can save a significant amount of time performing common, repetitive tasks. You can also secure Excel and your computer system from the outside threats posed by macro viruses. The next chapter focuses not on the threats posed by outside sources, but on the Excel features that enable you to share your worksheets on the Internet and access resources that are available on the Internet.

# USING EXCEL ON THE WEB

# Transforming Worksheets into Web Pages

Though printing is still the most common way to "publish" Excel worksheets, more and more users are choosing to publish their worksheets on the Web, a paperless medium. Excel features several tools that enable you to transform your Excel worksheets into Web pages, add hyperlinks to worksheets, import data from the Web into your worksheets, and email your worksheets over the Internet, as you will see throughout this chapter.

One of the first steps you want to take to publish a worksheet on the Web is to convert the worksheet from Excel's native format into a Web page format (also called *HTML* or *HyperText Markup Language*).

To convert a workbook, worksheet, data range, and/or chart into a Web page, take the following steps:

1. Open the workbook that contains the data you want to transform into a Web page.

2. Take one of the following steps to designate the portion of the workbook you want to convert into a Web page:

   To convert the entire workbook, skip to step 3.

   To convert a single worksheet into a Web page, click the worksheet's tab.

   To convert a portion of a worksheet into a Web page, select the desired range of cells.

   To convert a chart into a Web page, select the desired chart.

3. Open the **File** menu and choose **Save as Web Page**. The Save As dialog box appears, as shown in Figure 14.1. Note that the Selection option button displays a different option depending on what you selected in step 1. If you selected a worksheet, the option is *Selection: Sheet*; if you selected a range, the option is *Selection: Range*; if you selected a chart, the option is *Selection: Chart*.

**note**

As shown in these steps, you can choose to convert a worksheet into a *static* Web page, in which case the person who opens the Web page can only view the worksheet (not change it), or you can convert your worksheet into a *dynamic* Web page by turning on the Add Interactivity option. For example, if you create a worksheet that calculates a loan payment amount, you can turn on the Add Interactivity option to enable people to open the Web page in their browsers and enter the necessary details about their loans. This option does not enable the user to change the worksheet and save changes.

Choose to save the whole workbook or a portion of it

**FIGURE 14.1**

Use the Save As
dialog box to
save a workbook
as a Web page.

Choose
a location for
your Web page

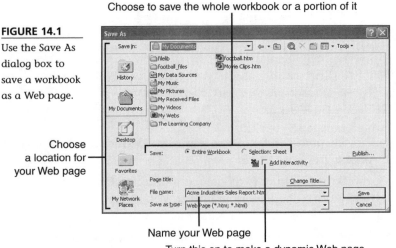

Name your Web page

Turn this on to make a dynamic Web page

4. Click the desired **Save:** option—**Entire Workbook**; **Selection: Sheet**; **Selection: Range**; or **Selection: Chart**.

5. In the **File name** box, edit the Web page filename, if desired. (Don't type the .htm filename extension; Excel adds it for you.)

6. Take one of the following steps to specify where you want the Web page file saved:

   To save the Web page to a folder on your computer's hard drive, open the **Save In** list (near the top of the dialog box) and choose the desired disk drive. Then double-click the desired folder in the folder list.

   To save the Web page directly to your company's Internet or intranet site or to a Web site you already set up as a Web folder in Windows, click **My Network Places**, and navigate to the Web folder you set up. (See "Setting Up a Network Place or Web Folder," later in this chapter, for details.)

   To save the Web page to an FTP (File Transfer Protocol) server on the Internet, open the **Save In** list, choose **FTP Locations**, and choose the desired FTP location. You can set up an FTP location by clicking the Add/Modify FTP Location option and following the onscreen instructions. (See "Uploading Files to an FTP Server," later in this chapter, for details.)

7. To give your Web page a title, which will appear centered at the top of the page, click the **Change Title** button. The Set Page Title dialog box appears, as shown in Figure 14.2.

Web page title

**FIGURE 14.2**

You can give your Web page a title.

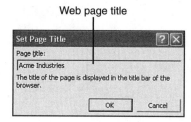

8. Type the desired title and click **OK**. Excel returns you to the Save As dialog box, which you saw in Figure 14.1.

9. To make your worksheet data or Excel database dynamic, click **Add Interactivity** to place a check mark in its box. With this option on, viewers of your Web page can enter their own data into the worksheet.

10. Click the **Save** button. Excel converts the worksheet data, as specified, into a Web page and saves the Web page to the specified drive and folder.

# Inserting Links on Your Worksheets

No Web page is complete without links that point to other Web pages or to other areas of your Web site. With Excel's Insert Hyperlink button, you can quickly transform any data entry, chart, or graphic into a live link that a user can click to obtain additional information or send an email message.

To quickly transform normal text into a link, drag over the text you want to use as the link. To transform a chart or other image into a link, click the chart or image to select it. Then click the **Insert Hyperlink** button in the Standard toolbar. The Insert Hyperlink dialog box appears, as shown in Figure 14.3, allowing you to enter preferences for the link.

The Insert Hyperlink dialog box provides the following Link To options:

- **Existing File or Web Page**—Lets you point the link to a recently opened file, a page you have recently opened in Internet Explorer, or a Web page address. You can also add a ScreenTip to the link that displays a description of the link when a visitor rests the mouse pointer on the link.

- **Place in This Document**—Inserts a link that points to a worksheet or cell address referenced in this worksheet.

- **Create New Document**—Inserts a link that points to a workbook you have not yet created. Type a name for the new workbook and select the folder in which you want the workbook stored. Excel creates a new blank workbook.

You can then add and format entries, insert formulas, and perform other tasks, as described in this book, to complete the workbook.

Text that appears as a link in the worksheet

**FIGURE 14.3**

Use the Insert Hyperlink dialog box to transform text or graphics into links.

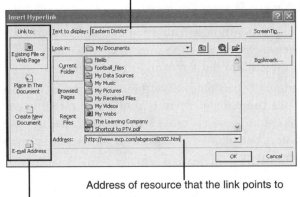

Address of resource that the link points to

You can link to another Web page, a worksheet in this workbook, a new file, or an email address

■ **E-mail Address**—Inserts a link that points to an email address. A person visiting your page can then click the link to run his email program and quickly send you a message. The message will automatically be addressed to the email address you specify.

After entering your preferences for the link, click **OK**. When you click **OK**, the selected text is transformed into a link and appears blue (or whatever color your system uses for displaying links).

If you decide to remove the link from your page, right-click the link, point to **Hyperlink**, and click **Remove Link**.

> **caution**
>
> Before you place a page on the Web, test its links to make sure they work. You don't want to point your visitors down a dead-end street.

# Publishing Your Worksheets on the Web

When you have completed your Web page, you must place it on a Web server so that other people can open and view it with their Web browsers. In the past, the only way to place a page on a Web server was to use a separate FTP (File Transfer Protocol) program. Excel simplifies the process by featuring a couple of tools that enable you to save your Web page(s) directly to a Web folder or a folder on the FTP server simply by using the File, Save as Web Page command.

The following sections lead you through the process of finding a home for your Web page and setting up Excel to upload your Web page and any associated files to the Web.

## Finding a Home for Your Page

If you work at a big corporation or institution that has its own Web server, you already have a Web server on which to store your Web pages. Just ask your Web administrator for the path to the server and write it down.

For the less fortunate, the best place to start looking for a Web server is your Internet service provider—the company you pay, typically on a monthly basis, to connect you to the Internet. Most providers make some space available on their Web servers for subscribers to store personal Web pages. Call your service provider and obtain the following information:

- Does your service provider make Web space available to subscribers?
- How much disk space do you get, and how much does it cost (if anything)? Some providers give you a limited amount of disk space, which is usually plenty for several Web pages, including images, assuming you don't include large audio or video clips.
- Can you save your files directly to the Web server, or do you have to upload files to an FTP server?
- What is the address or URL (uniform resource locator) of the server to which you must connect to upload your files? Write it down.
- What username and password do you need to enter to gain access to the server? (This is typically the same username and password you use to connect to the service.)
- In which directory (folder) must you place your files? Write it down.
- What name must you give your Web page? In many cases, the service requires you to name your opening Web page (your home page) index.htm or default.htm.
- Are there any other specific instructions that you must follow to post your Web page?
- After posting your page, what will its address (URL) be? You'll want to open it in your Web browser as soon as you post it to check it out.

## Setting Up a Network Place or Web Folder

If you have access to a Web server that supports Web folders, you should set up a Network Place or Web folder in My Network Places for convenient access to the folder where you will publish your Web pages. If your company or your Internet Service Provider uses a different server type to store Web pages, you might not be able to take advantage of the convenience offered by Network Places or Web folders.

If your computer is running Windows XP, you can set up a Network Place for any folder on your network, any Web folder, or any folder on an FTP server, assuming you have permission to access that folder. To set up a Network Place in Windows XP, take the following steps:

1. Open the Windows **Start** menu and choose **My Network Places**. The My Network Places window appears, as shown in Figure 14.4.

Click Add a Network Place

**FIGURE 14.4**

The My Network Places window.

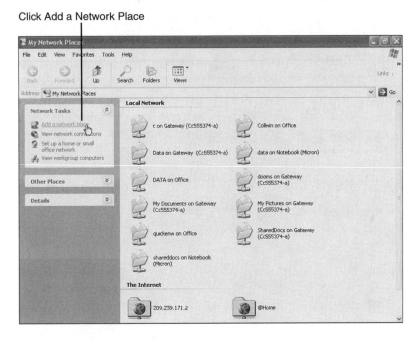

2. Click **Add a Network Place**. The Welcome to the Add Network Place dialog box appears, displaying a brief description of this feature.

3. Click the **Next** button. Windows connects to the Internet and gathers any information it needs about Microsoft's own Web services. The Add Network Place Wizard then displays a list of options, as shown in Figure 14.5.

4. Click **Choose Another Network Location** and click the **Next** button. The Wizard prompts you to type the address specifying where the folder is stored, as shown in Figure 14.6.

**FIGURE 14.5**

You can publish
a page to an
MSN community
or to another
network or
Internet location
of your choice.

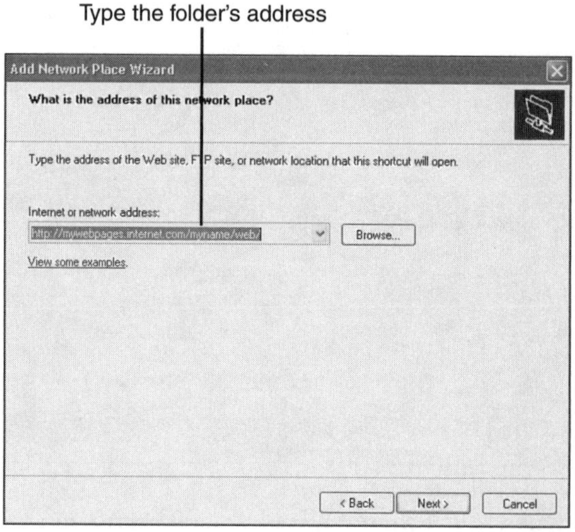

Choose another network location

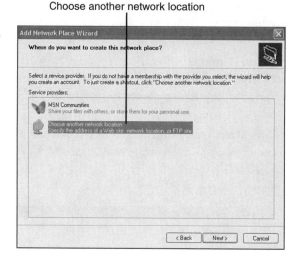

Type the folder's address

**FIGURE 14.6**

Specify the
folder's location
on the Web or
FTP server.

5. Type the address that specifies the folder's location on the network, Web,
   or FTP server. For example, you might type `http://www.internetsite.com/`
   `personal/folder` to specify a folder on the Web. (Click the **View Some
   Examples** link for more examples.)

6. Click the **Next** button. Windows attempts to establish a connection to the
   specified folder. If Windows succeeds, it displays a dialog box asking you to
   enter your username and password.

7. Enter the requested information and click the **Finish** button.

To save your Web page(s) to your Web folder, select the **File**, **Save as Web Page** command. Then click the **My Network Places** icon, double-click the Web folder you just set up, as shown in Figure 14.7, and click the **Save** button.

Double-click the folder you just set up

**FIGURE 14.7**

You might be able to save your Web page(s) directly to a folder on the Web server.

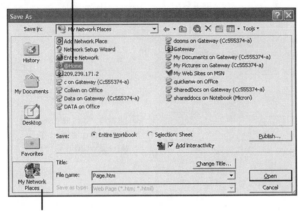

Click the My Network Places icon

To set up a Web folder in Windows Me or Windows 98, take the following steps:

1. Run My Computer, double-click the **Web Folders** icon, and then double-click the **Add a Web Folder** icon.

2. In the **Type the Location to Add** text box, type the address of the Web server, complete with a path to the directory in which you want your new folder created (for example, `http://www.internet.com/public`).

3. Click the **Next** button.

4. Type the name for the folder in which you intend to publish your Web pages.

5. Click the **Finish** button.

To save your Web page(s) to your Web folder, select the **File**, **Save as Web Page** command. Then click the **Web Folders** icon, double-click the Web folder you just set up, and click the **Save** button.

## Uploading Files to an FTP Server

Many Internet service providers still require that you upload Web pages to an FTP server to place them on the Web. Fortunately, Excel simplifies the process, allowing you to perform FTP uploads with the File, Save as Web Page command. Take the following steps:

1. Open the page in Excel.

2. Open the **File** menu and select **Save as Web Page**.

3. In the Save As dialog box, open the **Save In** drop-down list, and select **Add/Modify FTP Locations**. This opens the Add/Modify FTP Locations dialog box, shown in Figure 14.8, that prompts you to enter the address of the FTP site, your username, and your password.

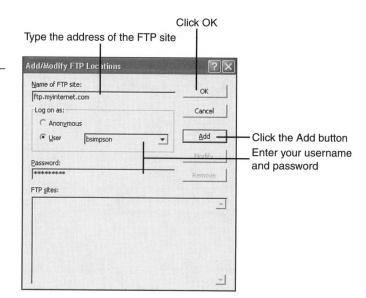

Click OK

Type the address of the FTP site

Click the Add button

Enter your username
and password

**FIGURE 14.8**

You can set up Excel to save Web pages directly to an FTP server.

4. Enter the requested information and click the **Add** button. (In the **Name of the FTP Site** text box, type only the address of the FTP site. Don't include the path to the folder.)

5. Click **OK**. This returns you to the Save As dialog box, which now contains the address of the FTP site.

6. Click the address and click **Open**.

7. If you are not connected to the Internet, the Connect To dialog box appears; click **Connect**. After you are connected, the Save As dialog box lists the directories (folders) on the FTP server.

8. Change to the folder in which your service provider told you to save the Web page file and then click the **Save** button.

# Importing Data from the Web into Your Worksheets

Excel 2002 is fairly Web savvy, enabling you to copy and paste data from Web pages into your worksheets and have that data automatically updated when it changes on the Web. You can, for instance, create a worksheet that tracks your investments. By copying and pasting stock prices from the Web into your worksheet and telling Excel to set up a Web query, you can have Excel create a live link between your worksheet and the Web page. Here's what you do:

1. Start your Web browser and open the page that has the data you want.

2. Highlight the data and press **Ctrl+C** to copy it.

3. Click in the worksheet cell in which you want to paste the data.

4. Press **Ctrl+V**. The Paste icon appears outside the lower-right corner of the cell, as shown in Figure 14.9.

**FIGURE 14.9**

The Paste icon lets you create a live link between the pasted data and its source.

Paste icon —

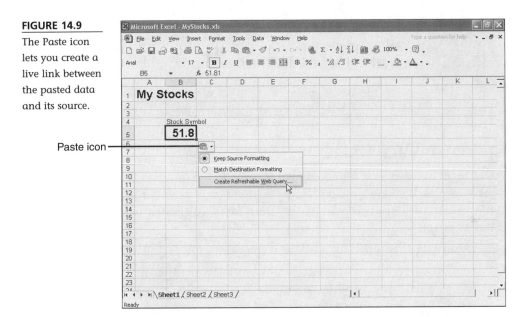

5. Click the **Paste** icon and click **Create Refreshable Web Query**. The New Web Query dialog box appears, displaying the Web page from which you copied the data.

6. Click the yellow-boxed arrow icon next to the table of data you want to import, as shown in Figure 14.10.

7. Click the **Import** button.

To insert the latest data from the Web page into your worksheet, open Excel's **Data** menu and click **Refresh Data**.

**FIGURE 14.10**
Click the arrow
next to the table
you want to
import.

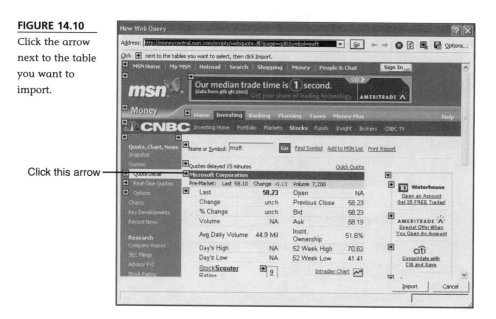

Click this arrow

# Emailing Your Worksheet

If you're on a network or your computer is wired to the Internet, you can send your workbook files to others via email, and you don't even need to run your email program. You can email workbooks directly from Excel. To email a workbook, take the following steps:

1. Run Excel and open the workbook you want to send.

2. Click the **E-mail** button in the Standard toolbar. An email bar appears, as shown in Figure 14.11, displaying text boxes for addressing the message.

3. Type the recipient's email address in the **To** text box.

4. Type a brief description of the message in the **Subject** text box.

5. Click the **Send This Sheet** button. Your default email program sends a copy of the document to the recipient as an HTML-formatted message, and the email bar disappears.

**note**

If, before you send your email, you decide to cancel the operation, simply click the E-mail button again. This removes the bar for addressing the message, returning you to a normal Excel screen.

Type the recipient's address

Click Send this Sheet

**FIGURE 14.11**

You can email a copy of a workbook directly from Excel.

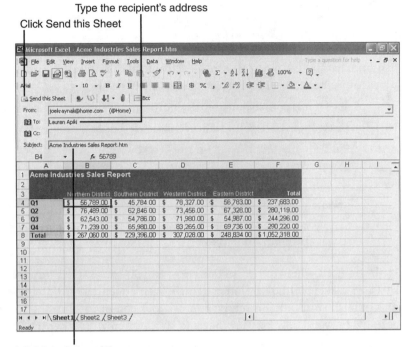

Type a brief description of the message

# THE ABSOLUTE MINIMUM

When you decide to forego paper copies of your worksheet and opt instead to publish and distribute your worksheets electronically on the Web, turn to this chapter for a brief refresher course. In this chapter, you learned how to

Transform a workbook or any portion of it into a Web page.

Insert links that point to other files, Web pages, or email addresses.

Publish your worksheets on the Web by saving them directly to a network server, Web server, or FTP server.

Import data from other Web sources and have that data automatically updated when the Web source data changes.

Send your worksheets or workbooks via email to friends, relatives, clients, and colleagues.

With the skills you acquired in this chapter, you can convert any workbook, worksheet, or range of data into an attractive Web page; add links to other Web pages; and publish your data on the Web or on your company's intranet. You can also email your workbooks or worksheets to share them with other users.

In the next chapter, we shift gears and look at another exciting, high-end Excel feature that enables you to enter commands and data orally, rather than by typing or using your mouse.

**15**

# USING EXCEL'S SPEECH AND HANDWRITING RECOGNITION FEATURES

# Making Sure You Have the Essential Equipment

One of the most significant additions to Excel in version 2002 is that it recognizes voice commands and can take dictation. Instead of meandering through Excel's menus and dialog boxes to enter a command, you simply *tell* Excel what to do. Do you want this worksheet printed? Say, "File, print, worksheet, okay," and your printer prints the worksheet. Do you need to transfer data from a printout to a worksheet? Then read the entries from the printout into a microphone and have Excel "type" them for you.

Before you try to use Excel's speech recognition feature, make sure your computer system is properly equipped. Work through the following checklist and examine your computer to make sure it meets the minimum requirements:

- **Processor**—Pentium II 400MHz or faster. Trying to run speech recognition on anything slower than a Pentium 400MHz machine will slow down your system to a crawl. (To view information about the processor, right-click **My Computer** and choose **Properties**. The System Properties dialog box appears, as shown in Figure 15.1.)

- **Memory**—128MB RAM (memory). If your system has less than 128MB of RAM, the speech recognition feature will slow down your computer and cause it to crash. (Again, display the System Properties dialog box to determine the amount of memory installed.)

- **Sound card**—Most computers come equipped with a 16-bit SoundBlaster-compatible sound card or better. A 16-bit sound card is sufficient for voice commands and dictation. If your computer has speakers, it has a sound card.

- **Close-talk microphone**—A close-talk microphone is positioned a couple inches from your mouth and is designed to block out background noise. If your computer has a built-in microphone or a microphone that sits on your desk, you must buy a better microphone, specifically a close-talk microphone.

**tip**

Get a microphone with a headset mount and position the microphone about one inch from the corner of your mouth. Do not position the microphone directly in front of your mouth; the puffs of air your mouth emits during normal speaking will cause erratic results. Try to mount the microphone in the same position each time you use it.

**FIGURE 15.1**

Display the System Properties dialog box for information about your computer.

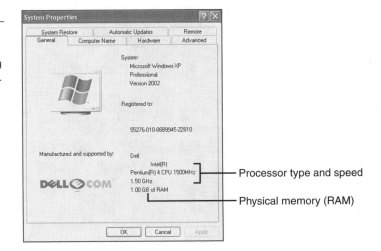

— Processor type and speed

— Physical memory (RAM)

# Checking Your Sound System

Before you install the speech recognition feature, you should make sure your sound system is working properly. Take the following steps to test your computer's sound system in Windows:

1. Double-click the **Volume** icon in the Windows taskbar. (The Volume icon is in the lower right corner of your screen—it looks like a speaker.) This opens the Volume Control window.

2. Open the **Options** menu and click **Properties**. The Properties dialog box appears, as shown in Figure 15.2.

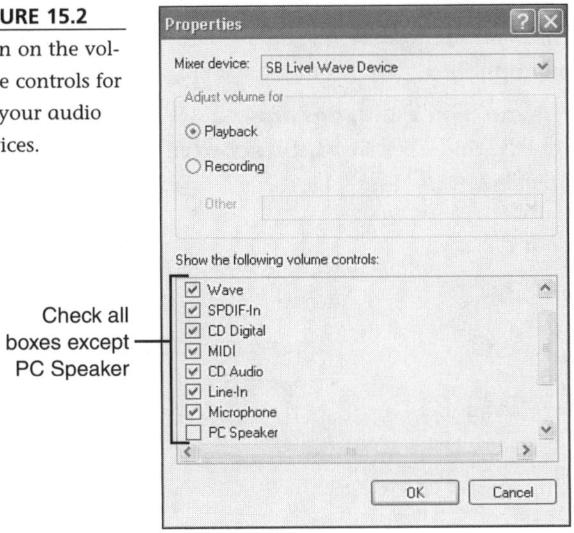

**FIGURE 15.2**

Turn on the volume controls for all your audio devices.

Check all boxes except PC Speaker

3. In the **Show the Following Volume Controls** list, make sure all the check boxes (except the one next to PC Speaker), are checked. If a check box is blank, click it to place a check in the box.

4. Click **OK**. This returns you to the Volume Control window, as shown in Figure 15.3.

Drag sliders up to increase volume

**FIGURE 15.3**

Make sure no volume control is muted and that all are turned up at least halfway.

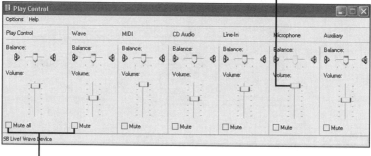

Make sure Mute checkboxes are clear

5. At the bottom of each volume control is a Mute option. Make sure the **Mute** check boxes are blank, NOT checked. If a Mute check box has a check mark in it, click the check box to remove the check mark.

6. Drag the **Microphone** volume control slider to the top to maximize the microphone volume.

7. Click the **Close (X)** button, in the upper-right corner of the Volume Controls window, to save your settings and close the window.

Now you are ready to test your microphone to determine whether it's working. Take the following steps to test your microphone:

1. Open the Windows **Start** menu, point to **Programs** or **All Programs**, **Accessories**, **Entertainment**, and click **Sound Recorder**. This starts the Windows sound recorder, as shown in Figure 15.4.

**FIGURE 15.4**

The Windows Audio Recorder.

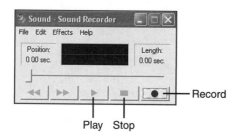

Play  Stop

2. Click the **Record** button (the one with the big red dot on it) and say a few words into your microphone.

3. Click the **Stop** button (the square block next to the Record button) to stop recording.

4. Click the **Play** button to play back your recording.

If you hear your computer talking back to you in your own voice, your microphone is working properly. If you don't hear your voice, check the following:

■ Make sure your microphone and speakers are plugged in to the correct jacks on your sound card. It's easy to mix up the connections.

■ If your sound card has a volume control on the card itself (typically where the microphone and speakers plug into the card), make sure the volume for your sound card is turned up.

■ If your microphone has a power switch, make sure the switch is in the On position. (Some close-talk microphones have a switch and a volume control on the cable.)

■ If your speakers have a power switch, make sure the switch is in the On position.

■ If your speakers have a volume control, make sure the volume is turned up.

**note**

Windows has several troubleshooters that can lead you through the process of tracking down common hardware problems. Open the **Start** menu and click **Help**. In Windows 98, click the **Contents** tab, click **Troubleshooting**, click the option for the **Windows Troubleshooters**, and click **Sound** in the list of troubleshooters. In Windows Me, click **Troubleshooting**, click **Audio-Visual Problems**, and click **Sound Troubleshooter**. In Windows XP, click **Fixing a Problem**, click **Games, Sound, and Video Problems**, and click **Sound Troubleshooter**. Follow the instructions that appear in the right pane to track down the problem.

# Installing Speech Recognition

The speech recognition component is not installed by default. Fortunately, all you need to do to initiate the installation is try to use the feature. In Excel, open the **Tools** menu point to **Speech**, and click **Speech Recognition**. If you don't see the Speech option, click the double-headed arrow at the bottom of the **Tools** menu to expand the menu.

Excel displays a dialog box indicating that it cannot run the speech feature because it has not been installed and giving you the option of installing it. Click the **Yes** button to initiate the installation. If the required Office CD is not in the CD-ROM drive, another dialog box appears, telling you which CD is needed. Insert the requested CD, wait about 10 seconds, and then click **OK**. When the installation is complete, Excel displays a dialog box indicating that it will lead you through the process of setting up your microphone and training speech recognition to recognize your voice. Click **OK** and then move on to the next section.

# Training Excel to Recognize Your Voice

To achieve success with speech recognition, you must train the speech recognition tool to recognize your voice and train yourself to speak clearly and consistently into the microphone. Unlike a person, who can interpret a word or phrase both by its sound and by its context, speech recognition is literal and requires a clear articulation of every phrase. Consistent, clear speech is essential to achieve any sort of accuracy.

**note**

After you install speech recognition, a language bar appears at the top of your screen. To disable the feature and hide the bar, right-click the bar and click **Close the Language bar**. To display the bar again, open the **Tools** menu in your Office application, point to **Speech**, and click **Speech Recognition**. To completely remove speech recognition from your system, run the Office setup again. In Chapter 12, "Customizing Excel," review the section named "Installing Optional Components" to learn how to install and remove various feature sets.

Assuming you just installed Speech, the Microphone Wizard should appear on your screen, as shown in Figure 15.5, providing instructions on how to position your microphone for best results. If the Wizard is not onscreen or if you ran it and want to run it again, open the **Tools** menu in the Language Bar and choose **Options**. The Speech Properties dialog box appears. Click the **Configure Microphone** button to display the Microphone Wizard. Follow the Wizard's instructions to position your microphone properly and test it.

**FIGURE 15.5**

The Microphone Wizard shows you how to position your microphone for best results.

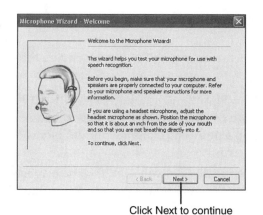

Click Next to continue

**caution**

If the Language bar is not displayed, open Excel's **Tools** menu, point to **Speech**, and click **Speech Recognition**. If the Language bar appears but has no Tools button, click the little down arrow on the right end of the Language Toolbar and click **Speech Tools**.

After you complete the microphone setup, the Voice Training Wizard should appear. If the Voice Training Wizard is not onscreen, or if you already ran it and want to run it again (to fine-tune its operation), you can run it from the Language bar. Click the **Tools** button in the Language bar and click **Training**. Follow the Wizard's instructions to complete the training session. The Wizard displays a series of dialog boxes that require you to read sentences into your microphone, as shown in Figure 15.6.

Read the sentence aloud

**FIGURE 15.6**

The Voice Training Wizard prompts you to read aloud.

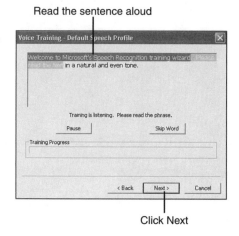

Click Next

The entire session takes about 15 minutes. Here are some tips to make the training session more successful:

■ Shut yourself in a quiet room, turn off the radio, unplug the phone, and tell anyone who might interrupt you to leave you alone for 20 minutes.

■ Speak in a level tone. Don't whisper, yell, or use a great deal of intonation.

■ Read the sentences at a consistent rate of speed. Don't pause between words; the speech recognition feature can translate phrases more accurately than it can interpret single words.

■ Articulate (sound out) the words clearly, but don't go overboard. The speech recognition feature has an easier time if you say "enunciate" as you normally would rather than saying "EEE-nun-see-ate."

■ Keep the microphone in a consistent position.

If you share a computer with other users, a computer trained for your voice obviously will be less responsive to other voices. Fortunately, each user can train speech recognition for his or her own voice by creating a separate profile. To create a profile, perform the following steps:

1. Open the Language bar's **Tools** menu and click **Options**. The Speech Properties dialog box appears, as shown in Figure 15.7.

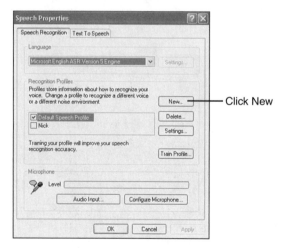

**FIGURE 15.7**

The Speech Properties dialog box.

— Click New

2. Under Recognition Profiles, click **New**. The Profile Wizard appears, prompting you to type your name.

3. Type your name and click **Next**. The Microphone Wizard appears, followed by the Voice Training Wizard.

4. Follow the Wizard's instructions to set up your microphone and train speech recognition to identify your voice.

[Tools] After you have set up two or more recognition profiles, you easily can switch from one profile to another. Simply open the Language bar's **Tools** menu, point to **Current User**, and click the name of the desired user (or click **Default Speech Profile** to use the profile you created when you ran and trained speech recognition for the first time).

# Dictating Your Entries

After you have trained speech recognition, the process of using the feature to convert your spoken words and numbers into typed text and values is a snap. The key is to know how to use the Language bar and to keep an eye on the selected cell, as shown in Figure 15.8. The Language bar contains several buttons that control your microphone and let you switch between dictation and voice command mode.

[Microphone] [Dictation] To start dictating text, make sure the **Microphone** button and the **Dictation** button are on (shaded light blue, instead of gray). If the Microphone button is off, both the Dictation and Voice Command buttons are hidden; click the **Microphone** button and then click the **Dictation** button. If the Microphone button is on and the Voice Command button is on, click the **Dictation** button to change to Dictation mode. Then click the cell where you want your entry inserted and start talking. Remember to speak clearly and at a steady pace.

As you speak, speech recognition displays a light blue bar with little dots in it in the selected cell, indicating that it is currently trying to convert your spoken words into text and values. When it has successfully translated a bit of text, the text or value pops up in place of the blue bar. (It can take several seconds to convert your spoken words into entries. Even though you cannot immediately see what you're saying, just keep talking.)

> **note**
>
> When you install speech recognition, the Office or Excel installation places an icon in your Windows Control Panel for the Speech Properties dialog box. In Windows XP, open the Start menu and click Control Panel. In earlier versions of Windows (Me or 98), open the Windows **Start** menu, point to **Settings**, and click **Control Panel**. Click the **Speech** icon to view the Speech Properties dialog box.

> **tip**
>
> Instead of clicking a button to change from Dictation to Voice Command mode (or vice versa), just say the word. To dictate text, say "Dictation." To enter a command, say "Voice command."

As you speak, keep an eye on the selected cell

Click Microphone to toggle the microphone on or off

Click Dictation to type

Click Voice Command to issue menu commands

**FIGURE 15.8**
Know your Language bar and keep an eye on the selected cell.

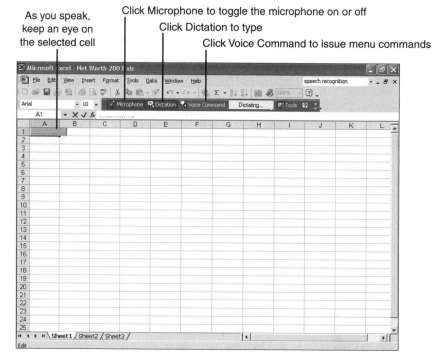

When you finish speaking an entry, pause for a second or two and say "Enter" to move to the next cell down or "Tab" to move one cell to the right.

If speech recognition inserts an incorrect word or value, double-click the word or value and type the correction or speak the word or value again.

# Entering Voice Commands

Speech recognition is very impressive at taking dictation, but it's also very competent when it comes to understanding and executing spoken commands. Open a workbook you previously saved. Strap on your microphone and then click the **Voice Command** button in the Language toolbar. Say "Save." Speech recognition passes your command along to Excel, which saves your workbook file to disk. Click a cell that contains a label, and then say "Bold." The entry becomes boldfaced. Say

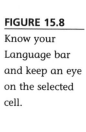

**note**

Try to keep your microphone as far away as possible from other electrical devices, including your computer. These devices emit EMF noise (electromagnetic frequencies), which can cause a low hum that might interfere with your dictation. Special noise-reduction microphones also can help reduce background noise. You might want to stay clear of chatty officemates, as well.

"Italic." The entry becomes italic. (To remove bold or italics, select the cell again and repeat the command.)

In addition to those basic commands, following is a list of keyboard commands you can use:

"Return" or "Enter" to accept the current cell entry and move the cell selector down to the next cell

"Tab" to accept the current cell entry and move the cell selector to the next cell (to the right)

"Shift tab" to accept the current cell entry and move the cell selector to the previous cell (to the left)

"Backspace" to delete the character to the left of the insertion point

"Delete" to delete the character to the right of the insertion point or delete the contents of the selected cell(s)

"Space" or "Spacebar" to insert a space

"Escape" or "Cancel" to close a menu or dialog box

"Right-click," "Right-click menu," "Show Right-click menu," "Context menu," or "Show context menu" to show a context menu

"Home" or "Go home" to move the cell selector to the first cell in the current row

"Up" or "Go up," to move the cell selector up one cell

"Down" or "Go down," to move the cell selector down one cell

"Left" or "Go left," to move the cell selector one cell to the left

"Right" or "Go right," to move the cell selector one cell to the right

Of course, you must be able to punctuate your text as you dictate. Punctuation is fairly intuitive. For a period, say "Period" or "Dot." For a comma, say "Comma." For a semicolon, say "Semicolon."

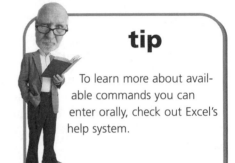

**tip**

To learn more about available commands you can enter orally, check out Excel's help system.

**note**

If you minimize the Language bar, it appears in the Windows taskbar at the bottom of the screen or EN appears in the system tray (at the right end of the Windows taskbar), indicating that you're in English mode. (Of course, if you're using a language edition of Excel other than English, other characters appear.) Click **EN** and click **Show the Language Bar** to display the Language bar, or right-click it for additional options.

# Handwriting Your Entries

Excel offers another feature to help you avoid typing: handwriting recognition. With handwriting recognition, instead of typing away on a keyboard, you can jot down entries by using a special stylus or even a standard mouse and have Excel's handwriting recognition feature convert your written entries into typed text.

This feature also provides an onscreen keyboard you can use to hunt and peck with your mouse pointer or other device. This makes an excellent alternate input device.

## Installing the Handwriting Recognition Feature

Handwriting recognition is not installed during a standard installation. You must run the Excel or Office installation again and choose to add the Handwriting Recognition component. Here's what you do:

1. Insert the first Excel or Office installation CD into your CD-ROM drive.

2. If a My Computer window does not open showing the CD's contents, double-click **My Computer** on the Windows desktop or open the **Start** menu and click **My Computer**, and click the icon for your CD-ROM drive.

3. Click or double-click the **Setup** icon to start the installation routine.

4. Click the **Add or Remove Features** option and click **Next**.

5. Click the plus sign next to **Office Shared Features**, as shown in Figure 15.9.

**FIGURE 15.9**

You must install the handwriting recognition feature before you can use it.

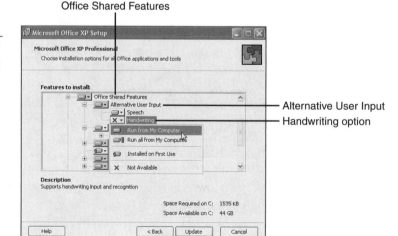

Office Shared Features

Alternative User Input
Handwriting option

6. Click the plus sign next to **Alternative User Input**.

7. Click the icon next to **Handwriting** and click **Run from My Computer**.

8. Click **Update**. The Excel or Office installation routine transfers the necessary program files to your computer.

## Penning Your Entries by Hand

After you install Handwriting recognition, a new Handwriting button pops up on your Language bar, as shown in Figure 15.10. Click the **Handwriting** button to display a list of options for writing onscreen. For example, click the **Handwriting** button and click **Writing Pad** to display an onscreen notepad.

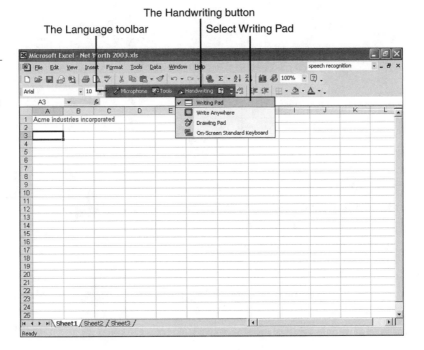

**FIGURE 15.10**
Click the Handwriting button and click Writing Pad.

Click the **Text** button, as shown in Figure 15.11, if it is not already on. When the mouse pointer is over the notepad, the pointer becomes a pen, allowing you to write on the pad. Use your mouse or whatever handwriting input device you have to handwrite your text as you write naturally—print, write in cursive, or use a combination of the two styles.

Click the Ink button to add your signature to a document

Handwriting recognition converts
your writing into typed text

Click the Text button to have your
handwriting converted to typed text

**FIGURE 15.11**

The handwriting recognition feature is enabled.

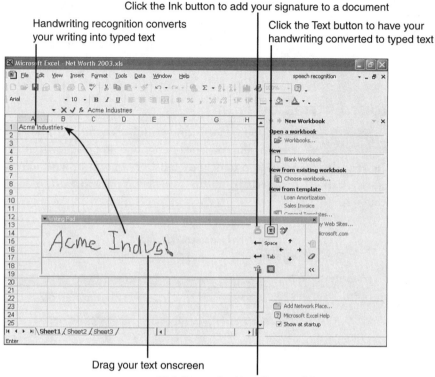

Drag your text onscreen

Click Recognize Now, if some delay occurs

The handwriting recognition feature automatically recognizes your text and inserts it into your document whenever you write enough information that can be recognized as text, run out of room onscreen, or pause for a time after writing some text. If you write some text and the application fails to recognize it, click the **Recognize Now** button.

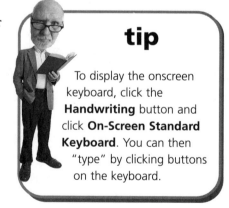

# tip

To display the onscreen keyboard, click the **Handwriting** button and click **On-Screen Standard Keyboard**. You can then "type" by clicking buttons on the keyboard.

# THE ABSOLUTE MINIMUM

As you saw in Chapter 4, the single most important and most time-consuming chore you face when you create a worksheet or workbook is *data entry*, and now that you have completed this chapter, you have one more tool for entering data in Excel. You now know how to

> Make sure your system can handle Excel's speech recognition feature and that your computer's sound system is in good working order.
>
> Install and set up the speech recognition feature on your computer.
>
> Train the speech recognition feature to recognize your voice and train yourself to speak in a way that ensures success with the feature.
>
> Dictate entries and have the speech recognition feature translate your oral input into typed entries.
>
> Switch to command mode and enter voice commands by speaking them into a microphone.
>
> Install and use the handwriting recognition feature to handwrite entries rather than type them.

With the skills you acquired in this chapter, you can take a more hands-off approach when creating and formatting your worksheets. These skills might also help prevent repetitive stress injuries, such as carpal tunnel syndrome, by limiting the amount of typing and mouse clicking you do in a day. At this point, you have completed this book and can consider yourself a true Excel master. Congratulations!

To become even more proficient, check out the appendixes to hone your Excel vocabulary and become a more efficient user by memorizing the most important shortcut keys.

**A**

# Excel Shortcut Keys

| To | Press |
|---|---|
| Select entire worksheet | Ctrl+A |
| Copy selection | Ctrl+C |
| Insert page break | Alt+Enter (when cell, row, or column is selected) |
| Find text or format | Ctrl+F |
| Replace text | Ctrl+H |
| Insert hyperlink (on a Web page) | Ctrl+K |
| Create new file | Ctrl+N |
| Open file | Ctrl+O |
| Print file | Ctrl+P |
| Save file | Ctrl+S |
| Copy format of the selection | Ctrl+Shift+C |
| Paste format | Ctrl+Shift+V |
| Paste selection | Ctrl+V |
| Cut selection | Ctrl+X |
| Cancel last undo action | Ctrl+Y |
| Undo last action | Ctrl+Z |

| To | Press |
| --- | --- |
| Delete selection | Delete |
| Get help | F1 |
| Check spelling | F7 |
| Activate menu bar | F10 |
| File/Save As command | F12 |
| End an entry you typed | Enter (or Arrow key) |
| Cancel an entry you typed | Esc |
| Create a new line in a cell | Alt+Enter (when entering or editing an entry in a cell) |
| Edit a cell entry | F2 |
| Edit a cell comment | Shift+F2 |
| Fill a cell entry into cells below | Ctrl+D |
| Fill a cell entry into cells to the right | Ctrl+R |
| End cell entry and move to the next cell to the right | Tab |
| Select entire column | Ctrl+Spacebar |
| Select entire row | Shift+Spacebar |
| Move one screen to the right | Alt+Page Down |
| Move one screen to the left | Alt+Page Up |
| Flip to the next worksheet page | Ctrl+Page Down |
| Flip to the previous worksheet page | Ctrl+Page Up |
| Go to a specific cell or named range | F5 or Ctrl+G |
| Recalculate all formulas | F9 |
| Paste a function into a formula | Shift+F3 |
| Insert the AutoSum formula | Alt+= (equal sign) |
| Insert the date | Ctrl+; (semicolon) |

# GLOSSARY

**absolute**   A cell reference that does not change when you move or copy the formula that contains the cell reference.

**address**   The column letter and row number that specify the cell's location.

**alignment**   The position of an entry inside a cell. Entries can be aligned left, center, or right, and positioned in relation to the cell's top and bottom.

**argument**   A statement that follows a function and contains the values or cell references the function needs to perform its calculations. See also *syntax*.

**arithmetic operator**   A symbol in a formula that tells the formula which mathematical operation to perform.

**ascending order**   An arrangement of entries from the lowest to the highest value or in alphabetical order from A to Z. See also *descending order*.

**AutoFill**   Excel feature that copies an entry from a cell into one or more neighboring cells or fills the neighboring cells with a logical series of entries, such as Monday, Tuesday, Wednesday, Thursday, Friday.

**AutoFit**   Excel feature that automatically resizes a column or row to make room for the largest entry in the column or row.

**AutoFormat**   Excel feature that adds formatting to a worksheet based on an existing worksheet design. The formatting includes number formats, cell shading, and borders.

**AutoSum**   Excel feature that automatically determines the total value of two or more values in a row or column.

**axis**   A straight line in a chart that represents a standard point from which all other points in the chart are measured. Most charts consist of a horizontal X axis and a vertical Y axis that intersect at the 0 (zero) point.

**block**   Another name for a cell range, or a selection of neighboring cells in a worksheet. See *range*.

**border**   A line that runs along any or all of the gridlines that define a cell's perimeter. Borders are commonly used to provide visual breaks in a worksheet.

**cell selector**   The box that appears around a cell when the cell is selected.

**cell**   In a worksheet, a box that is formed by the intersection of a row and a column.

**chart**   A graphic representation of values. Charts are useful for illustrating the change in values over time, the comparison of two or more sets of values, and for showing how a particular amount is divided up into portions.

**clear**   To remove the contents of cells without removing the cells themselves.

**clip art**   Professionally drawn illustrations that are included with Microsoft Excel, Microsoft Office, and many other programs, or are sold separately as collections.

**Close button**   The X button that appears in the upper-right corner of a program or workbook window and enables you to close the window.

**collapse dialog box**   To minimize a dialog box, thus making it easier to select cells in a worksheet.

**column heading**   The letter that appears at the top of a column.

**column label**   Text that you type in the topmost cell in a column that identifies the entries in that column.

**column**   In a worksheet, the vertical arrangement of data. Columns intersect with horizontal rows to form boxes, called cells, into which you type entries. See also *row* and *cell*.

**comment**  A note that appears outside the cells only when you choose to have the comment displayed or printed.

**comparison operator**  A symbol that signifies a range of values based on a specific value or entry. For example, the < (less than) operator can be used to define a range of values less than zero (<0) or entries less than "L" (<L)—in other words, entries starting with A through K.

**conditional format**  A font or cell format that Excel automatically applies to a particular cell when that entry matches a specified entry or falls within a specified range. For example, Excel can display a value more than $1,000,000 in blue with a pink background, or however else you want it displayed.

**context menu**  A list of options available for only the currently selected object. You typically display a context menu by right-clicking the desired object.

**context-sensitive**  Any feature that applies to only the currently selected object or the current task. If you press the F1 key when performing a task, for instance, Excel displays context-sensitive help for that task.

**data area**  The rectangular portion of a worksheet that contains data. If you choose to print a worksheet, Excel prints only the entries in the data area. Excel does not print the blank cells that fall outside the data area.

**data entry**  The process of typing labels, values, and formulas into blank cells to create a functioning worksheet.

**data list**  A collection of records, each of which is entered in its own row. When you create a worksheet to store records, such as names and addresses, rather than to perform calculations, Excel refers to the records as a data list.

**data series**  Related data points plotted in a chart. For example, if a chart contains sales amounts for two different years, the sales data for each year would be plotted as separate data series.

**database**  A collection of records, each of which is made up of two or more field entries. A phone book, collection of recipes, or a membership list are all examples of databases.

**default**  An original setting. In Excel, for instance, the default font is Arial 10-point type. Unless you change the setting, everything you type will appear in Arial 10-point type.

**delete**  To remove selected cells and their contents from a worksheet. Compare to *clear*.

**dependent**  A cell that contains a formula or function that depends on this cell to supply a value. Compare to *precedent*.

**descending order**   An arrangement of entries from the highest to the lowest value or in alphabetical order from Z to A. See also *ascending order*.

**dialog box**   A box that appears when you enter a command that requires additional input. If, for instance, you enter the Format, Cells command, the Format Cells dialog box appears, prompting you to enter the desired format settings.

**docking area**   A place in the Excel program window where you can drag toolbars to "lock" them in place. See also *floating toolbar*.

**email**   Messages you send and receive electronically, rather than through the postal service. You can send and receive email over a network connection, an online service connection (such as America Online), or an Internet connection.

**field**   A blank on a fill-in-the-blanks form. See also *data list* and *record*.

**file format**   Any unique way of encoding information in a file. Each program uses a unique file format for the files it saves. Excel workbook files, for example, use a different encoding method than Microsoft Word files, Windows Paint files, and so on.

**fill color**   The color used to shade a cell or graphic object.

**fill handle**   The tiny square that appears in the lower right corner of the currently selected cell. When you drag the fill handle over neighboring cells and release the mouse button, Excel copies the entry from this cell into the neighboring cells or fills the neighboring cells with a series of entries based on the entry in the selected cell. See also *AutoFill*.

**filter**   To display only a select group of records in a data list. A filter might filter out all records except those that have a particular city name in the City field.

**floating toolbar**   A toolbar that is not anchored to any part of the Excel window. Floating toolbars typically "float" above the worksheet area. See also *docking area*.

**font**   The type style and size that define the appearance of text.

**footer**   Text that appears at the bottom of every printed page of a worksheet or workbook. See also *header*.

**format**   Any setting that controls the appearance of a cell or the appearance of the cell's contents. Formatting includes cell shading and borders, font, font color, and number format.

**Format Painter**   A feature that enables you to copy the formatting from one or more cells (without copying the cell contents) and apply that same formatting to other cells.

**formula bar**   The area just above the worksheet that contains a box in which you can type and edit an entry for the currently selected cell. The formula bar also displays the address of the currently selected cell or range and buttons for accepting or canceling the current entry.

**formula**   A mathematical statement that tells Excel how to perform a particular calculation or series of calculations. Formulas typically contain cell addresses that pull values from other cells into the formula, and mathematical operators that tell Excel which operations to perform. Formulas may also contain values.

**function**   A ready-made formula that performs a mathematical operation on a set of values. The simple function SUM, for instance, determines the total of a set of values.

**graph**   Another name for a *chart*. See *chart*.

**graphic object**   Electronic art, including clip art, charts, and drawn objects.

**gridlines**   The non-printing lines that define column, row, and cell boundaries.

**handles**   Small squares or circles that surround a graphic object and enable you to resize and reshape the object.

**handwriting recognition**   A feature that transforms handwritten text into typed text.

**header**   Text that appears at the top of every printed page of a worksheet or workbook. See also *footer*.

**horizontal page break**   A page division that divides pages between rows. When Excel divides a long, wide worksheet into pages, it uses both horizontal and vertical page breaks. Excel prints all pages from top to bottom that are to the left of the vertical page break and then it moves to the right of the vertical page break and prints all those pages from top to bottom. Excel continues in this way until the entire worksheet is printed. See also *vertical page break*.

**HTML**   Short for *HyperText Markup Language*, a system of encoding a file so that it can be displayed properly in a Web browser. Excel provides a feature that can convert worksheets into HTML-encoded Web pages.

**interactive Web page**   A worksheet Web page that enables users to not only view the worksheet, but also to enter data, sort records, and use the worksheet as if they were working on it in Excel. See also *static Web page*.

**Internet**   A global system of interconnected networks that enables anyone with a computer and a modem or other Internet connection to open multimedia Web pages, exchange email, chat, and much more.

**label**   Text entries that are typically used to identify other entries on the worksheet. Labels are commonly used at the top of each column and to the left of each row to indicate the type of data entries in each column and row.

**landscape orientation**    A way of printing on a page so that when you hold the page to read it, the page is wider than it is tall. Wide worksheets are commonly printed in landscape orientation to fit more of the worksheet on a page. See also *portrait orientation*.

**legend**    A component of a chart that indicates what each data series on the chart represents. See also *data series*.

**macro**    A collection of two or more commands you can play back by selecting the macro from a list, pressing a special keystroke, or clicking a button assigned to play the macro.

**macro recorder**    A tool used to record a series of commands and actions as you perform a particular task and then save the commands and actions so you can play them back later. See also *macro*.

**marquee**    An animated dotted border that appears around a selection when the selection is cut or copied, to indicate the selection that has been cut or copied.

**Maximize button**    A button that appears in the upper-right corner of every non-maximized window and enables you to quickly make the window full-screen.

**menu bar**    A strip near the top of a program window that contains the names of the menus on which commands and other options are listed.

**menu**    A list of available commands or options.

**merge**    To combine two or more cells, thus creating one larger cell.

**Minimize button**    A button that appears in the upper right corner of a window and enables you to tuck the window offscreen. When a program window is minimized, a button for the program appears in the Windows taskbar. When a workbook window is minimized, its title bar appears in the lower-left corner of Excel's program window.

**Name Box**    The rectangle on the left end of the formula bar that displays the address of the currently selected cell or of the currently selected range. See also *formula bar*.

**operator**    A mathematical symbol that specifies that a certain operation be performed. Operators include + (addition), - (subtraction), * (multiplication), and / (division).

**order of operations**    The sequence in which a string of mathematical operations are performed. Unless parentheses are used to group mathematical operations, Excel performs exponential equations first, followed by multiplication, division, addition, and then subtraction.

**organization chart**    A schematic diagram that illustrates the hierarchical structure of a business or organization.

**page break**    A code that indicates to Excel where one page ends and the next pages begins. See also *horizontal page break* and *vertical page break.*

**pattern**    A combination of two colors arranged in any number of ways and used as the background for a cell or a worksheet.

**pivot table**    A report that consolidates data in worksheets and databases and enables you to restructure the data to compare and analyze it.

**portrait orientation**    A way of printing on a page so that when you hold the page to read it, the page is taller than it is wide. Most magazines are printed in portrait orientation, but landscape orientation often is more accommodating for wide worksheets. See also *landscape orientation.*

**precedence**    In formulas, the operations that Excel performs before performing other operations. Excel performs mathematical operations in a predetermined sequence called the order of operations: exponential equations first, followed by multiplication, division, addition, and then subtraction. Exponential equations are said to have "precedence" over all other operations. See also *order of operations.*

**precedent**    A cell that the current cell relies on to supply a value used in the current cell's formula. Compare to *dependent.*

**print preview**    A feature that shows onscreen how an Excel worksheet will appear in print.

**range**    Two or more cells. A range can be referred to using cell addresses, such as A3..H12 or by giving the range a name, such as "Sales."

**record**    A collection of information that applies to an individual person, place, or thing in a database. In an address book, for instance, a record might consist of a person's name, address, phone number, and email address.

**relative**    A cell reference, typically used in a formula or function, that Excel automatically changes when you cut or copy and then paste the formula or function to another cell.

**Restore button**    A button that appears in the upper-right corner of a maximized window and enables you to restore the window to the size it was before you maximized the window.

**row**    In a worksheet, the horizontal arrangement of data. Rows intersect with vertical columns to form boxes, called cells, into which you type entries. See also *column* and *cell.*

**row heading**    The number that appears to the left of each row.

**row label**    Text that you type in the leftmost cell in a row that identifies the entries in that row.

**scenario**  A set of values you can plug in to a worksheet to determine how the values affect the end result. When you play with sets of values in this way, you are said to be playing "What If?"

**ScreenTip**  A brief description of an object, button, or option that pops up when you rest the mouse pointer on the object, button, or option.

**scroll bar**  A strip on the right side or bottom of a window or to the right of a list that enables you to bring the contents of the window or list into view.

**select**  To choose an option or highlight one or more cells.

**Shortcut bar**  A strip of buttons that appear on the Windows desktop and provide quick access to the Microsoft Office applications. The Shortcut bar also enables you to perform common tasks, such as creating a new document or recording an appointment.

**smart menu**  A menu that displays only the most commonly selected options and automatically rearranges commands to place the commands you most commonly use near the top of the menu.

**smart tag**  An icon that automatically appears in a worksheet to provide additional instructions, list common commands or options, or display links to related data on the Web or in other Microsoft Office applications.

**sort**  To rearrange a series of records in alphabetical or numerical order based on the entries in a given column (or field).

**speech recognition**  A feature that enables you to dictate text and values and enter commands orally rather than by using the keyboard or mouse.

**split bar**  A small bar near the scroll bars that enables you to split a window into two panes. In two-pane view, you can see two parts of the same worksheet at one time.

**spreadsheet**  Synonym for "worksheet." See *worksheet*.

**static Web page**  A Web page that a user can view but not change. Excel provides a feature for saving a worksheet as a static Web page to make data available on the Web. See also *interactive Web page*.

**status bar**  The area near the bottom of the program window that contains information about the currently active document. Excel's status bar displays "Ready" when it is ready to accept an entry into the current cell and "Enter" as you type an entry, to help you remember to press the Enter key when you're finished. If you press the Caps Lock key to uppercase all characters, the status bar displays CAPS. If you press the Scroll Lock key, the status bar displays SCRL.

**style**   A collection of format settings that you can apply to selected cells by entering a single command. If you change any of the style's format settings, all entries formatted with that style are reformatted to reflect the change.

**syntax**   The order in which the items in a function's argument must be entered. In the function =PMT(rate,nper,pv,fv,type), for instance, the loan rate must be entered first, followed by the number of payment periods, the present value of the loan, the future value of the loan, and then the payment type.

**task pane**   A window frame that appears on the right side of the Excel program window and presents options for the task you are currently performing. If you select Insert, Picture, Clip Art, for instance, the Insert Clip Art task pane appears, providing options for searching for a specific image and inserting the image.

**taskbar**   The bar at the bottom of the Windows desktop that enables you to switch back and forth between applications or launch applications with the Start button.

**template**   A pattern for a workbook or worksheet that controls fonts, shading, borders, and other format settings for the worksheet. Templates can also contain macros and styles.

**tick mark**   A short line on a chart's axis, typically used to mark incremental values along the axis.

**title bar**   The colored band (typically dark blue) at the top of a program or workbook window that displays the program's name or the workbook's name (or both). On the right end of all title bars are the Minimize, Maximize/Restore, and Close buttons, used to control the window.

**toolbar**   A strip of buttons that usually appears at the top of an application's window just below the menu bar. With a toolbar, you can bypass the pull-down menus by clicking a button.

**truncated**   Chopped off at the end. When you type a wide entry into a cell, Excel typically runs the entry over the next cell to the right. However, if that cell contains an entry, Excel truncates the wide entry, displaying only the portion of the entry that fits in the cell.

**value**   A number, as opposed to a text (label) entry.

**vertical page break**   A page division that divides pages between columns. See *horizontal page break* for more information about how Excel divides a long, wide worksheet into pages and then prints those pages.

**Visual Basic Editor**   A programming tool that enables you to open and edit macros.

**Web**   Short for World Wide Web, a collection of pages that are stored on computers all over the world and are linked to one another with hyperlinks. Excel offers several features to help you convert worksheets and workbooks into Web pages and publish those pages on the Web.

**workbook**   A collection of Excel worksheets. Every file you create in Excel is a workbook file.

**worksheet**   A page in an Excel workbook on which you enter labels, values, dates, formulas, and functions. You can use a worksheet to arrange data in rows and columns, to perform calculations on numerical entries, and to analyze data through charts. "Worksheet" is Excel's name for a spreadsheet.

**worksheet auditor**   An Excel tool that inspects a worksheet's formulas and functions and highlights any potential errors.

**worksheet tabs**   Tags at the bottom of a workbook window that enable you to flip from one worksheet to another in a workbook.

**wrap**   To place an entry on two or more lines inside a cell. Unless you specify otherwise, Excel places each entry on a single line inside a cell. With wrapping, Excel creates additional lines, as needed, to fit a wide entry in a narrow cell.

# Index

*How can we make this index more useful? Email us at indexes@quepublishing.com*

*How can we make this index more useful? Email us at indexes@quepublishing.com*

WITHDRAWN FROM THE COLLECTION OF WINDSOR PUBLIC LIBRARY